The Daily Walk
365 Daily Devotions for Life's Journey

Dr. Mark Denison

The Daily Walk
365 Daily Devotions for Life's Journey

Author: Mark Denison

Published by Austin Brothers Publishing
Fort Worth, Texas
www.austinbrotherspublishing.com

ISBN: 978-0-9891027-7-3

Austin Brothers
Publishing

This and other books published by
Austin Brothers Publishing
can be purchased at -
www.austinbrotherspublishing.com

Printed in the United States of America
2013 -- First Edition

What Others are Saying...

I've been reading Mark's daily online devotions for years. These 'Daily Walk' devotions are concise and engaging. They propel me into the Word every day. I highly recommend this book to all my friends.

Rick Perry
Governor, State of Texas

Mark Denison has been my pastor and friend for ten years. I read his devotions every day. I take the 'Daily Walk' with me wherever I go. They lift me and challenge me to live the Christian life.

Terry Bradshaw
NFL Hall of Fame
Broadcaster, Fox Sports

These devotions are interesting, brief, and relevant. Mark Denison has assembled 365 inspiring stories that will help you start your day off right.

David Murrow
Author, *Why Men Hate Going to Church*

'A Daily Walk' is a great way to start your day off in devotional time with Jesus. Short devotionals that are sure to instill God's word in us and for us to carry throughout our daily walk.

Andy Pettitte
Pitcher, New York Yankees
Five-time World Series Champion

I love 'The Daily Walk!' This is a useful resource in getting my day off to a great start. I highly recommend it to you!

Don Piper
Author, *90 Minutes in Heaven*

Mark Denison has written a gem of encouragement. For those who want to start your day with an uplifting word and a Scripture that you can meditate on the entire day, reinforced by humorous stories and relevant quotes, this is the book.

Dr. Robert Sloan
President, Houston Baptist University

These devotionals will enlighten, encourage, and inspire you from God's Word. I read it every day. You'll love it!

Bobby Richardson
New York Yankees, 1955-1966
MVP, 1960 World Series

Here are gems of insight that will inspire you to apply the Bible to everyday life. With colorful stories, winsome humor, and practical wisdom, Mark will get you started each day on God's path.

Lee Strobel
Author, *The Case for Christ*

I dedicate this book to Beth,
my partner in ministry,
very best friend,
and the love of my life.
She has taught me,
more than anyone else,
how to live
'The Daily Walk.'

Forward

Uncle Billy was known as the "nickel uncle." Every time he came to visit, little Timmy got another nickel. He followed Billy around the house. Every time they were together for even a few seconds, Uncle Billy gave Timmy another nickel.

One day, Billy took Timmy to see his trunk, filled with an almost unlimited supply of nickels.

"Every time I'm with you, Timmy, I will give you another nickel."

After that, Timmy rarely left Uncle Billy's side. A few days passed, and Timmy offered a proposal. "Uncle Billy, I can see where this is headed. Every time I am in your presence, you give me another nickel. Eventually, I'll have all the nickels. So why don't you go ahead and give them to me now, and you can go back to wherever you came from."

"That's the problem, Timmy. That's precisely why I don't give you all the nickels now. I want to bless you with nickels, but I'm more interested in enjoying your company."

Most of us have been guilty of chasing after a "nickel God." He says to us, "I'd much rather you chase after me than my nickels." God wants time with us each day.

That is a lesson I learned as a new convert under the ministry of the most amazing pastor I have ever known, Dr. Cecil Sewell. That lesson came home even more as I grew in my faith, mentored by Jimmy McGowan. Some 35 years later, I still enjoy

God's nickels. But I'm learning to enjoy the God of the nickels more than the nickels of God.

My prayer is that this devotional book won't just sit on your shelf or desk. I have written it to be simple, encouraging, and applicable. Seventy-two percent of Jesus' words were application. So find one truth each morning from each lesson that applies to your life. I hope you will laugh some days, cry others, but find the God of the nickels always.

I am grateful for three incredible churches that have blessed me more than I could have ever blessed them. We planted Baybrook Baptist Church in Friendswood, Texas, in 1984. For nearly 18 years, this loving congregation put up with a young pastor still finding his way.

From 2001-2010, I was blessed to pastor the First Baptist Church of Gainesville, Texas. It was there that I began writing a daily newspaper column that gave inspiration to this project. I am forever grateful for the life-long friends I have from this wonderful church.

In 2010, I was honored to be called to one of the warmest churches I know. First Baptist, Conroe, Texas, has a heart for her community and her God. This church has been chasing the God of the nickels for generations. I am grateful to serve with an amazing staff and among an amazing people.

We were never called to a daily sprint with God, but a daily walk. My prayer is that your daily walk with be enhanced as you read the Scriptures and inspiration found on the 365 pages of this *Daily Walk*. Join me for the journey that ends with a chest-full of eternal nickels. Until then, may we be filled with the grace and love of our Savior as we chase after Him.

As you read these pages, be encouraged by the word of God, filled with the Spirit of God, and blessed by the presence of God. Join me for *The Daily Walk*.

January 1

A New Year

Do you know the difference between an optimist and a pessimist? An optimist will stay up until midnight to welcome the New Year. A pessimist will stay up to make sure the old one leaves.

I like the way an elderly man prayed for the New Year. "Lord, grant me the senility to forget the people I never liked anyway, the good fortune to run into the ones that I do, and the eyesight to tell the difference."

Are you a "resolution" person? I always set New Year's resolutions.

One guy was worried about his weight. His New Year's resolution that year was to get his weight under 180 pounds. The next year, his resolution was to get his weight under 200. And the year after that, he resolved, "to develop a realistic attitude about my weight."

Last year, he resolved to join a gym. And this year's resolution is, "to drive by the gym at least three days a week."

I like what Mark Twain said. "New Year's Day is the accepted time to make your regular annual good resolutions. Next week you can begin paving hell with them as usual."

The Bible says life is really short, like a vapor. You really don't have the promise of a New Year, but of a new day. So celebrate that promise. And if you're really serious, go drive by a gym.

"Teach us to number our days, that we may gain a heart of wisdom."

Psalm 90:12

January 2

Microwaved Years

Welcome to the second day of a brand new year! There is still time to set those resolutions you will take all year to break. This is the season to watch football, celebrate family, play golf, start putting up Christmas decorations, and eat turkey sandwiches three meals a day. And it's time to plan for the next twelve months. Life is busy. Don't get behind.

As someone put it, "This is the age of the half-read page and the quick hash and the mad dash, the bright night with the nerves tight, the plane hop and the brief stop, the lamp tan in a short span, the big shot in a soft spot, the brain strain and the heart pain, and the catnaps 'til the spring snaps, and the fun is done."

Don't microwave the New Year. Instead of texting your mother, call her. Instead of giving your friend a tweet, give her a hug. Blow off the newest technology. Communicate your affections to those you love the way we did when we were kids. Send them an email. Slow down. Don't microwave the New Year. Save the microwave for home-cooked meals as God intended it.

"You don't even know what will happen tomorrow. You are a mist that appears for a little while and then vanishes away."

James 4:14

January 3

Father Damien

Tourists travel to the Hawaiian Island of Molokai for its quiet charm, gentle breezes, and soft surf. But Father Damien came for a different reason. He came to help people die. He came to Molokai because leprosy came here first. It started about 1840.

Because of their gross disfigurement, lepers were outcasts placed on a small piece of land called Kalaupapa. There they lived out their lives in isolation and poverty. Then, in 1873, Father Damien stepped into the picture. He pled with his supervisors, "I want to sacrifice myself for the poor lepers."

Father Damien entered their world, dressing their sores, hugging their children, and burying their dead. He sang to them and taught them about God's love.

He didn't just join them; he became one of them. Due to his constant contact with them, he became a leper. He wrote to his friends, "It is one thing to treat a leper, but far better to become one."

On April 15, 1889, Father Damien died of leprosy. But he made a difference. He did what Jesus did. Not content to simply "treat" man, Jesus became a man. And he died a man. He has been where you are. And now, he is where you can be.

> *"He appeared in the flesh, was vindicated by the Spirit, was seen by angels, was preached among the nations, was believed on in the world, was taken up into glory."*

1 Timothy 3:16

January 4

The Toy Boat

A little boy had a toy boat that he played with at the pond. One day his boat drifted away from him, and he tried everything he could to get it back, but he couldn't reach it. All of a sudden, as he was watching the boat and trying to figure out what to do, he saw a man throwing rocks at the boat.

The little boy turned around in anger and said, "What are you trying to do, sink my boat? What are you doing?"

The man just smiled and kept throwing rocks.

The little boy yelled, "Quit it!"

Finally he ran to the man. "What are you doing?"

The man replied, "I'm trying to help you."

"What do you mean you are trying to help me? You're going to wreck my boat."

The man said, "Look at your boat."

As the boy looked at his little boat, he realized that the man was throwing the rocks over his boat. The ripples of the water were bringing his boat back to the shore.

The boy wasn't tall enough to see what the man could see. You aren't tall enough to see all that God is up to. Those rocks that are falling around you may rock your boat. But be patient. God may be the one throwing the rocks. He knows what he is doing.

> "I form the light and create darkness, I
> bring prosperity and create disaster; I, the
> Lord, do all these things."

Isaiah 45:7

January 5

Sermon on the Mound

Baseball manager Tommy Lasorda came to the mound to speak to his young, skinny, timid pitcher who was getting shelled. He looked into Leonard's face and said, "I don't see a skinny, scared, uncertain kid. I see a fighter. From now on your name will be 'Bulldog.'"

Leonard went on to win a Cy Young award in 1989. He set the all-time record for consecutive scoreless innings pitched. Leonard's full name is Orel Leonard Hersheiser IV. To this day, when asked the key to his success, he points back to what he calls Lasorda's "Sermon on the Mound."

Isn't it amazing, what a little encouragement can do? A national survey concluded that the average person needs to hear 17 words of encouragement every day, and for every criticism, we need 13 instances of encouragement.

I have never met a person who said, "Please don't encourage me. I get too much encouragement." We all need encouragement. You and I need to hear what Leonard heard, "The Sermon on the Mound."

*"And we urge you, brothers and sisters,
encourage the disheartened."*

1 Thessalonians 5:14

January 6

Lucy's Bad Day

In a classic Peanuts comic strip, Lucy announces, "Boy, do I feel crabby!"

Her little brother, Linus, always anxious to relieve tension at home, responds, "Maybe I can be of help. Why don't you just take my place here in front of the television while I go and fix you a nice snack? Sometimes we all need a little pampering to help us feel better."

Then Lunus brings her a sandwich, a few chocolate chip cookies, and some milk. "Now, is there anything else I can get you?" he asks. "Is there anything I haven't thought of?"

"Yes, there's one thing you haven't thought of," Lucy answers. And then she suddenly screams, "I don't want to feel better!"

For the forty years the late Charles Shultz drew Peanuts that always seemed to be one of Lucy's problems. She didn't want to change in the areas where she had a bad attitude, and she had a lot of them!

There are a lot of people like Lucy. You can't choose your birth place, your family, your gender, or your race. But you can choose your attitude. I agree with Chuck Swindoll, who said, "Life is ten percent what happens to you and 90 percent how you respond."

You can't determine your circumstances. But you will determine your attitude. And then your attitude will determine you.

"Finally, brothers, whatever is true, whatever is noble, whatever is right, whatever is pure, whatever is lovely, whatever is admirable, if anything is excellent or praiseworthy, think about such things."

Philippians 4:8

January 7

Men Can Fly

Larry Walker wanted to fly. It was his greatest passion and dream. Not born with wings, he had to become rather creative. So he hitched up 45 helium-filled balloons to his lawn chair. He strapped himself in, with a snack, soft drink, and pellet gun. His plan was to rise 30 feet into the air, then shoot the balloons to bring about a slow, gentle landing.

He overshot his target. Larry's lawn chair rocketed to heights of 16,000 feet! He then shot his balloons until he landed in some power lines. On his way to the police station someone asked why he had done this. He responded with brilliance. "A man can't just sit there!"

Now, I'm too afraid of heights to recommend the helium balloon route. But let's give Larry some credit. At least he tired of just sitting there.

What about your life? Are you content living life as you always have, or do you want more?

That great philosopher, Yogi Berra, was fond of saying, "If all you do is what you've done, then all you'll get is what you've got." Yogi was right. So take a risk. Do something big. Do something so big that if God doesn't come through, you will fail. Live life on the edge. Buy a lawn chair.

"The Lord had said to Abram, 'Leave your country, your people and your father's household and go to the land I will show you.'"

Genesis 12:1

January 8

Running Backwards

She was gorgeous. She was the most beautiful woman I had ever seen. She was 13. So was I. It was seventh grade, and the boys were running track. The one mile race started, and I fired into the lead. I wanted to be sure "she" was watching. So after we had passed our cheering fans, I turned and ran backwards, waving to my dream girl as I stumbled and fell.

I finished last. She finished the "relationship." I learned two lessons that day. I learned that girls can be trouble for any 13-year-old boy. And I learned that you can't win the race by looking back.

I know what kind of car you drive. Let me guess. I bet it is the kind of car that has a really big windshield and a really small rear view mirror. You know why? It's simple. While it is good to glance back occasionally, it is more important to look forward.

Keep your eye on the road. Keep looking forward. And if you are a 13-year-old boy, beware of 13-year-old girls! God has a big plan for your life. But you'll never get to where you're going by focusing on where you've been.

"Brothers, I do not consider myself yet to have taken hold of it. But one thing I do: forgetting what is behind and straining toward what is ahead, I press on toward the goal to win the prize for which God has called me."

Philippians 3:13-14

January 9

Joe DiMaggio

As World War II ended in the summer of 1945, all the soldiers were coming back, including many professional athletes who had been drafted to serve. Joe DiMaggio was among the returning soldiers, and though he hadn't been playing baseball, he took his four-year-old son, Joe, Jr., to a Yankees game, and slipped quietly into his seat.

Two or three fans soon recognized him, despite his ball cap that was intended to cover his identity. They called out, "Joe, Joe DiMaggio! Joe, Joe DiMaggio!"

Eventually, the whole stadium picked up on the chant and said as one, "Joe, Joe DiMaggio!"

Hearing the thunderous crowd, Joe, Jr. looked up at his dad and said, "See, Daddy, everyone knows me here!"

Of course, the adulation was intended for Joe, Sr., the father. But his little boy was like most of us. We are happy to enjoy the blessings of our Father, as Joe, Jr. enjoyed the opportunity to attend the game. But then we step out of his shadow and into his glory. And that is a dangerous place to stand. When the crowd throws praise in your direction, remember that all honor and adoration goes to your Father.

"So whether you eat or drink or whatever you do, do it all for the glory of God."

1 Corinthians 10:31

January 10

What Does God Look Like?

A child asked her mother, "What does God look like?" That's a good question, isn't it? What is your image of God? Some see him as a Scorekeeper God, one who keeps tabs on everything we do right and wrong, especially wrong. To others, he is the Stained Glass God, a rather formal impersonal deity. Still others see him as the Absentee God. He wound up the universe and let it go. He stands back and watches. To a lot of men, he is the Onstar God, the one we look to when we are lost. And to some, he is Grandpa God, a nice Creator full of wisdom, but not always real accessible.

A poor boy was begging for food or money. A nice man walked up and gave him $100, plus a great sack meal.

The boy asked the man, "Are you God?"

"Am I God?" Why would you think that?" was the man's reply.

"Because," the boy said, "I thought only God did things like that. So tell me, are you God?"

That's a great lesson. We never look more like God than when we do something nice for someone who cannot do anything to repay us.

"When a wicked man dies, his hope perishes. All he expected from his power comes to nothing."

Proverbs 11:7

January 11

The Scorpion and the Frog

There is an old fable about a scorpion and a frog. The scorpion asked the frog to carry him on his back across a creek. The frog said no, fearing the scorpion would sting him. The scorpion swore he would not, and so the frog warily allowed the scorpion to hop on, and started across the stream. Sure enough, when they were halfway across, the scorpion stung the frog.

"Why did you do that?" yelled the frog.

"Now I will die and you will drown, too!"

"I know," replied the scorpion. "It's just my nature to sting."

Satan is pictured several different ways in Scripture: as Lucifer, the accuser, a prowling lion. But they all have one thing in common. Satan's nature is to destroy.

J. I. Packer said, "Satan has no constructive purpose of his own; his tactics are simply to destroy the lives of men."

Satan and his minions have one goal: to destroy.

Jesus said, "I have come to give you life, and life more abundantly." But he also said, "The devil has come to destroy."

God created you for a great life. But in order to enjoy that life, get one thing right. Don't make the same mistake the frog made. Avoid riding with the devil.

"Take the helmet of salvation and the sword of the Spirit, which is the word of God."

Ephesians 6:17

January 12

The Farmhouse

There was a preacher who saved up enough money to buy a few inexpensive acres of land. A little run down, weather beaten farmhouse sat on the acreage, a sad picture of years of neglect. The land had not been kept up, either, so there were old tree stumps, rusted pieces of machinery, and all sorts of debris strewn here and there, not to mention a fence in need of repair.

The whole scene was a mess. During his spare time and on his vacations, the preacher rolled up his sleeves and went to work. He hauled off the junk, repaired the fence, pulled away the stumps, and replanted new trees.

Then he refurbished the old house into a quaint cottage with a new roof, windows, walkway, and paint job. It took years to finish, but was certainly worth the effort.

One day, when he was trimming the newly planted hedges, a neighbor walked over and said, "Well, preacher, I have to hand it to you. It looks like you and the Lord have done a pretty good job with this place."

The preacher wiped the sweat from his brow and said, "Yeah, I suppose we have. But you should have seen it when the Lord had it all to himself."

An old evangelist used to say, "Pray as though it all depends on God, but work as though it all depends on you."

God wants to enter into a partnership with you. Together, you can do amazing things.

"We are God's fellow workers."

1 Corinthians 3:9

January 13

Standing Still

The Tartar tribes of central Asia spoke a certain curse against an enemy. They didn't call for their enemy's swords to rust or for their people to die of disease. Instead they said, "May you stay in one place forever."

The best way to assure yourself that you will never get better is to stand still. Jim Rohn said, "In order to *do* more, you first have to *be* more."

Peter Drucker, the father of modern management, said, "The great mystery isn't that people do things badly but that they occasionally do a few things well. The only thing that is universal is incompetence."

Drucker's point is that we all have flaws, and that's okay. What's not okay is standing still, not doing anything to improve.

I read a story about a St. Louis doctor who met a young man in high school who had lost his hand at the wrist. When the doctor asked about his handicap, the teenager responded, "I don't have a handicap, sir. I just don't have a right hand."

It turns out the boy was the leading scorer on his basketball team. He learned to focus on what he had left rather than on what he had lost. He learned to not stand still.

"But as for you, be strong and do not give up. Your work will be rewarded."

2 Chronicles 15:7

January 14

Because I Love Her

A six-year-old girl became deathly ill. To survive, she needed a blood transfusion from someone who had already conquered the same disease. Her situation was complicated by her rare blood type. Her nine-year-old brother qualified as a donor, but they were hesitant to ask him, since he was so young. Finally, they had a doctor ask the boy if he would donate blood to his sister.

He didn't understand the details, but was quick to respond. "Sure, I'll give my blood for my sister!"

The day came for the procedure, and he lay down next to his sister and smiled at her as they pricked his arm with the needle. Then he closed his eyes and lay silently on the bed as the pint of blood was taken.

The doctor came in to thank the lad. The boy responded, "Doctor, when do I die?"

At that, the doctor realized the boy thought that by giving his blood, he was giving up his life. He assured the boy that he would be fine. Then he asked him, "If you thought you were going to die, why were you willing to give your blood for your sister?"

The boy said simply, "Because I love her."

Jesus gave his blood for you, for the same reason. He loves you.

"It was not with perishable things that you were redeemed, but with the precious blood of Christ, a lamb without blemish or defect."

1 Peter 1:18-19

January 15

For Men Only

I heard about a man who said to his wife, "I'm the boss here! I'm in charge! I am the leader and the man of the house!"

His wife responded, "You'd be more convincing if you came out from under the bed and said that!"

Most men are more consumed with leading than they are with loving. We need to learn from the affluent, older gentleman. They asked him why he went to visit his ailing wife of 55 years, every single day in the nursing home. "She doesn't even know who you are," they told him.

He replied, "No, but I know who she is!"

Men, do you know who she is?

Don't be like the man who took his wife to Hawaii for their twenty-fifth anniversary. When asked what he was going to do for his fiftieth, he said, "I may go back and get her!"

Your wife deserves better than that.

There once was a very wealthy king named Solomon. The Bible contains a book of love letters between Solomon and his wife. In just eight chapters, Solomon praised her 40 times. Focus less on leading and more on loving. And if you left your wife in Hawaii, don't wait another 25 years to go back to get her.

"Husbands, love your wives, just as Christ loved the church and gave himself up for her."

Ephesians 5:25

January 16

Nifty at Fifty

There are signs I'm getting older. Most of the time, I'd prefer a hot bath to a hot date. When I drive around with others, I point out the things that are no longer there. I feel like I'm on the Golden Pond and my boat is sinking. I still stay up for the news before I go to bed, but now it's the 6:00 news. My furniture is all antiques, but we bought it all brand new. The ceramic cats on my console television are even showing wear. I find myself saying things like, "It's coming a storm," and when a friend is recovering in a hospital, I say, "He's some better."

Now, I'm not wearing white tube socks with black shoes. Yet. But the socks are in my drawer for when I need them. I realize that some of my dreams from 20 years ago will never come true. And I can't remember the dreams I had last night.

But aging has benefits. I've got an AARP card. There are other benefits, as well. I just can't remember what they are.

But I do know this. I've never been as happy, healthy, hopeful, or hearty. I'm in the right place, have the right wife, and serve the right God. I'm nifty at fifty, or whatever I am this year. Yes, we're all getting older. But there's no sense crying about it.

Even Jeremiah, the "weeping prophet," didn't cry over this one. Celebrate life to its fullest. It is the gift of God.

*"Jeremiah said to himself, 'The Lord is my portion.
Therefore, I will wait for him.'"*

Lamentations 3:24

January 17

A Dog and a Lion

A little girl had developed a bad habit. She was always lying. Once when she was given a St. Bernard dog for her birthday, she went out and told all the neighbors that she had been given a lion.

Her mother took her aside and said, "I told you not to lie. You go upstairs and tell God you are sorry. Promise God you will not lie again."

The little girl went upstairs, said her prayers, then came down again.

Her mother asked, "Did you tell God you are sorry?"

The little girl replied, "Yes, I did. And God said sometimes he finds it hard to tell my dog from a lion too."

A school principal received a phone call. The voice said, "Thomas Bradley won't be in school today."

The principal was a bit suspicious of the young sounding voice. He asked, "Who is speaking?"

The voice responded, "My father."

Children learn how to tell lies early in life. I can't imagine where they pick up this nasty little habit! The worst thing we can do as parents is to tell our children to be honest while modeling dishonesty in our own lives. Make no mistake about it. Our kids know the difference between our words and our actions. And God knows the difference between a St. Bernard and lion.

"Simply let your 'Yes' be 'Yes,' and your 'No,' 'No.'
Anything beyond this comes from the evil one."

Matthew 5:37

January 18

Living Alone

Did you know that if you isolate yourself from others, you will be two to three times more likely to die an early death? You are more likely to contract terminal cancer if you are alone. If you are divorced, separated, or widowed, you are five times more likely to become mentally ill. Living alone can drive you crazy.

There are several ways to try to stay sane. You can go see a shrink and lay on a sofa and talk about your mother, you can get married (both are expensive), or you can have friends. God said it isn't good to be alone.

We need other people. Even when Simon was singing, "I am a rock, I am an island," he had Garfunkle singing back-up. The Lone Ranger wouldn't have made it without Tonto. We need friends.

A football coach was having a really bad year. It got so bad that when he confided to his wife, "I feel that my dog is my only friend, but a man needs at least two friends," she bought him another dog.

Yes, we all need friends. A friend is someone who walks in when everyone else walks out. A friend is there for you even when you mess up. David would become king. But it wasn't enough, unless he had a true friend. God created you for relationships. Yes, everyone needs a friend.

> *"After David had finished talking with Saul,*
> *Jonathan became one in spirit with David."*

1 Samuel 18:1

January 19

Not Far Away

Dr. Tony Compolo says that when he was a boy growing up in a bustling city, his mother arranged for a teenage girl to walk home with him at the end of the day. For this, she was paid a nickel a day. But Tony rebelled in the second grade and told his mother, "I'll walk myself to school, and if you give me a nickel a week, I will be extra careful. You can keep the other 20 cents and we'll all be better off!"

After a period of pleading and begging, little Tony finally got his way. For the next two years, he walked himself back and forth to school. He was careful and didn't talk to strangers or get distracted along the way.

Years later, he bragged about how he had taken care of himself as a boy. His mother laughed and asked, "Did you really think you were alone? Every morning when you left for school, I left with you. When you got out of school, I was there. You never saw me, but I was there, watching after you until you got home."

And that's the kind of God we have. You may not always see him, but he is there. He will watch over you, every step of the way, until you make your way home.

"Have I not commanded you? Be strong and courageous. Do not be terrified; do not be discouraged, for the Lord your God will be with you wherever you go."

Joshua 1:9

January 20

Crash Landing

Two hunters flew deep into the backwoods of Canada to hunt elk, and they bagged six. The pilot told them his plane could only carry four of the elk out. One of the hunters protested, "But the plane that carried six out last year was exactly like this one. That plane had the same horsepower, the weather was the same, and we carried out six last year."

Hearing this, the pilot reluctantly agreed to try. The hunters and their six elk were piled into the small craft, and the plane was soon airborne. But just as the pilot had predicted, there was insufficient power to lift the plane out of the valley, and the plane crashed.

As the men stumbled from the wreckage, one of the hunters asked the others if they knew where they were. Another hunter replied, "Well, I'm not positive, but I think we are about a mile from where we crashed last year."

Iconic coach John Wooden used to tell his players, "Experience does you no good. It is learning from experience that does you some good."

The hunters had experience, but it did them no good. You need the right experience, with the right people. That was the key to Paul's success. We can't change yesterday's crash landing, but we can avoid the one tomorrow.

"Only Luke is with me. Get Mark and bring him with you, because he is helpful to me in my ministry."

2 Timothy 4:11

January 21

Comfort or Compassion?

There is a difference between compassion and comfort. Comfort is putting compassion into action. A little girl took first aid training. A few years later she burst into the house and said, "Mother, I saw a terrible accident and I used my first aid training."

Mother asked her what she did.

The girl responded, "I saw a lot of blood, so I sat down and put my head between my knees so I wouldn't pass out."

Well, that wasn't very comforting. Compassion leads to comfort. On 35 separate occasions, the Gospels tell us that Jesus had compassion. And in each incident, Jesus acted on his compassion. His compassion led to comfort.

Because Beethoven was deaf, he found conversation difficult. When he heard of the death of a friend's son, he hurried over to the house, overcome with grief. He had no words of comfort to offer, but he saw a piano in the room. For the next half hour, he played the piano, pouring out his emotions in the most eloquent way he could.

Job suffered unlike anyone else. His friends were useless to him. They may have had compassion, but they certainly offered no comfort.

Unless you live in a closet, I'm pretty sure you know someone who is hurting. They don't need your compassion. They need your comfort.

"Job replied, 'I have heard many things like these; miserable comforters are you all!'"

Job 16:1

January 22

In Every Church

Every church has a few. When we see them, we think of the old chorus, "I'm so glad I'm a part of the family of God." But we change the words to, "I'm surprised you're a part of the family of God."

They are fearfully and wonderfully weird. They have a gift for sucking the joy right out of the ministry. They are a French fry short of a Happy Meal, missing a few buttons off the remote. You know the type. The porch light is on but nobody is home. They even look funny, as they apparently shop at "Nerds Are Us." There is always something that is unbuttoned, undone, unzipped, or untucked. They are the Dagwoods of Simpletown.

When you see them, you want to ask, "Where are Moe, Larry, and Curly?" They stand when they should sit and speak when they should listen. They are everywhere. And they always find you, excited to tell you the same story they told you last week.

You find yourself avoiding them. And then it occurs to you that you, too, are weird. Your life is often untucked. But you realize and rejoice that God came to love untucked people. And when you mistreat these untucked people, you are really mistreating Jesus.

"Whatever you did not do for one of the least of these, you did not do for me."

Matthew 25:45

January 23

Burn the Ships!

It was a strange new world. Sure they had heard stories about riches and treasures, but when they stepped ashore, they didn't know what to expect. After a rendezvous in Cuba, Hernan Cortez led his 400 men to the coast of present-day Mexico. The men stepped onto Mexico's shore in February of 1519. As had been the case in Cuba, a group of men moved to take charge of the now emptied eleven ships, planning to do the normal thing, to guard the ships while Cortez led the rest in exploration of the interior.

This was the safe, sensible thing to do. In so doing, there would be a way to escape should Cortez run into a band of head hunting natives. Who wouldn't want a way out? Cortez didn't. He did something that had never been done before. He ordered his men to burn the ships, thus cutting off any possible avenue for a quick return home.

His message was clear: "No turning back. We're all in. We are pushing forward, no matter what."

That is the message of faith. "I'm all in. I'm following Jesus, no matter the cost."

The Christian life isn't complicated. It's just a matter of burning a few ships.

"Then the Lord said to Moses, 'Why are you crying out to me? Tell the Israelites to move on.'"

Exodus 14:15

January 24

A Big Universe

Our solar system has a diameter of 7.5 billion miles. That means if you drove your space car 65 miles per hour around the clock, it would take 13,172 years to get across it. And there are over 100 billion stars in the Milky Way (galaxy, not candy bar). That's 100 billion solar systems in our galaxy. Astronomers estimate that there are 50 billion galaxies in the universe.

As I meet people I didn't know I knew, I often comment, "It's a small world."

But as I look to the sky, I conclude, "It's a big universe."

And call me simple, but I figure that if a watch must have a watch maker, then a universe must have a universe maker.

But the majesty of God is not that he is big. It is that he is small.

During WWII, Viktor Frankl was a prisoner in the infamous Auschwitz concentration camp. In his book, *Man's Search for Meaning*, Frankl chronicled his experience and found something outside of himself. He wrote, "Being human always points, and is directed, to something, or Someone other than oneself."

That was Frankl's way of saying the God of the universe wants to be the God of your heart.

"The Word became flesh and made his dwelling among us. We have seen his glory, the glory of the One and Only, who came from the Father, full of grace and truth."

John 1:14

January 25

Great Organization

In his book, *Harvest of Humility*, John Seamands told of a wounded German soldier who was ordered to go to the military hospital for treatment. When he arrived at the large and imposing building, he saw two doors, one marked "For the slightly wounded" and the other, "For the seriously wounded."

He entered the first door and soon found two more, one marked "For officers," and the other marked "For non-officers."

He entered through the latter and was suddenly faced with two more doors, marked "Party members" and "Non-party members."

He took the second, and then found himself standing back on the street.

When the soldier returned home his mother asked him, "How did you get along at the hospital?"

"Well, Mother," he replied, "to be honest, the people there didn't do anything for me, but they have tremendous organization!"

That is the picture of many modern churches. The people are busy, and things are well-organized. Things run well. But lives aren't being changed. The church has just one product: changed lives. Otherwise, it doesn't matter how organized we are.

"Offer right sacrifices and trust in the Lord."

Psalm 4:5

January 26

Decisions

A young man, known to be a bit of a trouble maker, walked into a blacksmith's shop shortly after the blacksmith had thrown a horseshoe on the ground so it could cool. Seeing it laying there, the young fellow reached down and picked it up. He instantly cast it aside, as it burned his fingers.

The blacksmith said, "It's kind of hot, isn't it, son?"

The brash kid responded, "No, it's not too hot. It just doesn't take me long to look at a horseshoe."

Despite his arrogance, the young man was quick on his feet. He knew when to pick something up and he knew when to let it go.

When Bill Hill, a Montana guide, killed a grizzly bear in a protected area, he offered the following defense. "When I saw that bear come rushing down on me, I didn't have any trouble deciding who was the endangered species."

Again, we see an example of quick decision-making. But too many of us suffer from a rabid disease I call "paralysis by analysis." There is a time to think and a time to decide. We face several important decisions every day: sweet or unsweetened, soup or salad, up or down, left or right, Leno or Letterman, Ginger or Mary Ann.

Start with a really important decision, taken from Joshua. "Choose who you will serve, but as for me and my house, we will serve the Lord."

"Commit to the Lord whatever you do, and your plans will succeed."

Proverbs 16:3

January 27

Going to Heaven?

A national poll asked an interesting question. What are the chances these people will go to heaven? Here is what you said, America. The chance these people will go to heaven is as follows: Mother Teresa – 79 percent. Oprah Winfrey – 66 percent. Michael Jordan – 65 percent. Colin Powell – 61 percent. Dennis Rodman – 28 percent. O.J. Simpson – 19 percent. But who got the most votes? Who is most likely to go to heaven? You have to read another 63 words to find out!

We all admire Mother Teresa. Nobody did more to promote peace and bless the unfortunate than she did. Michael Jordan was a great athlete in his prime. That should help, shouldn't it? Dennis Rodman suffers from the anti-tattoo lobby, I suppose. But guess who got the most votes, as the most likely to go to heaven, ahead of even Mother Teresa?

"Me" got 87 percent. That's interesting. 87 percent say they expect to go to heaven.

What about you? And, as good as 87 percent sounds, wouldn't it be even better if you could be 100 percent sure? The good news is, you can. Paul was talking to a bunch of jail workers one night. He told them how to be 100 percent sure. Notice the use of the word "will" in the following verse.

"Believe in the Lord Jesus Christ, and you will be saved."

Acts 16:31

January 28

Rich but Dead

In 1923 the world's most successful financiers met at the Edgewater Hotel in Chicago. Collectively, they had more wealth than the U.S. Treasury. Here's the rest of the story. Jesse Livermore, the greatest bear on Wall Street, committed suicide. Ivan Kruegar, head of the world's greatest monopoly, did the same. Charles Schwab, president of the largest steel company, lived on borrowed money the last five years of his life. Arthur Cutten, the great wheat speculator, died insolvent. Richard Whitney, president of NRSE, died in prison. Albert Fall, member of the president's cabinet, was pardoned from prison so he could die at home.

History is full of men and women who attained all this world offers, but it was never enough.

John Rockefeller was asked how much money it took to be happy. He said, "A little bit more."

Lucille Ball was asked how many actors she knew who were happy. She said, "None."

Adolf Hitler was the most powerful figure of his day. He ended his life on April 30, 1945, when he blew his brains out with a gun.

So much for money buying happiness! It's okay to pursue happiness. But it's better to pursue the God who gives happiness.

"Then my head will be exalted above the enemies who surround me; at his tabernacle will I sacrifice with shouts of joy; I will sing and make music to the Lord."

Psalm 27:6

January 29

Eternity

It was November, 1942. The city was Sydney, Australia. The man was Arthur Stace, a WWI veteran and a homeless alcoholic. On a Sunday night, Stace stumbled into a small church, where he heard a simple message on eternity from the pastor, John Ridley. That night, Stace made a course correction, with eternity on his mind. He dedicated the rest of his life to doing what he could to help people find the God who had found him.

Every day, for more than 25 years, he rose early, had a cup of tea, then went into the streets of Sydney with a piece of chalk, and he wrote the word "eternity" thousands of times. As the city awoke, they saw it everywhere.

Today, in a certain government building, you can still look up and still see "eternity" scribed inside a tower overhead.

Stace died in 1967 at age 83, but his legacy lives on. His gravestone reads, "Arthur Malcolm Stace – Mr. Eternity."

He wrote the word 500,000 times. And 30 years after his death, in his honor, Australia hosted the Olympics under the banner of the theme "ETERNITY."

This life is so short. What matters is eternity. Just ask Mr. Stace.

"He has made everything beautiful in its time. He has also set eternity in the hearts of men."

Ecclesiastes 3:11

January 30

Golfer's Timing

Arnold Palmer was invited to a convention of blind golfers. The golfers told how they were able to know what direction to hit the ball. One of them explained that the caddy went out ahead of him with a little bell, which he would ring as he stood near the hole. The blind golfer would then hit the ball toward the sound of the bell.

Arnold asked how well it worked, and the blind golfer said that it worked so well he was willing to take on Arnold Palmer for a round of golf, and just to make it interesting, was willing to bet Palmer $10,000 he could beat him. Palmer said, "Okay, what time do we tee off?"

And the blind man said, "11:00 tonight!"

Do you ever feel like you've been kept in the dark? Or, as the saying goes, the light is on but nobody is home.

One of the most wonderful claims Jesus ever made was this one: "I am the light." We need that light, because we live in a dark and fallen world. When you walk in darkness, you need the light. Don't take another step without it. Think of each morning as tee time. And think of Jesus as the only light that can help you find your way.

"This is the message we have heard from him and declare to you: God is light; in him there is no darkness at all."

1 John 1:5

January 31

Criticism

One of Aesop's fables tells of an old man and his son bringing a donkey to market. Passing some people on the way, they heard one remark, "Look at that silly pair, walking when they could be riding."

The old man thought about it, then he and the boy got on the donkey and continued on their way. Soon they passed another group. "Look at that lazy pair," a voice said, "breaking the back of that poor donkey."

At that the old man slipped off, but soon heard more criticism. "How terrible! The old man has to walk while the boy gets to ride."

They changed places, but soon heard, "What an awful thing! The big, strong man is riding, and making the little boy walk!"

The man came up with a final solution. He and the boy carried the donkey on a pole between them. But as soon as they crossed a bridge, the donkey broke loose, fell into the river, and drowned.

Aesop's conclusion: "You can't please everyone."

I love what Ed Young says about criticism. If one person says you're a donkey, ignore him. If two say you're a donkey, don't sweat it. But if three people say you're a donkey, it's time to buy a saddle.

Rarely is all criticism valid. And rarely is all criticism invalid. Knowing how to respond to criticism is one of the marks of a mature believer.

"A gentle answer turns away wrath, but a harsh word stirs up anger."

Proverbs 15:1

February 1

Passing the Exam

An attractive young college student was doing well in all her classes except Chemistry. She found that to be the most difficult class she had ever had. But she just had to pass, or she would lose her scholarship. So the student made an appointment to see her professor in his office.

"What can I do for you?" he asked her.

"I just have to pass your class," she said, "but I am really having a hard time. I will do anything, if you will pass me."

"Anything?" asked the professor. "You will do anything to pass my class?"

"Oh yes," she replied. "Use your imagination. I am willing to do anything you want, one time, if you will give me a passing grade."

Then, as she began to undress, the professor stopped her.

"Are you sure you mean this? You will do anything one time, if I pass you in my class?" he asked her.

"Yes, I said that. Now just tell me what you want me to do."

To that, he responded with one word: "Study!"

The Bible says we will face final exams one day. It is called the Great White Throne Judgment. But if you want to pass the exam then, you need to prepare now.

"Study to show yourself approved, a workman who does not need to be ashamed."

2 Timothy 2:15

February 2

You Choose the Ending

Not long ago, Beth and I watched a television show in which viewers were allowed to phone in their vote to determine how that episode would end. And that's how it is in life. We don't get to choose how we start, but we do get to choose how we end.

The ending didn't go well for these famous people: Ernest Hemingway, Marilyn Monroe, Jimi Hendrix, Janis Joplin, Kurt Cobain, River Phoenix, Heath Ledger, and Amy Winehouse. They all took their own lives.

They missed the truth that helped British preacher John Wesley soar through life, and then enjoy a great landing. Wesley lived from 1703 to 1791. He travelled 250,000 miles by horseback and preached 40,000 sermons. As he lay on his deathbed, he gathered his family around him and summoned the strength to speak his last words.

He sat up for his last 60 seconds of life and said, "Best of all, God is with us. Best of all, God is with us."

And then he died.

You didn't choose your journey's beginning, but you can choose how it ends. And you don't have to walk it alone.

Trust the words of a dying saint. "Best of all, God is with us."

"You were shown these things so that you might know that the Lord is God; besides him there is no other."

Deuteronomy 4:35

February 3

Deep in the Woods

An old man and his wife lived in the back woods. One day a peddler came by while the man was home alone.

He said, "My wife's gone to the crick to wash our clothes. She'll be back after a spell. Show me what you got."

The salesman offered some pots and pans, but the old man wasn't interested. Then, spotting a mirror, the old codger asked, "What's that?"

Before the peddler could say it was a mirror, he picked it up and looked into it.

He said, "My word! That's a picture of my Pappy," looking at his own image for the first time.

The man gladly paid full price for it, and the peddler went on his way.

He loved the "picture" so much, but didn't think his wife would approve of the purchase, so he hid the mirror in the barn, and would go out there to look at his "Pappy" every day, in secret.

One day, his wife got suspicious. She followed him to the barn, and yanked the mirror from his grasp. Seeing her image for the first time, she said, "Is this the old lady you've been foolin' around with?"

This old couple was a lot like us. We have a hard time seeing ourselves as we really are. That is where God's word comes in. It is our mirror. We look at it, find our flaws, then ask God to help us correct them.

"Anyone who listens to the word but does not do what it says is like a man who looks at his face in a mirror and, after looking at himself, goes away and immediately forgets what he looks like."

James 1:23-24

February 4

Semper Fi

The most tragic event during the Reagan presidency happened on a Sunday morning when terrorists attacked the Marine barracks in Beirut. Hundreds of soldiers were killed in their sleep.

A few days later, Marine Corp Commander Paul Kelly visited some of the wounded survivors in a Frankfurt, Germany hospital. Among them was Corporal Jeffrey Lee Nashton, with tubes running out of his body. As Kelly approached him, Nashton, struggling to move and racked with pain, motioned for a piece of paper and a pen. He wrote a brief note and passed it back to the Commander.

On the slip of paper were written only two words: "Semper Fi," the Latin motto of the Marines. It means "forever faithful."

With those two words, Nashton spoke for millions of Americans. Despite severe sacrifice, risking it all, he was "forever faithful."

There is no such thing as a former marine. So why don't you go thank a veteran today. The best way to thank them is to be like them, toward your husband, your wife, your church, and your God.

Two words say it all. Say it with me: "Forever faithful." Semper Fi.

"It will be good for that servant whose master finds him doing his work when he returns."

Matthew 24:46

February 5

Puddles

It was the most embarrassing moment any child can face. A little boy was suddenly aware of the puddle between his feet and that the front of his pants was all wet. How could it have happened? Embarrassed beyond measure, he wanted to die. The boys would never let him forget it, and the girls would never speak to him again.

"Please, God," he prayed, "I'm in big trouble here. I need help now!"

Suddenly, a classmate named Susie lost her grip on the goldfish bowl she was carrying. It tipped over, right in the boy's lap.

"Thank you, God," he silently prayed.

The boy pretended to be angry with Susie, and she became the center of classroom scorn. He rushed to the office for a pair of dry gym shorts.

After school, the two children were waiting for the bus. Susie was standing off by herself, but he went up to her and whispered, "You did that on purpose, didn't you?"

Susie whispered back, "Yeah, I wet my pants once, too."

Here is what the girl had come to understand. Comfort is not about arguing the facts. It is about acknowledging the feeling. If you know someone in need, remember, life is 80 percent just showing up. Whenever something great is done by God's people, it happens because someone is always there to help clean up the puddles.

"Then Zerubbabel son of Shealtiel and Jeshua son of Jozadak set to work to rebuild the house of God in Jerusalem. And the prophets of God were with them, helping them."

Ezra 5:2

February 6

Waterloo

This is how the message of victory at Waterloo arrived in England. They knew that Wellington was facing Napoleon in an epic battle. A ship signaled the news of the battle to the man on top of Winchester Cathedral. He then signaled to another man on a hill, and the news was relayed like this, from station to station until all England had received the news.

The first signal from the ship contained the word "Wellington."

Moments later, they signaled "Defeated."

Then the fog rolled in and the ship could no longer be seen. So the message that went across England was "Wellington defeated." Gloom swept the countryside.

But two hours later, the fog lifted. Then the full message could be seen: "Wellington defeated the enemy."

At that, all England rejoiced. In like manner, the message after the cross was this: "Christ defeated."

But three days later, the fog lifted. And the message has resonated ever since: "Christ defeated the enemy."

There once was a time in my life when I lived as though I was on the losing team. Then the fog lifted. And now I know who won the victory. The enemy is defeated.

"Give glory to him who is able to keep you from falling and to present you before his glorious presence without fault and with joy."

Jude 24

February 7

Just As I Am

Charlotte Elliott, of Brighton, England, was an embittered woman. Her disability had hardened her.

"If God loved me," she muttered, "he would not have treated me this way."

Hoping to help her, a Swiss minister named Dr. Cesar Malan visited the Elliotts on May 9, 1822. Charlotte went into a violent outburst.

Dr. Malan asked her, "You are tired of yourself, aren't you? You have become sour and bitter."

"What is your cure?" asked Charlotte.

"The faith you are trying to despise," he said.

Charlotte began to soften. "If I wanted to become a Christian and to share the peace you possess, what would I do?"

"Give yourself to God just as you are now," said the pastor.

"Are you saying I can come to God just as I am?"

"Yes, just as you are."

And so she did. Several years later, Charlotte wrote a poem, describing what had happened. She wrote, "Just as I am, without one plea, but that thy blood was shed for me, and that thou bidd'st me come to thee, O Lamb of God, I come! I come!"

And that has become a favorite hymn to millions. That is God's message for you today. "Come," God pleas, "just as you are."

"Come to me, all you who are weary and burdened, and I will give you rest."

Matthew 11:28

February 8

Getting Rid of Daddy

The family talked Mother into getting a hamster as long as they took care of it. They named their new pet "Danny." Two months later, when Mother was caring for Danny the hamster, she made some phone calls and found a new home for him. She broke the news to the children, and they took it quite well, but they did offer some comments.

One of the children remarked, "He's been around here a long time. We'll miss him."

Mom said, "Yes, but he's too much work for one person, and since I'm that one person, I say he goes."

Another child offered, "Well, maybe if he wouldn't eat so much and wouldn't be so messy, we could keep him."

But Mom remained firm. "It's time to take Danny to his new home now," she insisted "Go and get his cage."

With one voice the children shouted, "Danny? We thought you said 'Daddy'!"

Now they were really upset! It was bad enough to give away Daddy, but they couldn't imagine losing Danny. And that is the life of being a "Daddy." The kids love you, and they prefer to keep you around. But you may never receive the adoration of the hamster.

"He will turn the hearts of the fathers to their children, and hearts of the children to their fathers."

Malachi 4:6

February 9

Successful Failures

If you have never failed, you have not lived. Benjamin Williams said, "To live is to fail."

Actually, I said that. There is no Benjamin Williams. But it always sounds better to quote someone else. Forgive me. That was a failure on my part.

There's that word again: "failure." Do you know any successful failures? Let's consider a few. Paderewski, the great pianist, was told his hands were too small to play, by his music teacher. Henry Ford forgot to put a reverse gear in his first car. In 1902, the editor of The Atlantic Journal rejected every poem submitted by a 28-year-old aspiring poet named Robert Frost.

In 1905, the University of Bern turned down a Ph.D. dissertation as being irrelevant. Its author was Albert Einstein. A teacher at Harrow School in England told Winston Churchill he'd never amount to anything. Thomas Edison once spent $2 million on an invention that flopped.

That's just a few examples. I failed to mention my seventh grade teacher who said I'd never make an "A."

I failed to mention a lot of things. Because I fail a lot. I hope you do, too. Otherwise, you'll never succeed. It's not about being great. It's about not giving up.

"Diligent hands will rule, but
laziness ends in slave labor."

Proverbs 12:24

February 10

Advice from Charlie Brown

Lucy says to Charlie Brown, "You know what I don't understand? I don't understand love!"

He says, "Who does?"

She says, "Explain love to me, Charlie Brown."

He says, "You can't explain love. I can recommend a book or a poem or a painting, but I can't explain love."

She says, "Well, try, Charlie Brown, try."

Charlie says, "Well, let's say I see this beautiful, cute little girl walk by."

Lucy interrupts, "Why does she have to be cute? Huh? Why can't someone fall in love with someone with freckles and a big nose? Explain that!"

Charlie: "Well, maybe you are right. Let's just say I see this girl walk by with this great big nose."

Lucy: "I didn't say GREAT BIG NOSE!"

Charlie: "You not only can't explain love, you can't even talk about it."

Let's talk about it. The ancient Greeks had three words for love, meaning sensual love, friendship love, and sacrificial love. God has one word for love: the sacrificial kind. The most famous verse in the Bible begins, "God so loved." God loves with a sacrificial love that cost him his son. He loves us all, including those of us with a big nose.

"For God so loved the world that he gave his one and only Son, that whoever believes in him shall not perish but have eternal life."

John 3:16

February 11

Manipulation

Five-year-old Susie asked her dad for a Twinkie.

He responded, "No, darling. Supper will be in ten minutes."

Susie stomped here feet. She cried in agony. She begged for the Twinkie, as she said she would starve without one. Dad said "no" several times, and each time, Susie pouted just a little bit louder.

Dad decided to use psychology. He picked up his girl and asked her, "If I don't give you your Twinkie, you will still be my sweet precious love and my little angel, won't you?"

Susie responded, "I ain't gonna be your nothin' if you don't give me a Twinkie!"

It is scary how much most of us are like little Susie. We say we love God. We wear our Christian cross, our Christian shirt, and our Christian bumper sticker. We listen to our Christian music and love our Christian church. We wouldn't think of denying our heavenly Father. Sure, Peter did, but we will never deny him.

And then, one day, God decides to not give us our Twinkie. He recognizes that our version of a Twinkie isn't good for us. And just like that, we stomp and pout. We love God, but we only follow him if he is giving us a Twinkie.

"Four things on earth are small, yet they are extremely wise. Ants are of little strength, yet they store up food for the summer."

Proverbs 30:24

February 12

Staying Warm

In the sheep country of New Mexico, shepherds were losing lots of lambs in the winter time. The problem was, the ewes were taking their lambs out to graze late in the day, and when it started to snow, the temperatures would drop below freezing. But the ewes were unaware of the danger to the young lambs and would continue to graze, and many of the lambs froze to death.

The shepherds came to realize the problem. The ewes were unaware of the danger because they were covered in such thick wool that they didn't feel the drop in temperature. The shepherds came up with a unique solution. They sheared the top of the ewes' heads. That way, when the temperature would drop, the ewes felt it and headed back to the barn, with their lambs following behind.

The first step in helping others is to feel what they are feeling. There is an old adage that says, "People don't care how much you know until they know how much you care."

The key to changing your world is simple. It's all about feeling what others feel. That is what gets sheep to the barn and people to the shepherd.

"Be kind and compassionate to one another, forgiving one another, just as in Christ God forgave you."

Ephesians 4:32

February 13

The Previous Pastor

The new pastor wasn't at all like the former pastor. He didn't care to do the repairs and mowing around the church and parsonage. He hired someone to do these chores. The additional cost concerned the church elders. One of them approached the new pastor and addressed this issue.

"Our previous pastor mowed the lawn himself. Have you considered this approach?"

The new pastor responded, "Yes, I'm aware of this. And I asked him. But he doesn't want to do it anymore!"

Here's where we get into trouble. We do things God intended someone else to do. That leads to misery every time. You need to figure out what you are especially good at and called to do.

Find your personal SHAPE. Let me help.

S = Spiritual gifts. What are the gifts God has uniquely given you?

H = Heart. Where is your passion?

A = Abilities. What are you naturally good at doing?

P = Personality. Are you outgoing or introverted?

E = Experiences. What have you done in the past?

Do what only you can do. Let others do the other stuff. If you are like me, this isn't so hard, because I'm not good at too many things.

"The body is a unit, though it is made up of many parts; and though all its parts are many, they form one body."

1 Corinthians 12:12

February 14

Unsticky Stamps

The leader of a small country was disappointed that nobody used the postage stamps bearing his image. The postmaster explained that the stamps were not sticking. Seizing a stamp, the dictator licked it and stuck it onto an envelope.

"Look!" he shouted. "It sticks perfectly!"

The postmaster then explained, "Well, sir, the truth is that the stamps would work, but the people keep spitting on the wrong side!"

You can identify the leader in any crowd. He's the one with an arrow in his back. Critics abound everywhere, even in church. But they sit so far back, by the time they hear anything it's already a rumor. They weren't born again; they were born against.

Sometimes I feel like the guy who said to an acquaintance, "I wish I had two more critics just like you."

"Why?" asked his critic.

"Because I have ten. I wish I had just two."

One day, Winston Churchill received a standing ovation. That night he told a friend, "That was nice, but if it had been my hanging, we would have doubled the crowd."

If you have critics, you're in good company. The most persecuted man in the world was the Son of God.

> *"Love your enemies and pray for those who persecute you, that you may be sons of your Father in heaven."*

Matthew 5:45

February 15

Forgiveness

Two little brothers, Harry and Jimmy, had finished supper and were playing until bedtime. Somehow, Harry hit Jimmy with a stick, and tears and bitter words followed. Charges and accusations were still being exchanged as Mother prepared them for bed.

She said, "Now, Jimmy, before you go to bed you're going to have to forgive your brother."

Jimmy was thoughtful, and then replied, "Well, okay, I'll forgive him tonight, but if I don't die before I wake up, he'd better look out in the morning."

Martin Luther's colleague, Philip Melanchthon, vexed his more ebullient friend by his quiet and virtuous ways. "For goodness' sake, why don't you go and sin a little?" cried Luther in exasperation. "Doesn't God deserve to have something to forgive you for?"

I love what Philip Yancey says about the Sermon on the Mount. "God has set the bar so high no one can get over it, and has set grace so low that no one is too low for it."

Indeed, God has much to forgive you for. But he still likes to hear it from you. And rejoice that God doesn't forgive like little Jimmy did. What God forgives, he forgets.

"Do not gloat when your enemy falls; when he stumbles, do not let your heart rejoice."

Proverbs 24:17

February 16

A Few Good Men

One of the great movies of recent years was *A Few Good Men*. Jack Nicholson played the role of Colonel Nathan R. Jessup. In a courtroom scene, he bellowed to Tom Cruise, "You can't handle the truth!"

The same could be said to the modern church. You want the truth? I'm afraid most of us can't handle the truth. But here it is. Forty-six percent of people in their twenties say Christians get on their nerves. And only five percent of them are drawn to a church that bears a denominational name.

But most churches fall into one of two categories. We are a "checkmark church," where we check off "I went to church today." Or we are a "clown church," driven by entertainment. And as a result, the church is losing ground.

We are like the Black Plague. In 1664, only a few cases were reported. By 1665, 590 died. And within a few years, 100 million were dead. Disease is like decay. It happens slowly.

The modern church must awaken to today's reality. The world is hungry for Jesus. It's not Jesus they don't like; it's the church. The way most of us are "doing church" isn't working anymore. Does that make you angry? I told you, "You can't handle the truth!"

"Then you will know the truth, and the truth will set you free."

John 8:32

February 17

Know Fear

James Smith wrote, "Strange fears possess the souls of many."

Even some great men have not been free from them. Dr. Samuel Johnson, with all his philosophy, was very careful not to enter a room with his left foot. If by any chance he did so, he would immediately step back and re-enter with his right foot. He was terribly afraid of death, too, and would not suffer it to be mentioned in his presence.

Julius Caesar, to whom the shouts of thousands of the enemy were but sweet music, was mortally afraid of the sound of thunder and always wanted to be underground to escape the dreadful noise.

When crossing a bridge, Peter the Great would cry out with fear.

Martin Luther said, "The Lord allows us to have fear so he can bring us comfort. The devil, on the other hand, attacks our comfort so we might have fear."

Do you know fear? I love the old proverb: "Fear knocked on the door. Faith answered, and there was no one there."

Face your fears with faith. But it must be faith in God. Do that, and you can do what Peter the Great couldn't do. You can cross life's bridges with confidence.

"The Lord is my rock, my fortress and my deliverer; my God is my rock, in whom I take refuge. He is my shield and the horn of my salvation."

Psalm 18:2

February 18

Honesty

There was an elderly lady who said to a little girl, "How do you do, my dear?"

The girl replied, "Quite well, thank you."

After a long pause the woman asked, "Why don't you ask me how I am doing?"

The child paused and then said calmly, "Because I don't care how you're doing."

There is another story about two women who were riding together on a bus. One of them suddenly realized that she had not paid the fare. "I will go right up to the driver and pay it now," she said.

Her companion replied, "Why bother? You got away with not paying. So why pay now, if you don't have to?"

The first woman said, "I have found that honesty always pays. It is a virtue. I couldn't live with myself if I did not pay the fare." At that, she went up to the front of the bus to pay the driver.

When she returned, she said to her new friend, "See, I told you honesty pays! I handed the driver a quarter, and he gave me 50 cents in change!"

Sometimes it is inconvenient to be honest. But it is always right. I don't ever remember telling a lie, and looking back on it as a good idea. Be a truth teller. God will bless you for that. Honestly!

"Above all else, guard your heart, for it is the wellspring of life."

Proverbs 4:23

February 19

Clowns

Joseph Grimaldi lived from 1778 to 1837. He is still recognized as history's greatest clown. Grimaldi was exclusively a theatrical clown, and is considered the "Father of Modern Clowning" because he is the entertainer who elevated the whiteface clown to a starring role. He performed for the King of England, among others, and literally made the whole world laugh. Thousands would travel great distances to see him, just to get a laugh and forget the problems of life.

Grimaldi was so good and so famous that a doctor once gave an unusual prescription to one of his patients, who complained of great depression. The doctor told him to go to the Music Hall that Friday night and see the great Grimaldi perform. "That will be your best medicine for depression," said the physician.

"There is one problem with that," said the patient. "You see, I am Grimaldi."

Behind every mask is a real person. We only let people see what we want them too see. You probably know someone like Grimaldi. On the outside, they appear happy. But on the inside, there is a God-shaped emptiness that only God can fill.

> *"But he said to me, 'My grace is sufficient for you, for my power is made perfect in weakness.' Therefore, I will boast all the more gladly about my weaknesses."*

2 Corinthians 12:9

February 20

I'm Trying My Best!

There once lived a man who was trying his best. But his best was never good enough. Those around him had their own opinions of what his life was supposed to look like. They had their opinions on how he was to live, speak, drive, text, tweet, laugh, cough, sneeze, run, smile, shave, dress, sing, think, act, sleep, shop, jump, snore, listen, work, organize, play, lead, read, walk, and talk. And just as he pleased one group, another was upset.

So he tried to please that group, but offended the first group. He worked harder, tried harder, and prayed harder. But while it was enough for God, it was never enough for some of them. So one night he screamed, "I'm trying my best!"

Then a stranger came to town. The man who was trying his best became friends with the stranger. The stranger accepted him as he was. He didn't care how he lived, spoke, drove, texted, tweeted, laughed, coughed, sneezed, ran, smiled, shaved, dressed, sang, thought, acted, slept, shopped, jumped, snored, listened, worked, organized, played, led, read, walked, or talked. He was loved and accepted by God. And that made him good enough.

"Do not judge, or you too will be judged."

Matthew 7:1

February 21

Who Killed the Cat?

Stephen Pile has written a book titled *The Book of Failures*. It's got unbelievable stuff in it. For example, back in 1979, during the fireman's strike in England, one of the greatest animal rescue attempts was made. Valiantly, the British Army had taken over emergency firefighting. On January 14, they were called out by an elderly lady in South London, to rescue her cat. They arrived with impressive haste. Then they proceeded to cleverly and carefully rescue the lady's cat. Then they started to drive away. But the lady was so grateful that she invited the squad of heroes in for tea. After their time with the appreciative woman, they bid farewell. Off they drove, waving to the lady. And in the process, they ran over her cat and killed it.

Now, this is either a sad story or a happy one, depending on your view of cats. But don't miss the point. We can go to a lot of trouble doing everything right, and we should. But one mistake can be deadly.

Think of the ones you love the most. Then be reminded daily, that in one moment, by one bad choice, you can destroy the very lives you have spent years building up.

> *"But Lot's wife looked back, and she became a pillar of salt."*

Genesis 19:26

February 22

Life's a Gamble

A pastor felt sorry for the old man in the park. So one day, he handed him an envelope with $10 in it, and a simple message: "Never Despair."

The next day, the old man handed the pastor an envelope with $60 in it.

"What is this for?" asked the pastor.

"I bet the $10 at the horse race on Never Despair, just like you told me. You won. Here's your money."

I heard about a guy who tried to sell a raffle ticket to his buddy. "We're having a raffle for a nice young lady who is down on her luck. Would you like to buy a ticket?"

"No," replied his friend. "Even if I won, my wife wouldn't let me keep her."

Life is a gamble. A young couple went to Las Vegas on their honeymoon. They gambled $100 in the casino, and lost $98. That night, the man went out on his own, to see what he could do with the remaining $2. He won big, and increased it to $1,000. Then he turned the $1,000 into $40,000. But then, sadly, he bet the whole thing on "black" at the roulette table and lost.

He went back to his room. His wife asked how he had done. He said, "I lost the $2." Yes, life is a gamble. Unless you bet on God, in which case you will always win. You may think you can achieve joy and peace on your own, apart from God. But if I were you, I wouldn't bet on it.

"Trust in the Lord with all your heart and lean not on your own understanding."

Proverbs 3:5

February 23

The Rabbi's Wisdom

A troubled man went to see a wise Rabbi.

"Rabbi," he said, wringing his hands, "I am a failure. More than half the time I do not succeed in doing what I must do."

"Oh?" said the Rabbi.

"Please say something wise, Rabbi."

After much pondering, the Rabbi spoke as follows: "Ah, my son, I give you this wisdom. Go and look on page 930 of the *New York Times Almanac* for the year 1970, and you will find the peace you are looking for."

This is what the man found on page 930. It was a story about Ty Cobb, arguably the greatest hitter in the history of baseball, with a career batting average of .367. The story emphasized that, though Cobb had the highest career batting average of any player in history, he made an out nearly two-thirds of the time.

The man returned to the Rabbi, filled with wisdom and thanksgiving. "Thank you, Rabbi," he said. "I see your point. Though I don't always succeed, I succeed some of the time. I will take heart, and rejoice in my successes, rather than dwelling on my failures." The next time you step into the batter's box and take a swing at life, remember Ty Cobb. And remember the wisdom of the Rabbi.

> *"If we claim we have not sinned, we make him out to be a liar and his word is not in us."*

1 John 1:10

February 24

Trust Him Anyway

Helen Roseveare, British missionary in Conga, survived the uprising that resulted from the invasion of the Mau-Mau revolutionaries. This godly, gracious lady was raped, assaulted, and humiliated. But she never abandoned her faith.

While recovering from the horrible attack, Helen and the Lord grew closer together than they had ever been. She wrote a statement in the form of a question that every person needs to ask himself, from God's perspective. "Can you thank me for trusting you with this experience, even if I never tell you why?"

Golfer Bernhard Langer had one putt that would decide the Ryder Cup winner, between Europe and the United States. He missed the putt. But he told a reporter afterwards, "If I had made that putt, it wouldn't have made God love me more. And by missing it, it didn't make God love me less."

God's love is perfect, whether our shots go in or not. It's one thing to trust him when you miss a putt. But when you go through a truly horrific experience, listen to God's voice. "Can you thank me for trusting you with this experience, even if I never tell you why?"

"Samuel asked, 'What have you done?' Saul replied, 'When I saw that the men were scattering, and that you did not come at the set time, I felt compelled to offer you a burnt offering.'"

1 Samuel 13:11

February 25

Little Engine that Could

A man went to a fortune teller to hear about his future. She looked into a crystal ball and said, "You will be poor and unhappy until you are 45 years old."

"Then what will happen?" asked the man hopefully.

"Then you'll get used to it."

In their book, *The Answer*, businessmen-authors John Assaraf and Murray Smith talk about the negative messages children receive growing up. They write, "By the time you're 17 years old, you've heard 'No you can't' an average of 150,000 times. You've heard 'Yes you can' about 5,000 times. That's thirty 'no's for every 'yes.' That makes for a powerful belief of 'I can't.'"

When I was a child, one of my favorite stories was *The Little Engine that Could*. Why? Because I found it so encouraging! I used to read it over and over, and think, "That's me! I can do that too!"

If you aren't where you want to be in life, you have two choices. You can be like the 45-year-old man who opted to just get used to his plight. Or you can be like the little engine that could. Let God fuel your tank. If the little engine could do it, so can you!

"You have too many men. I cannot deliver Midian into their hands, or Israel would boast against me."

Judges 7:2

February 26

Heaven and Hell

This is a condensed version of an old story. A man wanted to see the difference between heaven and hell. The angel took him to hell first. There, he saw a large pot of delicious stew in the middle of a room. Around the pot were hungry people, each with a spoon. But each spoon was longer than their arms. So, they were able to dip their spoons into the stew, but unable to bring it up to their mouths. For eternity, they would see the stew, smell the stew, and desire the stew. But they would not be able to enjoy the stew.

The scene in heaven was surprisingly similar. Again, there was a large pot of delicious stew. And again, the people had long spoons. But they were well fed. What was the difference? They had learned servanthood.

Each person would dip his spoon into the pot, and then feed someone else. By serving others, they were feeding themselves. That's how it works in life. You can spend your time only caring for yourself. But you will die from spiritual malnutrition.

It was only after the 12 disciples fed the 5,000 that they received baskets full of food for themselves. The choice is yours. Serve or starve.

"The Son of Man has not come to be served, but to serve, and to give his life as a ransom for many."

Mark 10:45

February 27

Perspective

One day, Linus found Charlie Brown to tell him about the greatest football game ever played. He told Charlie about an amazing comeback. With the score 6-0 and three seconds left on the clock, the home team had the ball. They were on their own one-yard-line. The quarterback called the play, and then he took the snap. He broke three tackles in his own end zone. Then he made the perfect pass to his wide receiver, going over the middle. The receiver broke seven tackles and ran all the way for a touchdown. The extra point was good. The home team won, 7-6.

Linus described the game with great celebration. He concluded, "You should have been there, Charlie Brown! It was fantastic!"

To that, Charlie Brown responded, "How did the other team feel?"

When we go to the church, we park in the same old spot, sit in the same old pew in the same old building next to the same old people, as we sing the same old songs. But do we ever stop to ask ourselves, as the "home team," how the other team feels?

This Sunday, follow the advice of Charlie Brown. Think about the visiting team (guests) first.

"Accept the one who is weak, without quarreling over disputable matters."

Romans 14:1

February 28

Direction

Pastor Clifford Stewart, of Louisville, Kentucky, sent his parents a microwave oven for Christmas one year. This is how he recalls the event. "They were excited to join the instant generation. When my dad unpacked the microwave and plugged it in, within seconds it transformed my parents' smiles into frowns! Even after reading the directions, they couldn't make it work.

Two days later, my mom was playing bridge with a friend and confessed her inability to even get the microwave to boil water. Her friend asked her, 'What is the problem?'

My mom responded, 'The problem is, my son knows how to work it. What I need is for my son to come along with the microwave.'"

When God gave us the gift of salvation, he didn't send a complicated booklet to give us directions to figure things out. He sent his Son. Life is complicated. We have the Bible as our manual. But even that is not enough, because until you know the Author, it is difficult to understand his Book. But God left nothing to chance. For your salvation, there is no assembly required, for one simple reason. God has given us his Son.

"They asked each other, 'Were not our hearts burning within us while he talked with us on the road and when he opened the Scriptures to us?'"

Luke 24:32

March 1

Death of Payne Stewart

The 1999 crash of golfer Payne Stewart's plane was a bizarre incident. He and five companions boarded a twin-engine, $2.4 million Learjet, which left the runway at 9:19 a.m. There were two pilots, and all seemed fine when they checked in with air traffic controllers. But the pilots lost consciousness shortly before they were to turn west toward Dallas, and when they couldn't be raised by air traffic controllers, two Air Force jets went aloft to investigate.

No one was at the controls. There was no movement in the cockpit, and the windows were fogged, suggesting that the cabin had depressurized and become chilled with stratospheric air some 45,000 feet above the earth.

One of the Air Force pilots said, "It was a very helpless feeling to pull alongside that aircraft and realize there was nothing we could do."

Picture humanity on a runaway airplane, on a collision course, with only moments remaining. Yet people are so caught up in their pleasures and pressures and pursuits that they don't realize the urgency of their plight. They are about to crash, all because the great Pilot is not at the controls.

"You diligently study the Scriptures because you think that by them you possess eternal life."

John 5:39

March 2

First in Line

President Woodrow Wilson was known for his great sense of humor. In those days, you could call the White House with some chance of actually speaking to the President. One night, at 3:00 a.m., a New Jersey man telephoned the White House. He asked to speak to the President on a matter of national importance. The White house operator woke Wilson, and he took the man's call.

The caller said, "The collector of customs here in New Jersey has died."

Mr. Wilson replied, "I am very sorry to hear that, but why are you calling to tell me that at 3:00 in the morning?"

The fellow replied, "Because I want to replace him."

President Wilson responded, "Well, if the undertaker has no objection, neither do I."

There is one thing worse than losing a friend or family member to death. That is losing them to eternal death. The Bible says, "It is appointed to man once to die, and then the judgment."

There are no do-overs. You cannot take their place. Someone already did that 2,000 years ago. But we must accept that gift before we see the undertaker. Sorry, but after that, it is simply too late.

"Abraham believed the Lord, and he credited it to him as righteousness."

Genesis 15:6

March 3

Galileo

There are few more tragic records of the struggle of the human mind and spirit against bigotry than this text of Galileo's recantation before the Holy Inquisition. "Because I have been enjoined by this Holy Office to abandon the false opinion which maintains that the sun is the center and immovable, and forbidden to hold, defend, or teach the said false doctrine in any manner, and after it had been signified to me that the said doctrine is repugnant with the Holy Scripture, I abjure, curse, and detest the said heresies and errors. And I swear that I will never more in future say or assert anything verbally, or in writing, which may give rise to similar suspicion of me."

The problem, of course, was that Galileo had proclaimed that the sun was the center of the solar system, rather than the earth. The words above were written in the 1630s, and are therefore difficult to follow.

Galileo was brilliant. Not just anybody could invent the telescope. And the world was fine with Galileo, right up until the day when he suggested man was not the center of the universe. We've been struggling with that ever since.

"He sits enthroned above the circle of the earth, and its people are like grasshoppers."

Isaiah 40:22

March 4

Smart Kids

We can learn so much from children. There was a little girl who was discussing that day's Sunday School lesson with her mom. She said that they had talked about Jesus going to heaven, where he was now sitting beside God. Then her mom commented on the beautiful rainbows God has drawn across the sky.

The girl said, "Yes, mom, and just think! God did that with just his left hand!"

"Just his left hand?" her mother asked. "Why wouldn't God use both hands?"

"Because, we learned today that Jesus went to heaven and sat on the right hand of God."

While that's a cute story, here's a really good lesson from children. It happened in 1964. A first-grader went on her first day to a newly integrated school. Her anxious mother welcomed her home at the end of the day.

"How did it go?" she asked.

"Oh, Mother, it was wonderful! A little black girl sat next to me!"

Expecting trauma, the mother asked, "And how did that go?"

Her girl replied, "We were so scared that we held hands all day."

Now, that's a great lesson! Find someone who is different from you in some way. Then, don't judge them. Hold their hand.

"So in Christ we who are many form one body, and each member belongs to all the others."

Romans 12:5

March 5

The Family Parrot

Here's some great advice I read somewhere. Live in such a way that you wouldn't be ashamed to sell the family parrot to the town gossip. Little Johnny was struggling to live his life in such a way. His report card included a notation from his teacher, which said he was very adept in the "creative use of visual aids for learning."

Johnny's father called the teacher and asked, "What does that mean, the creative use of visual aids?"

The teacher responded, "That means Johnny copies from the kid in the next seat!"

In Woody Allen's movie, *Annie Hall*, Woody has his protagonist say, "I was thrown out of New York University for cheating on a metaphysics test. The professor caught me looking deeply into the soul of the student seated next to me."

Studies show that students continue to cheat at an alarming pace. But, of course, they were taught by the best, their parents.

Here's my advice to you, mom and dad. If you don't want to read about your kid's "creative use of visual aids," set the example yourself. Live in such a way that you wouldn't be ashamed to sell the family parrot to the town gossip.

"The man of integrity walks securely, but he who takes crooked paths will be found out."

Proverbs 10:9

March 6

John Quincy Adams

In his extreme old age, John Quincy Adams was slowly and feebly walking down a street in Boston. An old friend accosted him, and while shaking his trembling hand, asked, "And how is John Quincy Adams today?"

"Thank you," said the ex-President. "John Quincy Adams is well, quite well, I thank you. But the house in which he lives at present is becoming quite dilapidated. It is tottering upon its foundations. Time and the seasons have nearly destroyed it. Its roof is pretty well worn out. Its walls are much shattered, and it trembles with every wind. The old tenement is becoming almost uninhabitable, and I think John Quincy Adams will have to move out of it soon. But he himself is quite well, quite well."

I love Revelation 22 because it tells me what heaven will look like. But I also like Revelation 21, because it tells me what heaven will be like. I especially like the "not to be" part. It says there will not be any death, tears, pain, or sorrow there.

The "house" you live in will wear out. But that is not a bad thing. It just means there is coming a day when you will upgrade to a better neighborhood.

"After this I looked, and there before me was a door standing open in heaven. And the voice I had first heard speaking to me like a trumpet said, 'Come up here, and I will show you what must take place.'"

Revelation 4:1

March 7

The Lord's Prayer

Harry Cohn, head of Columbia Movie Studios, tells the following story. In the early days, Harry's brother came out from New York and was criticizing the way Harry did things. They got into a heated argument one day.

Harry said, "I bet you don't even know the Lord's Prayer."

His brother replied, "What's that got to do with anything?"

Harry said, "I just bet you don't know the Lord's Prayer."

His brother responded, "Of course I do. It goes like this: 'Now I lay me down to sleep, I pray the Lord my soul to keep. If I should die before I wake, I pray the Lord my soul to take.'"

To that Harry replied, "Wow! My apology! I really didn't think you knew it!"

Do you know The Lord's Prayer? How does it start? If you said, "Our Father, who art in heaven," you would actually be wrong! The correct answer is, "Father, the time has come. Glorify your son."

You see, the "Father who art in heaven" prayer was our model prayer. But to hear Jesus' actual prayer, The Lord's Prayer, turn to John 17. You will never know a man better than when you hear him pray. Read John 17 today. Listen to Jesus pray.

"Jesus looked toward heaven and prayed, 'Father, the time has come. Glorify your son that your son may glorify you.'"

John 17:1

March 8

A Matter of Perspective

Sugar Ray Leonard was one of the greats of boxing. He was asked to speak to the intellectual crowd of Harvard.

"I consider myself blessed. I consider you blessed. We've all been blessed with God-given talents. Some of you have the talent to create rockets that will inhabit the universe. Others can cure disease. My God-given talent happens to be beating people up."

That's an interesting perspective.

Agatha Christie once offered this perspective on marriage. "An archaeologist is the best husband a wife can have. The older she gets, the more interesting she will be to him."

The great Picasso once asked his friend Rodin if he liked Picasso's latest painting that was yet unsigned. Rodin studied the painting from all directions and, only after careful deliberation answered Picasso. "Whatever else you do, sign it. If you do that, we will know which way to hold it."

God has signed his handiwork with a sunrise, a rainbow, a gentle breeze. But until you recognize the hand of God, you will never know which way is up.

The Old Testament tells us of a man named Ahithophel, who killed himself simply because he never discovered the right perspective. Only a close walk with the Creator can give you the perspective you really need.

"When Ahithophel saw that his advice had not been followed, he saddled his donkey and set out for his house in his hometown. He put his house in order and then hanged himself. So he died and was buried in his father's tomb."

2 Samuel 17:23

March 9

How to Preach

One day, St. Francis of Assisi said to one of the young monks at the Portiuncula, "Let us go down to the town and preach!"

The novice, delighted at being singled out to be the companion of Francis, obeyed with excitement. They passed through the principal streets, turned down many of the byways and alleys, made their way into the suburbs, and at great length returned by a circuitous route to the monastery gate.

As they approached it, the younger man reminded Francis of his original intention. "You have forgotten, Father, that we went to the town to preach!"

"My son," Francis replied, "we have preached. We were preaching while we were walking. We have been seen by many; our behavior has been closely watched; it was thus that we preached our morning sermon. It is of no use, my son, to walk anywhere to preach unless we preach everywhere as we walk."

The unknown writer said it well. "I'd rather see a sermon that hear one any day. I'd rather one would walk with me than merely show the way."

Your job is to preach every day. And on a few occasions, this may even involve words.

"In the same way, let your light shine before men, that they may see your good deeds and praise your Father in heaven."

Matthew 5:16

March 10

Banks

A farmer who had experienced several bad years went to see the manager of his bank. "I've got some good news and some bad news to tell you. Which would you like to hear first?" asked the farmer.

"Why don't you tell me the bad news first, and get it over with?" the banker replied.

"Okay. With the bad drought and inflation and all, I won't be able to pay anything on my mortgage this year, either on the principal or the interest."

"Well, that is pretty bad."

"It gets worse," continued the farmer. "I also won't be able to pay anything on the loan you gave me for all that great machinery I bought."

"Wow, is that ever bad!" said the banker.

"It's worse that than. You remember I also borrowed to buy seed and fertilizer and other supplies? Well, I can't pay anything on those things, either."

The banker said, "That's enough! Tell me what the good news is."

"The good news," replied the farmer, "is that I intend to keep on doing business with you."

You and I have the greatest Banker in the universe. Despite our defaults and faults, debts and moral bankruptcies, he still does business with us."

"Jesus Christ is the faithful witness, the firstborn of the dead, and the ruler of the kings of the earth."

Revelation 1:5

March 11

Tired of You

A golden anniversary party was thrown for an elderly couple. The husband was moved by the occasion and wanted to tell his wife just how he felt about her. She was very hard of hearing, however, and often misunderstood what he had to say.

With many family members and friends gathered around, he toasted her: "My dear wife, after fifty years, I've found you tried and true!"

Everyone smiled their approval, but his wife said, "Eh?"

He repeated his compliment louder, to which his wife again responded, "Eh?"

So he shouted it at her. "AFTER FIFTY YEARS, I'VE FOUND YOU TRIED AND TRUE!"

His wife bristled and shot back, "Well, let me tell you something! After fifty years, I'm tired of you, too!"

Count Herman Keyserling said, "The essential difficulties of life do not end, but rather begin with marriage."

My grandparents were married 57 years. We have a couple in our church who come every Sunday. They have been married nearly 80 years. Sometimes the key is love. Other times, the key is patience. Always, the key is Christ, and sometimes, a poor sense of hearing."

"If a man has recently married, he must not be sent to war or have any other duty laid on him. For one year he is to be free to stay at home and bring happiness to the wife he has married."

Deuteronomy 24:5

March 12

Texas v. White

This was a landmark decision of the U.S. Supreme Court in 1869, that decreed by law what the Union's victory in the Civil War had established by force; namely, that the United States is an indestructible union from which no state can secede. In 1850 the State of Texas had received $10 million in federal bonds in settlement of boundary claims. In 1862 these bonds, which lacked the necessary signature of the Governor, were transferred to pay for Confederate supplies. At the war's end, Texas brought a suit in the Supreme Court, to recover the bonds.

The defendants claimed that because Texas had seceded from the Union, it could not sue. The court upheld the right of Texas to sue and recover the bonds. The ruling stated, "The unsuccessful effort of Texas to secede may temporarily have lost the state the privileges of membership in the Union, but not membership itself."

Now, what is the point of this history lesson? The Bible says believers are "adopted" into God's family. Even if they wanted to "secede," they could not. Our membership in God's Union is secure.

Make no mistake. Saved people act differently than those who are unsaved. But their relationship with the Father is secure.

"Why do you call me, 'Lord, Lord,' and do not do what I say?"

Luke 6:46

March 13

Taste of Power

A first-grade boy was told by his mother to return home directly after school was dismissed, but he got home as much as 20 minutes late almost every day. His mother asked him, "You get out of school the same time every day. Why can't you get home at the same time?"

He said, "It depends on the cars."

"What do cars have to do with it?" his mother asked him.

The youngster explained, "The patrol boy who takes us across the street makes us wait until some cars come along so he can stop them."

When I was in elementary school, I was a crossing guard for both of my fourth grade years. I loved the power. The whole universe would stop on my command. I felt in charge. I had the pole, the orange vest, and a whistle. And I knew how to use it.

It was a real rush, controlling when others could walk, drive, or stand still. But there was one problem. At the end of the day, I put my whistle back in the box and returned my snappy vest and pole. Then I had to walk home. And there was no one to help me.

I learned a hard lesson. It's a lot easier to tell others how to walk than it is to get it right yourself.

"Do not judge, and you will not be judged. Do not condemn, and you will not be condemned."

Luke 6:37

March 14

Attitude

John Maxwell says, "Your attitude will determine your altitude."

It's true. If a man has limburger cheese on his upper lip, he thinks the whole world smells.

I love the story that former NBA coach Johnny Kerr tells. His biggest test came when he coached the Chicago Bulls and his biggest player was 6'8" Erwin Mueller. "We had lost seven in a row, and I decided to give a pep talk before a game with the Celtics," Kerr said.

"I told Bob Boozer to go out and pretend he was the best scorer in basketball. I told Jerry Sloan to pretend he was the best defensive guard. I told Guy Rodgers to pretend he could run an offense better than any other point guard, and I told Mueller to pretend he was the best center in the game. Then we went out and lost the game by 17 points.

"I was pacing around the locker room afterward, trying to figure out what to say, when Mueller walked up, put his arm around me, and said, 'Don't worry about it, Coach. Just pretend we won.'"

Here's the good news for the believer. Jesus said, "It is finished." He won. We reap the benefits of eternal and abundant life. There is no need to pretend.

"But in your hearts set apart Christ as Lord.
Always be prepared to give an answer to
everyone who asks you to give a reason for
the hope that you have."

1 Peter 3:15

March 15

Stuck

The 19th century evangelist, D. L. Moody, loved to tell the story of a man who was asked by his ten-year-old son, "Daddy, why don't you ever go to church with us?"

The father replied, "I don't need to go to church, son. My faith is established."

Later that same day the man drove his horses out of the barn and hitched them to the buggy. As he and his son drove out of the yard, the horses became mired in a mud hole. The man tried in vain to extricate them, whereupon the boy observed, "They're not going anywhere, Daddy. I believe they're established."

The Bible warns us, "Do not forsake the assembling of yourselves together, as has become the habit of many."

In America, that is so true! Most Americans skip church religiously. They come to church disguised as empty pews. I was raised going to church consistently, every Christmas and Easter.

Most of us think we are "established," but we are really "mired in a hole." We aren't going anywhere. This Sunday, that can change for you. If you like, you can even come on your horse.

"Let us not give up meeting together, as some are in the habit of doing, but let us encourage one another."

Hebrews 10:25

March 16

Shopping Carts and Marriage

The great Charlie Brown commented on what it meant to have a good day. "I know it's going to be a good day when all the wheels on my shopping cart turn the same way."

Don't you love it when you get the one cart that has one wheel that is not aligned?

If ever we need our wheels aligned, it is in marriage. I heard about one couple who could never get aligned with their schedule. Bob called his wife from work in the middle of the afternoon. "I'm able to get two tickets for the show we wanted to see. It's playing now. Do you want to go?"

Martha answered, "Oh, yes! I'll get ready right away!"

"Perfect," said Bob. "The tickets are for tomorrow night."

Another couple was not aligned. The Vermont farmer was sitting on the porch with his wife. He looked over at her and thought about all the ways she had blessed him in 42 years of marriage.

Then he spoke, "Wife, you've been such a wonderful woman that there are times when I can hardly keep from telling you."

To have a really great marriage, we need all wheels headed the way. Then it is okay to tell your spouse you love them. Read the Song of Solomon, in the Bible. You will find a modern romance story. You will find two mates whose carts are fully aligned.

"His mouth is sweetness itself; he is altogether lovely. This is my lover. This is my friend."

Song of Solomon 5:16

March 17

Shoe

Jeff MacNelly used to write an old comic strip called *Shoe*. In one of the comic strips, Shoe is pitching in a baseball game. In a conference on the mound, his catcher says, "You've got to have faith in your curve ball."

Shoe grumbles, "It's easy for him to say. When it comes to believing in myself, I'm an agnostic."

Unfortunately, that is the way a lot of people think about themselves.

I love the words of Charles Schwab. "When a man has put a limit on what he *will* do, he has put a limit on what he *can* do."

Let me suggest you follow the advice of Jack Canfield. In his book, *The Success Principles*, he recommends the following four steps to transform limiting beliefs into empowering beliefs. First, identify a limiting belief that you want to change. Second, determine how the belief limits you. Third, decide how you want to be, act, or feel. Finally, create a turnaround statement that affirms or gives you permission to be, act, or feel this new way.

Leadership expert John Maxwell says it like this. "Practice a small discipline daily in a specific area of your life."

Great advice! Don't be an agnostic. Don't be the Shoe.

> "In his heart a man plans his course, but the Lord determines his steps."
>
> Proverbs 16:9

March 18

Political Correctness

Do you know how to never offend anyone with what you say? It's simple. Never talk about religion, politics, or cats. The one exception is that in most circles it is okay to criticize Christianity, but not other religions. Avoid attempts at humor at all cost. It is acceptable to laugh at anything crude, but don't "force" your morality on anyone. The phrase for today is "political correctness." If you are new to the game of political correctness, let me help.

We don't "man" an office or position. We "person" it. We don't allow our children to play Cowboys and Indians. They are to play Cowpersons and Native Americans. As Vice President Al Gore taught us, "My mother always made it clear to my sister and me that men and women were equal, if not more so."

You have your assignment. May all mankind and womankind strive for equality, if not "more so." Strive for non-offensive, non-controversial speech in everything you say. But if it is political correctness you want, you may want to avoid the Scriptures. The Scriptures are all about truth, whether it stings or not.

"May these words of my mouth and this meditation of my heart be pleasing in your sight."

Psalm 19:14

March 19

Etiquette

One day, Donald Trump was being interviewed by Larry King on King's radio show. At one point during the interview, and not waiting for a commercial break, Trump said to King, "Do you mind if I move back a little? Your breath is really bad."

In 1961, Sam Rayburn, the Speaker of the house, was hosting Frank Sinatra in Texas, at a black tie dinner. Late in the program, Rayburn leaned over to Sinatra and asked, "Are you going to sing 'The Yellow Rose of Texas' for us, Frank?"

Sinatra replied, "Get your hands off my suit, creep." That's bad etiquette.

I was raised by the queen of etiquette. My mother knew all the rules. She taught me how to set a table. I learned where to put the napkin, knife, spoon, salad fork, regular fork, and dessert fork. I learned how to hold my glass, and how to cut my meat. The only thing I had to learn on the street was how to hide my peas in the mashed potatoes.

But I'm thankful. Good etiquette is all about learning to not offend needlessly. The master of good etiquette was a carpenter from Bethlehem. But keep reading for the best etiquette rule of all.

"If anyone causes one of these little ones who believe in me to sin, it would be better for him to have a large millstone hung around his neck and to be drowned in the depths of the sea."

Matthew 18:6

March 20

1929

Have you ever seen those little booklets that tell you everything that happened in a particular year? It's fun to browse through the one that highlights the events that took place in the year of one's birth. They sell them at a certain restaurant in town. I will not endorse a restaurant here, even the one near League Line Road in Conroe with rocking chairs on the front porch.

If you turn 85 in 2014 or 86 in 2015, there's an excellent chance you were born in 1929. Of course, 1929 is best known for the crash of the Stock Market, which ushered in the Great Depression.

But other things, really good things, happened in 1929. That was the year the Grand Tetons became a national park. The Vatican City became a sovereign State. New York's Museum of Modern Art opened. And Al Capone cleaned up the streets of Chicago with the St. Valentine's Day Massacre.

Here's the point. In bad times, God is there. When we see the negative, God shows up. Do you think you're having a bad year? I suggest you aren't qualified to make that judgment.

"Even though I walk through the valley of the shadow of death, I will fear no evil, for you are with me."

Psalm 23:4

March 21

Phone Booths

Today, let's talk about phone booths. If you are too young to know what they are, borrow your parents' book of ancient American history. There used to be a wonderful activity we would engage in as kids. It taught us fellowship, teamwork, and tolerance of body odor. It was called "seeing how many people you can cram into a phone booth."

This critical American pastime had its origins in South Africa, dating back to the mid-1950s, when students there claimed to have fit 25 people in a space approximately three feet square and eight feet high. British students tried, but couldn't outdo the South Africans.

American and Canadian college students had a go at it, and the craze spread across the continent, with increasingly elaborate "rules" in phone booth stuffing. Lots of variations were tried, like stuffing people in a car or in a booth underwater. One of the shorter-lived fads of the 1950s and '60s, phone booth stuffing faded by 1970. But its basic premise was good. It is always a good thing when we can bring people together.

"For we were all baptized by one Spirit into one body, whether Jews or Greeks, slave or free, and we were all given the one Spirit to drink."

1 Corinthians 12:13

March 22

Clocks

What do Henry Ford, Robert Fulton, Eli Whitney, and Paul Revere have in common? The answer is so obvious! They all were clockmakers at one point in their lives. Levi Hutchins made the first modern alarm clock in 1787. Fastidious by nature, Hutchins fashioned a mechanical ringing bell clock so that he could arrive punctually at work each morning. He never bothered to patent or mass-produce his invention, which only went off at 4:00 a.m. Leonardo de Vinci invented and used an alarm clock in which water flowed in a thin stream from one receptacle to another.

Greek mathematician and scientist Heron of Alexandria invented a water clock during the reign of Alexander the Great. Its purpose was to limit the time a lawyer could speak in court.

We have had a fascination with time for centuries. The average American owns 3.7 watches. Did you know the average person looks at a watch or clock 452 times a day? On Sunday mornings at church, the number doubles. We always want to know the time. But God says "No one knows the time when Jesus will return." Instead of looking at your watch, just be ready!

"No one knows about that day or hour, not even the angels in heaven, nor the Son, but only the Father."

Matthew 24:36

March 23

Government "Competency"

An 18-month investigation by the Texas State Library and Archives Commission, reported by the Houston Chronicle on October 29, 2007, concluded that the state government requires too many reports. Approximately one-fourth of the more than 1,600 reports were duplicates of existing reports or were issued to agencies no longer in existence. In some cases, they were prepared annually even after evidence surfaced that they went unread. The commission published its conclusions in a 668-page report.

I love that! It took a government agency 668 pages to say they had nothing to say. That is easy to criticize. But ask yourself this. Of the 10-15,000 words you spoke yesterday, how many of them really mattered?

The Book of James says we need to listen much, but speak little. It says the tongue is a spark that causes great damage. Join me in laughing at the prolonged punditry of political people, but keep a close eye on what you say, as well. Make every word count. It is amazing what can be said in less than 668 pages.

For example, I said all of this with just 187 words!

"He who answers before listening, that is his folly and his shame."

Proverbs 18:13

March 24

Who Packs Your Parachute?

Charles Plumb, a U.S. Naval Academy graduate, was shot down over Vietnam. He ejected and parachuted into the jungle where the Viet Cong captured him and held him prisoner for six years. Today, Plumb lectures on lessons learned from that experience.

One day, he and his wife were sitting in a restaurant and a man from another table came over and said, "You are Charles Plumb, who flew jet fighters in Vietnam from the aircraft carrier Kitty Hawk. You were shot down!"

Plumb asked how in the world he knew that.

The man said, "I packed your parachute. I guess it worked!"

Plumb thanked the man. "If not for your work I wouldn't be here today."

And Plumb thought about that many times. The man who packed his parachute was just a sailor, but if he hadn't taken untold hours to weave the shrouds and fold the silks of each chute, Plumb would not have survived.

Now, Plumb asks his audience, "Who packed your parachute?"

In other words, who is making you look good? Who is supporting you, though unseen by many? When's the last time you thanked them for packing your parachute?

"He made himself nothing, taking the very nature of a servant, being made in human likeness."

Philippians 2:7

March 25

Howard Hughes

The world's most famous recluse, this hermit's hermit has grown to symbolize that subgroup of people who, for various reasons, prefer to navigate life in the singular, apart and aside from others. Howard Hughes was an aviator, industrialist, film producer, and one of the world's wealthiest men. He began to show signs of mental illness in his 30s. On thanksgiving Day in 1966, Hughes moved into a suite at Las Vegas' Desert Inn and dug in deep, rarely emerging from that point forward.

When hotel staff finally asked him to leave, he countered by buying the hotel. Hughes would dwell reclusively in the penthouses of many more hotels until his lonely death in 1976. By then Hughes' beard, hair, toenails, and fingernails were freakishly long, a situation that suggested that personal hygiene no longer carried much weight with the billionaire.

I've been to Hughes' burial plot. It is very nondescript. Howard Hughes had money, planes, hotels, even islands. What he didn't have was peace.

"I have told you these things, so that in me you may have peace. In the world you will have trouble. But take heart! I have overcome the world!"

John 16:33

March 26

A Sinking Sub

They thought it couldn't happen. The Russian Navy built their finest submarine, Kursk, a nuclear carrier. It was the best sub they had ever built, and one of the finest the world has ever seen. She was to begin her service on August 12, 2000. Five high-ranking naval officers journeyed to sea to witness a demonstration of her strength.

Then the unsinkable did the unthinkable. The naval officers witnessed two sudden explosions. The thundering booms registered 1.5 and 3.5 on the Richter scale. Something had gone dreadfully wrong.

The seven-ton vessel immediately took on water and plunged 350 feet to the seabed of the Arctic Ocean. Most of the 118 crewmembers died instantly. The others spent their dying hours in frigid, horrifying conditions.

I submit to you that this is a parable on life. We, like the sailors, are hopeless and helpless. The Book of Romans says none of us are sinless. We are not sinking in the ocean of saltwater, but the ocean of sin. But there is good news. In Christ, God has offered a life raft. But that's not enough. By faith, you must come aboard. To know this and not do it will give you a real sinking feeling for all eternity.

"Anyone who knows the good he ought to do and doesn't do it, sins."

James 4:7

March 27

Presumed Ignorant

It happened in a Houston courtroom in April, 1994. Arthur Hollingsworth was on trial for the armed robbery of a convenience store. Hollingsworth waived his constitutional right to remain silent and testified in his own defense. Harris County prosecutor Jay Hileman eventually got Hollingsworth to admit that he was, in fact, in the Sun Mart convenience store at the time of the hold-up. Hileman then got Hollingsworth to admit he had taken a gun into the store with him at the time it was robbed. Hileman then moved in for the kill.

Hileman asked, "Mr. Hollingsworth, you're guilty aren't you?"

Hollingsworth replied, "No."

Hileman repeated, "Mr. Hollingsworth, you're guilty, aren't you?"

Then Hollingsworth replied, "Yeah, I guess I am."

While Arthur Hollingsworth will forever be presumed ignorant in legal circles, I admire him for coming clean. You see, the God of the universe asks the same question of you today. He asks you, "You are guilty, aren't you?"

And until you admit the answer to that question, you are not eligible for the blessings of an eternal pardon by a benevolent Judge.

> *"If we confess our sins, he is faithful and just and will forgive us our sins and purify us from all unrighteousness."*

1 John 1:9

March 28

Worst Player Ever

A great argument for any occasion is, "Who was the greatest?" We talk about the greatest president, leader, entertainer, singer, and athlete. Well, my question today is this. Who was the *worst* basketball player of all time?

The answer is obvious. He missed more shots than anyone else (9,000). He lost over 300 games. By his own admission, "Twenty-six times, I took the game-winning shot and missed."

Let's talk about baseball. Who was the worst pitcher ever? That would be a fellow who lost nearly 400 games, a record. Who was the worst hitter? Well, that would be the guy who struck out more times than anyone else. In football, who was the worst quarterback to ever play? That would be the man who played 20 years, throwing more interceptions than anyone else.

The worst players in their sports are as follows: Michael Jordan, Cy Young, Babe Ruth, and Brett Favre.

Of course, they are not really the worst in their sports. They are among the very best. And what made them great will make you great: a willingness to risk failure in hope of success. So go ahead. Do what Jordan did. Give it your best shot.

"For God did not give us a spirit of timidity, but a spirit of power, of love, and of self-discipline."

2 Timothy 1:7

March 29

Mrs. Jones

Nancy Jones lived a rather non-descript life. And so, on her tombstone were written these words: "Here lie the bones of Nancy Jones; for her, life held no terrors. She lived an old maid, she died an old maid; no hits, no runs, no errors." It appears that Mrs. Jones was a fine lady, but she didn't grasp life at its fullest.

If you should die today, what would they say about your life? Les Moore is buried at Boot Hill Cemetery in Tombstone, Arizona. On his grave are written these words: "Here lies Lester Moore. Four slugs from a twenty-four. No Les. No more."

I love funny epitaphs. "Herein lies a man named Zeke. Second fastest draw in Cripple Creek."

"Here lies the body of Margaret Bent. She kicked up her heels and away she went."

"To follow you, I am not content, for I do not know which way you went."

But let's return to Nancy Jones. "No hits, no runs, no errors."

The fact is, if you swing the bat of life, you will make a few outs. But if you live your life where it's safe, in the stands, you'll never score any runs. Jesus didn't die just to give you life. He died to give you abundant life.

"The Son of Man is going to be delivered into the hands of men."

Matthew 17:22

March 30

Thomas Edison

American inventor Thomas Edison was an amazing man. He held over 1,500 patents, including those for the phonograph, kinetoscope, dictaphone, radio, light bulb, autographic printer, and tattoo gun. He produced the first film version of *Frankenstein*. It was a 15-minute silent "movie." We owe a lot to old Tom. Where would we be today, without the kinetoscope? And I don't know about you, but our family couldn't survive without our tattoo gun. Our church still relies on our autographic printer to run off Sunday's worship guides. But Mr. Edison did something else of interest. He did it by simply dying.

Henry Ford was enamored with Edison, so when the great inventor died, Ford captured his last breath in a bottle. Why would he do that? Ford never said. That question will always be pondered along with the other great questions of history, such as who shot Kennedy, who shot J.R., and who watches Jersey Shore.

But one thing is clear. When Edison died, Ford was ready. What is not clear is whether or not Edison was ready. What about you? Are you ready for that moment when you take your last breath?

"Precious in the sight of the Lord is the death of his saints."

Psalm 116:15

March 31

All about Food

I love food. Food is a Denison tradition. It is our favorite thing to eat. I think I'll traverse the country, chasing after the great food festivals that are offered. Just reading this will make your stomach growl.

In May, I will look forward to the Rocky Mountain Oyster Festival, held in that great Rocky Mountain get-away, Throckmorton, Texas. In Pocahontas County, West Virginia, we can all look forward to the annual Roadkill Cookoff. For those who prefer the beauty of Hawaii, you can fill up at the Waikiki Spam Jam.

My personal favorite is the Bugfest in Raleigh, North Carolina. If you are from Oklahoma, I'm sure you are familiar with the Rattlesnake hunt they've been doing in Waurika for over 50 years.

Of course, Bell Buckle, Tennessee is best known for their annual Moon Pie Festival. And when in Freemont, Michigan, you will want to enjoy the fare at the National Baby Food Festival.

Having considered all these options, I may try fasting, reading Scripture, and prayer first. See ya in Waurika! Or better yet, enjoy the bread of life.

"I am the living bread that came down from heaven, which a man may eat and not die."

John 6:51

April 1

April Fool's Day

April Fool's Day began in England in 1614. King James had a dilemma. The queen would not make him the dinner of his choice. He insisted that she obey his orders and prepare his favorite meal. In desperation, he turned to his servants.

"What should I do?" he asked them. "How do I get the queen to follow my orders? She must learn to obey me!"

The leader among the king's servants was a man named Philo, who spoke on the servants' behalf. "Your majesty, you must not order the queen to do anything. She is your wife, not your servant. Treat her as an equal."

King James was outraged. "But I am the king!" Then he ordered the deaths of all his servants.

The next day, the queen prepared his meal, laced with poison. The king ate it, but soon died.

The queen said, at his death, "The king is a fool."

The date was April 1, 1614. And from that quote, "The king is a fool," came April Fool's Day.

Well, except for the fact that I just made up the whole story. Sorry. April Fools! But you should know by now that you can't believe everything you read, unless you read it in the Bible.

"When your words came, I ate them; they were my joy and my heart's delight."

Jeremiah 15:16

April 2

Build a Canal

When dealing with critics, learn some lessons from the building of the Panama Canal. The builder of the Panama Canal was besieged with criticism. When asked how he was going to handle his critics, he said, "I'm going to build the canal."

Don't get sidetracked if you are on the right track. Stay positive. One football coach says, "When you are out of town, go to the head of the line and look as though you are leading a parade."

There is nothing worse than poor leadership. Actually, there is one thing worse: no leadership. There are three keys to success in any organization: leadership, leadership, and leadership. To raise those around you, become a better leader.

If you're old enough to read this column on your own, you are old enough to know that every person who is attempting to achieve something worthwhile will meet the challenge of criticism. Washington, Lincoln, FDR - they all faced many critics.

So did a particular Messiah you've probably heard of. No, criticism is not a guarantee that you are off track. But a total lack of criticism certainly is! So go ahead! Build a canal.

"Whoever corrects a mocker invites insult; whoever rebukes a wicked man incurs abuse."

Proverbs 9:7

April 3

Initiative

General William Westmoreland was once reviewing a platoon of paratroopers in Vietnam. As he went down the line, he asked each of them a question. "How do you like jumping, son?"

"Love it, sir!" was the first man's answer.

"How do you like jumping?" he asked the next.

"The greatest experience in my life, sir!" exclaimed the paratrooper.

"How do you like jumping?" he asked the third.

"I hate it, sir," he replied.

"Then why do you do it?" asked Westmoreland.

"I want to be around guys who love to jump."

That's good initiative!

Here's a story of bad initiative. A store manager was walking through the packing room when he saw a man lounging on a shipping crate. He asked how much he was paid. The man said, "$500 a week."

At that the manager paid the man $500 and said, "Here's a week's pay. Get out!"

The manager went to the department head and asked why he had hired the man in the first place.

"We didn't, sir," he replied. "He was here to pick up a package."

Initiative can be good or bad. I'd go with the first kind. Find a group going places. Don't hold back. And at the right moment, jump! But don't jump alone. Find a church full of believers worth jumping with.

"From him the whole body joined and held together by every supporting ligament, grows and builds itself up in love, as each part does its work."

Ephesians 4:16

April 4

The Man We Want

Mike Kollin, former linebacker of the Miami Dolphins, was talking to Coach Shug Jordan, who wanted him to help with recruiting. Mike said, "Sure, Coach. What are you looking for?"

"Well Mike, you know there's that fellow, you knock him down, and he just stays down?"

Mike said, "We don't want him, do we, Coach?"

"No, that's right. Then there's that fellow, you knock him down and he gets up. You knock him down again and he stays down."

Mike said, "We don't want him either, do we, Coach?"

"No, but Mike, there's that fellow, you knock him down, he gets up. Knock him down again, and he gets up again. Knock him down, he gets up; knock him down, he gets up; knock him down, he gets up."

Mike said, "That's the guy we want, isn't it, Coach?"

Coach Jordan replied, "No, Mike. We don't want him either. I want you to find the guy who keeps knocking everybody down. That's the guy we want!"

The lesson isn't to knock people down. The lesson is, God is looking for people who go on the offensive for him. Step up. Go for it! Don't wait for life to knock you down. The best example is Peter. He got knocked down a lot early in his ministry. But then he went on the offensive and was a leader of the movement that rocked the world.

"I tell you that you are Peter, and on this rock I will build my church, and the gates of Hades will not overcome it."

Matthew 16:18

April 5

Pushing Trains

There was a pastor of a small church in a rural town. He was seen sitting by the train track each morning. A church member asked him what he was doing. "Why do you sit here each day, watching the train go by?" she wanted to know.

"It's simple," replied the pastor, "I enjoy watching something move that I don't have to push."

Can you relate? I bet there are things in your life that you really believe in, but you wish someone, anyone, would take the lead, so you don't have to push trains all the time.

I love it when church members recommend new ministries for the church. My most common reply is, "Great idea! When do you start?"

As leaders, we all want to do all the work. But that's not leadership. Being popular and being effective are two unrelated issues.

Casey Stengel offered this advice for managing a baseball team. He said, "The key is to keep the five people who hate you away from the four who are undecided."

Managing people is never easy. But it is necessary, as a pastor, or in any avenue of life. As tough as it is to manage others, it sure beats pushing trains.

"Obey your leaders and submit to their authority. They keep watch over you as men who must give an account. Obey them so that their work will be a joy, not a burden. For that would be of no advantage to you."

Hebrews 13:17

April 6

Rational Thinking

Darren Hardy wrote a great little book, *The Compound Effect*. In this treatise on instant gratification, he wrote, "We understand that scarfing pop tarts won't slenderize our waistlines. We realize that logging three hours a night watching *Dancing with the Stars* and *Bachelorette* leaves us with three hours less to read a book, walk a dog, or pray a prayer. We 'get' that merely purchasing a great pair of running shoes doesn't make us a runner. We're a 'rational' species. At least that's what we tell ourselves. So why are we so irrationally enslaved by so many bad habits? It's because our need for instant gratification can turn us into the most reactive, non-thinking animals around."

So much for rational thinking!

I love the way Eric Hoffer says it. "People will cling to an unsatisfactory way of life rather than change in order to get something better for fear of getting something worse."

We'd rather hang on to the problem we know than trade it for the solution we don't know.

God has a better plan. Give him what you can't keep anyway. And he will give you what you can never lose.

> *"See, I set before you today life and prosperity, death and destruction."*

Deuteronomy 30:15

April 7

Thanks a Lot!

Leslie Weatherford tells the story of a sailor who dove into the water to rescue a drowning boy. A few days later the boy and his mom were shopping and the boy saw the sailor and told his mom that he was the man who had saved his life. His mother walked up to the young man and asked if he was, indeed, the one who had pulled her son out of the water. The sailor confirmed that he was the one. He then anticipated a warm embrace, a heartfelt "thank you," and perhaps a reward, though he didn't seek any of those things.

What he got was far different: a question, not an affirmation. Said the boy's mother, "My son had a new cap on that day when he fell into the water. You were right there. Did you find it?"

People are funny. The man saved the boy's life, and all she cared about was a $10 cap. But think about it. A couple thousand years ago, Jesus dove into the lake of sin to pull you out. He did it to save your life forever. In response, do you thank him? Or do you ask for things as meaningless as a $10 cap?

He risked his life to save yours. Is it too much to whisper a simple "thank you"?

"Give thanks in all circumstances, for this is God's will for you in Christ Jesus."

1 Thessalonians 5:18

April 8

Just $5

It was one of the greatest Sunday sermons of all time. Just before our traditional service, a young girl came up to me. She said, "I have something to give you."

"What is it?" I asked.

She opened up her wallet and pulled out five $1 bills, all the money she had. She handed them to me and asked, "Can you give this to God for me?"

I handed the money back to her and had her follow me to one of our offering receptacles that sit in the back of the sanctuary. I said, "Here, why don't you give it to God yourself?"

At that, she pushed the money through the slot, into the receptacle.

Jesus tells us about the widow's mite. It seems the lady tossed into the offering the smallest coin minted in that day. At that, she received the commendation of the God of the universe. Jesus said, "She has given more than anyone, for she gave all she had."

God doesn't measure our gifts by their size. What matters is not how much we give, but how much we keep. On that Sunday morning, the greatest sermon in our church was preached by a little girl who gave God all she had.

"Everyone who was willing and whose heart moved him came and brought an offering to the Lord for the work on the Tent of Meeting, for all its service, and for the sacred garments."

Exodus 35:21

April 9

Little Jack Horner

Do you remember this old nursery rhyme? It goes like this. "Little Jack Horner sat in the corner eating a Christmas pie; he put in his thumb, and pulled out a plum, and said, 'What a good boy am I!'"

Now, I never met Jack Horner personally, but I grew up with a lot of boys that were like him. You see, we have no evidence that Jack Horner planted the plum tree or pruned it on a regular basis. There is no evidence that he picked the plums when they were ripe. Nor is there evidence that he cooked or even served the pie. All Jack Horner did was eat it and take credit for it. He stuck his thumb in the pie, pulled out a plum, and pronounced, "What a good boy am I!"

There is a little Jack Horner in all of us. We are good at receiving the blessings of God. We enjoy his benefits. But we fall short in the area of credit.

God blesses us bountifully in so many ways. Then we pull out a plum, lick our thumb, and tell everyone how great we are.

Read your Bible. It was God who gave the Promised Land, his only son, and the gift of life. Remember that the next time you are tempted to say, "What a good boy am I."

"And if by grace, then it is no longer by works; if it were, grace would no longer be grace."

Romans 11:6

April 10

The Christian Barber

There was a barber that thought he should share his faith with his customers more than he had been doing. So the next morning when the barber got out of bed he said, "Today I am going to witness to the first man that walks through my door."

Soon after he opened his shop the first man came in and said, "I want a shave!"

The barber said, "Sure, just sit in the seat and I'll be with you in a minute."

The barber went to the back and prayed a quick and desperate prayer. "God, the first customer came in and I'm going to witness to him. So please give me the wisdom to know just the right thing to say to him. Amen."

Then the barber burst out with his razor in one hand and a Bible in the other hand, and asked the man a direct question. "Good morning, sir. I have a question for you. Are you ready to die?"

There aren't many things in this life that are scarier than a barber with a sharp blade asking you if you're ready to die. I know what you are saying if you are a believer. It's good to share our faith, but I don't like the way he did it. So here's my question. How are you doing it?

"Therefore go and make disciples of all nations, baptizing them in the name of the Father, and of the Son, and of the Holy Spirit."

Matthew 28:19

April 11

Texan in London

The story is told of the Texan who visited the Summer Olympics in London. He was taking a taxi tour of London as he was in a hurry to see as many sites as he could in a short amount of time. As they passed the Tower of London, the cabbie explained what it was and that construction started in 1346 and continued until its completion in 1412.

The Texan replied, "Shoot, a little 'ol tower like that? In Houston, we'd have that thing up in two weeks!"

A few minutes later, they passed the House of Parliament. The driver explained that it was built from 1544 until 1618.

The Texan replied, "We built a bigger one than that in Dallas in less than a year!"

As they passed Westminster Abbey the cabbie was silent. The Texan asked, "Whoah! What's that over there?"

The cabbie scratched his head and said, "Now that, I don't know! It wasn't there yesterday!"

The Bible says that Jesus has been building a mansion for you ever since he returned to heaven. That is 2,000 years of construction. Even for a Texan, that will be an unbelievable place. I hope to see you there someday!

"For here we do not have an enduring city, but we are looking for the city that is to come."

Hebrews 13:14

April 12

A Sheep's Perspective

I love the old cartoon of the two sheep. They were laying in a pasture, talking about the temptations of life. One of them remarked to the other, "All we, like people have gone astray."

We have many versions of the Bible: KJV, NIV, NASB, and now the RSV (Revised Sheep's Version). Here's how it reads in the KJV: "All we like sheep have gone astray."

We see sheep as the ultimate example of straying off one's intended course. But sheep see us in that same light. And who can blame them? Think about it. Maybe their version is actually closer to the way life really is.

Father Scott Mansfield, a priest in St. Patrick's Catholic Church in Charma, NM, said at the funeral mass of Ben Martinez, that Martinez was a "lukewarm catholic living in sin."

Now, we can debate the merits of sharing that at a funeral service, but we all have strayed. The Bible refers to many ways we stray: gossip, lying, covetousness, jealousy, lust, etc. We all have strayed from God's intended path for our lives. We all have chosen our path over God's path from time to time. When you think about it, the sheep had a good point.

"You ignored all my advice and would not accept my rebuke."

Proverbs 1:25

April 13

Moving In

A sweet and very independent 92-year-old lady came to the point where she had to sell her house and move into a nursing home. Her husband of 70 years had passed away, and she was legally blind. Despite her wishes, this move had become her only option. She waited in the lobby of the facility for a long time before finally being told that her room was ready. As she was escorted down the corridor, her attendant described the room, down to the curtains hung on the windows. "Oh, I just love it!" the elderly lady enthused.

"But you haven't even seen the room yet. Just wait," the attendant responded.

"That doesn't have anything to do with it," she replied. "Happiness is something you decide on ahead of time. Whether I like my room or not doesn't depend on how you arrange the furniture. It's all about how I arrange my mind."

My old pastor used to say it like this. "I'd rather live in the outhouse with Jesus than in the penthouse without him."

You can spend the rest of your life trying to re-arrange everything. But until you rearrange your mind, you are wasting your time.

"But those who hope in the Lord will renew their strength. They will soar on wings like eagles; they will run and not grow weary, they will walk and not be faint."

Isaiah 40:31

April 14

The Day Lincoln Died

The date was April 14, 1865. Today marks the anniversary of that event that changed America. The sixteenth president of the United States sat in his private box, attending a performance at Ford's Theater in Washington. Seated with his wife, Mary Todd, Abraham Lincoln had earned a night out. After all, he had just preserved the Union and was about the business of rebuilding a nation. But John Wilkes Booth had other ideas. He burst into the President's box and fired one shot that would forever change history. Lincoln was declared dead at 7:22 the next morning. You knew that. But there's more.

When Lincoln died, he had five items in his pockets: an old eyeglass case, a handkerchief, a pocketknife given by his dad, five dollars (Confederate money), and newspaper clippings praising his presidency. According to presidential aides, Lincoln read the newspaper articles for one reason. Abraham Lincoln, the greatest man of his century, needed to hear the praise of man.

Imagine that! The greatest leader in America needed encouragement.

So here's your job. Find someone, anyone, and tell them how wonderful they are. With your encouragement, they just might make history.

"Therefore encourage one another and build each other up, just as in fact you are doing."

1 Thessalonians 5:11

April 15

One Night – 1,595 Dead

It was the greatest vessel ever imagined, a floating palace. She weighed 46,328 tons. She was indestructible. She was the Titanic. On her maiden voyage, the White Star liner churned from Southampton toward New York. The rich and famous were aboard. The band played, the people danced, and they all rejoiced. On the night of April 14, 1912 they had a party.

Then it happened. The unsinkable did the unthinkable. The great Titanic ran into an iceberg, as the band was playing *Nearer My God to Thee*. Two hours, 40 minutes later, of the 2,340 aboard, only 745 survived. 1,595 perished in the icy waters. Just a few years ago, the last survivor died.

What are the lessons from the Titanic? Captain Smith ignored numerous warnings of pending danger. The spotlight was not installed correctly. The lifeboats were too small and too few. They travelled faster than they should have. They didn't take icebergs seriously.

You know, all of our "ships" can sink. You need the right Navigator, One who sees the icebergs of life and knows how to deal with them. Your job is to obey his directions.

"We know that we have come to know him if we obey his commandments."

1 John 2:3

April 16

The Sin of Silence

Years ago, when Nikita Khrushchev visited America, he gave a press conference at the Washington Press Club. The first question from the floor, handled through an interpreter, was, "Today you talked about the hideous rule of your predecessor, Stalin. You were one of his closest aides and colleagues during those years. What were you doing all that time?"

At the height of his power Stalin was exterminating 40,000 people a month. Khrushchev's face got red. "Who asked that question?" he roared.

All 500 faces turned down. "Who asked that question?" he repeated.

There was still no response other than silence. Then Khrushchev answered. Referring to their silence, he said, "That's what I was doing."

It may be that our greatest sin is the sin of silence. Not speaking the message of good news is the sin of silence. Not affirming someone when they are down is the sin of silence. Not saying "good job" is the sin of silence. Failure to offer a word of encouragement is the sin of silence. Sometimes the silent response is the worst response of all. Sometimes silence is sin.

"All wrongdoing is sin."

1 John 5:17

April 17

Dream Girl

A young man excitedly called his mother to brag that he had finally met the girl of his dreams. "Now what should I do?" he asked her.

His mother offered him some great advice. "Why don't you send her flowers, and on the card invite her to your place for a home cooked dinner?"

Her son agreed that this was a good plan. He called the young lady and invited her over. He said, "Would you like to come over for a great home cooked dinner?"

She was pleased to accept. The day after their big date, the man's mother called him to see how things had gone.

"The whole date was a total disaster," he lamented.

"Why, didn't she come over?" asked his mother.

"Oh, she came over," he said. "But she refused to cook dinner."

The young man made one mistake. He falsely assumed the key to a good relationship was receiving rather than giving.

Let me say a word to the men. (Ladies, look away for a moment.) Guys, if you want a great wife, become a great husband. Be a godly man. Lead your family. Set the example. Mentor your kids. And if you want a great home cooked dinner, learn to cook.

"The Lord God said, 'It is not good for the man to be alone. I will make a helper suitable for him.'"

Genesis 2:18

April 18

History of Typing

I have always done my own typing. I type my own newspaper columns, daily online devotions, and radio devotions. I type my own papers when asked to write articles by desperate publishers. I enjoy typing.

For me, it goes back to the eighth grade, when my mother insisted that I learn to type. We used something called a manual typewriter then. Most of you also know how to type. But have you ever pondered the reasoning behind the placement of the keys? Why does one row read, "QWERTYUI-OP[]\"? How does that make sense to anyone? The answer is simple.

Keys on the machines of the 1800s jammed if the typist was too fast. So they placed the most common letters in the most difficult places. Then, about 40 years ago, a keyboard called the Dvorak Simplified Keyboard was developed. It rearranged the letters into an easier to use pattern. Tests showed typists increased their speeds rapidly, once adjusting to the new keyboard. But it never caught on.

To this day, we continue to use the outdated keyboard of ancient days, for one reason only. Nobody likes change, unless it jingles. The disciples disliked change as much an anyone. They couldn't imagine Jesus leaving them. But even that change was to be a good one.

> *"But I tell you the truth: It is for your good that I am going away. Unless I go away, the Counselor will not come to you, but if I go, I will send him to you."*

John 16:7

April 19

Family Tree

The great American novelist Mark Twain said that he spent a large sum of money to trace his family tree and then spent twice as much trying to keep his ancestry a secret!

He was like the family that reportedly wanted its history written up, so they hired a professional biographer to do it, but they were worried about how the document would handle the family's black sheep. Uncle George had been executed in the electric chair for murder.

"No problem," said the biographer. "I'll say that Uncle George occupied a chair of applied electronics at an important government institution. He was attached to his position by the strongest of ties, and his death came as a real shock."

We can't do much about our ancestors, but we influence our descendents greatly. I have often commented that I will change the world more by how I pastor my son than by how I pastor my church.

Even if you could change your ancestry, would it matter? Spend your time where you have the most influence, with your family. The seeds you plant today will bear fruit tomorrow. The Bible says your greatest inheritance is your kids.

"Sons are a heritage from the Lord, children a reward from him."

Psalm 127:3

April 20

We'll Never Fly!

Who said these words, in the late 1800s? "We'll never fly!"

Those words are attributed to a religious leader. He was a bishop on the East Coast. One day, he paid his annual visit to a small religious college. Engaging in conversation after dinner, the college president predicted that with the new millennium would come flight.

"Nonsense!" said the bishop. "Everything in nature has been discovered and all inventions have been made," he continued.

When the college president stated his case that God had given man the ingenuity to fly like the birds, the bishop chastised him. "Flight is reserved for the angels," he insisted.

The bishop's name was Wright. Bishop Wright had two sons. Perhaps you've heard of them: Orville and Wilbur. I'm glad the boys, in this case, didn't listen to their old dad.

But give the bishop a break. Not a lot of people saw this airplane thing coming. So keep that in mind the next time you say, "It can't be done."

God continues to inspire his creation with the ability to do truly amazing things. But the most amazing thing we can do is to chase after the God of the universe.

> *"Jesus replied, 'No one who puts his hand to the plow and looks back is fit for service in the kingdom of God.'"*

Luke 9:62

April 21

Comfort vs. Wisdom

I used to make the mistake of trying to fix everything. I felt the need to share my wisdom, whether it was wanted or not. Then I discovered that people would rather have a part of my heart than a piece of my mind. People want comfort, not answers. We have plenty of critics; we need encouragers.

When Robert Fulton showed off his new invention, the steamboat, the critics cried, "It'll never start! It'll never start!"

Once it started, they shouted, "It'll never stop! It'll never stop!"

It is easier to criticize than to comfort.

A football coach was having a bad year. It got so bad that he confided in his wife, "I feel that my dog is my only friend, but a man needs at least two friends."

So she bought him another dog.

Pooh bear was walking along the river bank. Eeyore, his stuffed donkey friend, suddenly appeared floating downstream, about to drown.

Pooh said, "You look like you are drowning."

Eeyore asked if he could save him.

Pooh hesitated, and then pulled him from the water.

"Thanks," said Eeyore.

"No problem," said Pooh. "You should have said something sooner."

Pooh offered his wisdom. But Eeyore, like us, needed comfort. I love the old song, *Rescue the Perishing*. I'm sure you have a lot of wisdom. But your drowning friends need rescuing. They need comfort.

"Comfort, comfort my people, says your God."

Isaiah 40:1

April 22

How People Pray

Let's tackle three issues about prayer. First, why do Christians put their hands together when they pray? This custom is not rooted in the Bible, but in Roman culture. In the ninth century, a man would put his hands together as a symbol of submission, and it was accepted by the Christian Church.

Second, did you know that people used to say "grace" before each meal? In ancient times, food spoiled quickly, sometimes causing death. Nomadic tribes were often poisoned from eating bad food. Before a meal, they would ask the gods to protect them, and after a meal, they thanked their gods for the "grace" by which they were still among the living.

Third, why do we say "amen" after a prayer? The word appears 13 times in the Old Testament and 119 times in the New Testament. The word originated in Egypt around 2500 B.C. It meant "hidden one." That evolved to mean "so it is," and was passed down to both Christians and Muslims.

And here's a fourth question. If we really believe in the power of prayer and in the God of the universe, why don't we pray more? I wish I had a good answer.

"Brothers, pray for us."

1 Thessalonians 5:25

April 23

Heal Thyself!

Johann Wolfgang von Goethe said, "I am fully convinced that the soul is indestructible, and that its activity will continue through eternity."

Philosopher Teilhard de Chardin said it like this: "We are not human beings having a spiritual experience. We are spiritual beings having a human experience."

The ancient Hebrews did not draw a sharp line between the physical and the spiritual. They understood the interplay between the two. Modern medicine is coming to the same conclusion.

A study by Purdue University found that people who practice their religion regularly develop only half as many medical problems as nonbelievers. "We have recently completed a systematic review of over 1,200 studies on the effects of religion on health," the study concluded. "The vast majority of these studies show a relationship between greater religious involvement and better mental and physical health, and lower use of health services."

This confirms what most of us already knew. Believers are happier, more at peace, and healthier. So if you are unhealthy, I suggest you visit the Great Physician.

"Dear friend, I pray that you may enjoy good health and that all may go well with you, even as your soul is getting along well."

3 John 2

April 24

Values

Sam Waksal, CEO of ImClone, pleaded guilty to securities fraud, bank fraud, and conspiracy to obstruct justice. He was ordered to pay $4.3 million in fines and back taxes.

Enron admitted to inflating its income figures by $586 million.

WorldCom admitted to overstating profits by $7.1 billion, costing 17,000 workers their jobs.

What do these stories all have in common? Values. Or lack of values.

George H. Lorimer, editor of the *Saturday Evening Post*, commented, "Back of every life there are principles that have fashioned it."

No one was more guided by his principles than Abraham Lincoln. He said, "When I lay down the reins of this administration, I want to have one friend left, and that friend is inside myself."

John Maxwell says it like this: "Methods are many, values are few. Methods always change, values never do."

What you accomplish during your life matters far less than the way you live your life. You can leave an incredible inheritance to your kids. It's called values.

To quote comedian Fred Allen, "You only live once. But if you work it right, once is enough."

"The integrity of the upright guides them, but the unfaithful are destroyed by their duplicity."

Proverbs 11:3

April 25

Enemy Attack

I loved an old comedy show, on in the 1970s when I was a baby. It was *The Flip Wilson Show*. The star of the show, surprisingly, was Flip Wilson. He did all sorts of silly stuff, and had some unique guests. But Wilson's mantra was to get in trouble, then say, "The devil made me do it." He was so funny that CBS kept him on the air for nearly two years. But let's talk about that statement. "The devil made me do it."

Do you believe in the devil? (I know, some of you ladies may think you are married to him.) Well, the Bible sure believes in the devil. St. Peter said, "Your adversary the devil, is a roaring lion, seeking whom he may devour" (1 Peter 5:8). Lions roar when they are hungry. The "roaring lion" (Satan) is roaring because he wants to devour you.

I heard about a hiker who came upon a lion, but was pleased to see him praying. Then he heard the lion's prayer. "Thank you, Lord, for this meal you have set before me."

When the devil looks at you, he sees a "meal set before him." But it doesn't have to end that way. Submit to God, and the devil can't make you do anything, despite what Flip Wilson says.

"Your adversary the devil, is a roaring lion, seeking whom he may devour."

1 Peter 5:8

April 26

Controlling Yourself

A man was standing in line at a grocery store check-out, when he witnessed a man and his son struggling for control. The boy, about two years of age, was whining and complaining. He was trying to capture everything in sight, to put in the shopping cart. He was making a public nuisance of himself, much to the embarrassment of his father. The dad kept repeating, "Just be calm, Albert. Don't act up, Albert. Don't make a scene, Albert. Control yourself, Albert. Don't act like a child, Albert."

The witness approached the man with praise, "Sir, I couldn't help but overhear you. I just want to say how impressed I am with the way you just dealt with little Albert."

The man responded, "Sir, the boy's name is Jimmy. My name is Albert."

What a lesson for all of us. You see, there is really only one person you can control. That person is you.

Don't give up on changing the world. But remember the lesson from Lucy, who told Charlie Brown she would change the world, starting with him. It doesn't start with Charlie Brown or the little boy. It starts with you.

"It is not honorable to seek one's own honor. We become like a city whose walls are broken down."

Proverbs 25:28

April 27

Luggage Handlers

One day a man arriving at the airport saw a well-dressed businessman yelling at a porter about the way he was handling his luggage. The more irate the businessman became, the calmer and more professional the porter appeared. When the abusive man left, the first man complimented the porter on his restraint.

"Oh, it was nothing," said the porter. "You know, that man's going to Miami, but his bags are now going to Kalamazoo."

What the disgruntled businessman failed to understand was that people who disrespect others always hurt themselves the most.

When it comes to respect, we need to learn two principles. First, give respect freely. Second, earn respect, in return. Don't expect respect. Earn it. Don't demand respect. Earn it.

Charles Spurgeon said it well, "Carve your name on hearts and not on marble."

He was simply saying that we need to constantly look for opportunities to be a blessing rather than to be blessed. You receive by giving. The respectful become the respected. And as an additional benefit, their luggage only ends up in Kalamazoo if they go there as well.

"Be devoted to one another in brotherly love. Honor one another above yourselves."

Romans 12:10

April 28

Crackers and Cheese

I heard the story of a guy who took a trip across the ocean. He saved just enough money for the trip and a barrel of crackers and cheese, so he'd have something to eat. Every day, he noticed another fellow eating steak: ribeyes, t-bones, and filets. With only a few days left on the trip, the cracker-eater tackled the steak-eater, took his steak and begged for a few bites.

"How do you afford the steak?" he asked his new friend. "Here I am, eating crackers and cheese every day, and you are eating steak."

"Check your ticket," came the reply.

He turned his ticket over and read these words: "Meals included."

God has a great trip planned for all of us. If you've ever taken a cruise you know how good the buffets are. Waiting at the end of life's cruise is a buffet for the ages. The end of the journey will be the best part. But we are to enjoy the ride right now, as well. We don't have to wait for the steak.

For each of us is the promise of incredible joy, peace, and blessing right now. So, when your ride gets a little bumpy, just remember the promise: "Meals included!"

"Seek first his kingdom and his righteous, and all these things will be given to you as well."

Matthew 6:33

April 29

17 Days

Two young blonde women were sitting in a coffee shop in a celebratory mood. A man drifted over, to buy them something to drink. When he got close, he heard one lady say to the other, "Here's to 17 days!"

Smiling, the man said, "Congratulations! But what's so special about 17 days?"

Eyes twinkling, one of the blondes explained, "Well, we've been spending our evenings working on a jigsaw puzzle! And we finished it in only 17 days!"

"What's so good about that?" asked the man.

The lady responded, "On the box, it said 3-5 years."

A famous Christian author wrote a book a few years ago. His premise was, "It all goes back in the box." He said that whatever you have in life, when this life is over, your toys all go back in the box.

A little boy stunned his dad by putting together a jigsaw puzzle of the world in just ten minutes.

"How did you do it?" asked his dad.

"It was easy," said the lad. "I turned the pieces over, and they formed a heart. When I got the heart right, the world fell into place."

Get your heart right today, because when it's over, it all goes back in the box.

"Blessed are the pure in heart, for
they will see God."

Matthew 5:8

April 30

C. S. Lewis

One of the most prominent minds of the first half of the twentieth century was philosopher and author C. S. Lewis. As a young man, he met Joy Greshem, a poet. They established a strong friendship that grew into love. They eventually married, then Joy was diagnosed with cancer. After a hard battle, she died. But there were many ups and downs along the way.

During a period when Joy was responding well to treatment, a colleague of Lewis' approached him with words of praise. "I know how hard you've prayed. God is answering your prayers," he said.

Lewis replied, "I didn't pray for that. I prayed because I can't help myself. The power of prayer isn't that it changes my circumstances, but that it changes my heart."

Most of us practice what I call "outcome prayers." We pray in order for God to change an outcome. But real spiritual maturity is marked by the man or woman who prays in order to get in touch with the Father out of a desire to change their heart.

Joy still died. But C. S. Lewis went on to change the world. But before he changed the world, God changed his heart.

"In the same way, the Spirit helps us in our weakness. We do not know what we ought to pray for, but the Spirit himself intercedes for us with groans that words cannot express."

Romans 8:26

May 1

Longest

The word for today is "longest." Do you know the longest movie ever? If you're a guy, that would be just about any romantic comedy. But in real time, the answer is *Berlin Alexanderplatz*, at 14 hours, 56 minutes. *War and Peace*, based on the book by the same name, was a mere seven hours, 22 minutes.

What was the longest song? Limiting our discussion to Top Ten hits, it would be *American Pie*, by Don McClean, at eight minutes. This song also gets the prize for strangest lyrics. I'm still not sure what to make of the Holy Ghost taking the last train for the coast.

The longest football game was the playoff adventure between the Dolphins and Chiefs in 1972.

The longest baseball game was the 26-inning affair between Brooklyn and Boston in 1920.

But my favorite is the world's longest banana split, constructed in Selinsgrove, PA on April 30, 1988. Consisting of 33,000 bananas, 2,500 gallons of ice cream, and 600 pounds of nuts, the all-you-can-eat dessert stretched 4.5 miles.

But here's something even longer than that: the distance between you and God apart from the gift of his Son. But because he came a really long way, all the way from heaven, we can spend a really long time with him in heaven.

"If you were of the world, the world would love its own. Yet because you are not of the world, but I chose you out of the world, therefore the world hates you."

John 15:19

May 2

Bureaucrats

I love bureaucracy. The Florida Department of Labor recently reported, "The increase in unemployment last month resulted from workers losing their jobs."

The Ohio Health Department stated, "Death certificates are to be ordered one week in advance of death."

A governmental fire prevention pamphlet states, "Exit access is that part of a means of egress that leads to an entrance to an exit." (Who can't understand that?)

But here is my favorite. The Ohio Department of Administrative Services sent a memo to explain how to figure out future Leap Years. "Leap Year is determined if the four-digit year can be divided by four unless the year can be divided by 100. Then it is not a Leap Year, unless the year can be divided by 400. Then it is a Leap Year, unless the year can be divided by 4,000. Then it is not a Leap Year, unless the year is 200 or 600 or after a year that is divided by 900. Then it is a Leap Year."

People are funny. We have an amazing ability to make the simple appear complex, while God does just the opposite. Life is about complexity. But God is about simplicity. And grace.

"And I will pour on the house of David and on the inhabitants of Jerusalem the Spirit of grace and supplication. Then they will look to me."

Zechariah 12:10

May 3

On Speed

One day, little Johnny was running through the halls at school. His third grade teacher ordered him to slow down. When he wanted to keep running, she made him sit still in a chair for two hours.

He said to the teacher, "I may be sitting on the outside, but I'm still running on the inside."

But Johnny really can't help it. It's no wonder people are always on the move. We are made to be active. Did you know your fingernails are always growing, at a clip of .004 millimeters per hour? Don't take my word for it. Measure them.

The human sneeze is much faster, traveling at 100 mph. Hair grows at a pace of .16 millimeters per hour. Blood traverses our veins at two mph. And the fastest among us can run at speeds up to 28 mph. People are always moving.

The only exception is the man sitting on the bench at the mall waiting on his wife. He hasn't moved in days.

But did you know the Bible has over 7,000 commands, and none of them says, "Hurry up!" So even if you're running on the inside, sit down on the outside.

"Be still, and know that I am God."

Psalm 46:10

May 4

A Couch Cat

Vickie Mendenhall, of Spokane, Washington, bought a used couch from a thrift store for $27 in 2009. Then the noises began. For several days, she heard strange sounds in the house, but couldn't figure out where they were coming from. Finally, Mendenhall's boyfriend was sitting on the couch one day watching television when he felt something underneath him. He lifted the couch up, and found a cat stuck inside it. The cat was in bad shape, so he took it to the animal shelter where they nursed it back to health.

Mendenhall contacted the thrift store, but they had no record of who had donated the couch. So she put notices in a paper, and Bob Killion contacted her.

He'd donated the couch to the store, and his nine-year-old cat had disappeared about the same time. She survived being stuck in the couch for 18 days, even without food and water. Killion loved his cat, and even though she was right there in his couch, he didn't know it.

What blessings are you surrounded by that you no longer notice?

"My God shall supply all your needs according to his riches in glory by Christ Jesus."

Philippians 4:19

May 5

No Cure

There was a farmer whose chickens were dying. He called an agriculture agent and said, "I had 600 chickens, but now I have just 300, as half of them died. What should I do?"

"It's simple," said the agent. "Give them penicillin."

A few days passed, and the farmer approached the agent again. "I tried penicillin, but now I'm down to 150 chickens. It didn't work."

The agent offered, "Give them castor oil twice a day. That should take care of your problem."

A few days later the farmer called again. "That didn't help. Now I'm down to fifty chickens."

The agent countered, "Here's your solution. Give them two aspirin each day. That should do it."

Two days later, the farmer was back on the phone. "All my chickens are dead!" he said.

"Oh, no! That's too bad," said the agent.

"Why are *you* so upset?" asked the farmer.

"Because I still had some more remedies we didn't get to try."

We all know people like the agriculture fellow. Sometimes, we are like him ourselves. We are surrounded by people with problems. We love to offer remedies.

In Jesus' day, they were called "Pharisees." Sometimes, it's okay to say, "I'm sorry. I don't have all the answers. But I know Someone who does." And when he doesn't make sense to us, he still makes sense.

"Behold, happy is the man whom God corrects. Do not despite the discipline of the Lord."

Job 5:17

May 6

Hear Charlie Brown

One day, Charlie Brown struck out on the baseball field. He returned to the bench. "Rats! I'll never be a big-league player. I just don't have it! All my life I've dreamed of playing in the big leagues, but I know I'll never make it."

Lucy replied, "Charlie Brown, you're thinking too far ahead. What you need to do is set more immediate goals for yourself."

"Immediate goals?" Charlie asked. Like most people, he had never considered such a thing.

"Yes," Lucy advised. "Start with the next inning. When you go out to pitch, see if you can walk to the mound without falling down!"

I can relate to Charlie Brown. Sometimes, a day when I don't fall down is a good day, simply on the merits of not falling down. And if you're like me, you are "blessed" with people in your life who will be happy to weigh in, when you do fall down. Perhaps they are even trying to trip you.

Industrialist Ian McGregor said, "It's important in management to never ask people to accomplish goals they can't accept."

What goals do you have? May God put people in your life who will help you get to the mound.

> *"The Lord is not slack concerning his promise, but is longsuffering toward us, not willing that any should perish."*

2 Peter 3:9

May 7

Bob Hope

Comedian Bob Hope once went to the airport to meet his wife, Dolores, who had been doing charity work for the Catholic Church. When her private plane pulled in, the first two people to step off the plane were Catholic priests. Then came Dolores, followed by four more priests. Hope turned to a friend near him and quipped, "I don't know why she doesn't just buy insurance like everybody else!"

What kind of "insurance" are you counting on? May I suggest that the only insurance God recognizes is the policy of faith.

St. Augustine said, "Faith is to believe what we do not see; and the reward of this faith is to see what we believe."

D.L. Moody, the nineteenth-century preacher, explained how his faith developed. "I prayed for faith and thought that some day faith would come down and strike me like lightening. But faith did not seem to come. One day I read in the tenth chapter of Romans, 'Faith comes by hearing, and hearing by the word of God.' I began to read my Bible, and my faith began to grow."

One day, your flight will end. When you step off the plane, do so by faith.

"We walk by faith, and not by sight."

2 Corinthians 5:7

May 8

Ouch!

In the middle of an October night in 2005, a mugger pulled a handgun on a man in Milwaukee. He demanded money. The victim gave him all he had. Then the getaway car rushed up to pick up the robber. But the driver failed to brake in time, and hit him. This having attracted attention, the driver fled the scene, leaving the robber behind. The thief tried to get away with the cash by limping into the street, but was hit by a woman driving a Lexus. She heard the bump, and backed up, hitting him again. The robber reached into his pocket for his gun and shot himself in the leg. The woman ran into him again, then drove off. Police showed up and arrested the robber, who was taken to the hospital with serious injuries.

I'm sure the thief thought he had considered every possibility. What he hadn't counted on was his own driver hitting him and a lady in a Lexus hitting him, and his pistol mishap.

But I have discovered sin is like that. You can never think of everything to cover it up. So the best thing to do is to not do it in the first place.

> *"If you sin against the Lord, take note. Your sin will find you out."*

Numbers 32:23

May 9

Climbing Mountains

A good friend, David Brooks, loves to climb mountains as a hobby. He has great stories. Then there was an amateur climber who scaled a great mountain with the aid of two guides. He climbed the shaded side to the top. As they reached the peak, the man was exhilarated and began to celebrate, jumping with glee. The gale-force winds almost blew him off the mountain. One of the guides grabbed him and said, "On your knees, get on your knees! You'll only be safe on your knees!"

That is great advice for life. The safest place to be, especially if you seek to scale mountains in your life, is on your knees. Prayer changes things, but it especially changes people.

Dr. Ed Young says, "Wherever you walk, do so on your knees."

A young girl heard the choir singing *God Is Still on the Throne*. On her way home from church, she told her mom, "I really like that song, God Is Still on the Phone."

That is funny, but it's really true! God is still on the phone! Give him a call. You don't need an operator or customer assistance. And the good news is, the toll has already been paid. Rejoice, for God is still on the phone!

"Therefore I say to you, whatever you ask for, when you pray, ask in faith and you will have it."

Mark 11:24

May 10

Snakebites

A Los Angeles police officer took training in how to deal with snakebite victims. The trainer even taught the police officers what to do if they were bitten by a snake but were unable to get medical attention. He explained in great detail that under extreme circumstances one would have to cut his or her skin with a sharp knife and suck out the venom by the mouth.

At that point the officer said, "What happens if I get bitten on my behind?"

After a long pause the instructor said, "Then you'll find out if you have any friends."

When life bites you from behind, you need friends.

A good friend will do five things for you. He will bring you good cheer. He will offer a listening ear. She will give a sensitive tear. When needed, they will kick you in the rear. And always, your friend will speak the truth in fear.

You will probably never have to suck snake venom from a friend. But when your friend needs a good cheer, listening ear, sensitive tear, kick in the rear, and truth in fear, what will you do?

A lousy friend will back away in times like these. But if you are a real friend, in their time of need, you will always be near.

"If they fall, one will lift up his companion."

Ecclesiastes 4:10

May 11

The First Billionaire

When Howard Hughes, Sr. died, his son became a millionaire. He inherited the Hughes tool Company, but decided to go into the moviemaking business. After marrying a Houston socialite, he threw himself into risky ventures.

In the late 1920s, Howard Hughes, Jr. turned his attention to aviation. He started his own aircraft company in 1932, Hughes Aviation. In 1940 he bought controlling interest in Trans World Airlines. He would buy RKO Pictures, several small airlines, television stations, and several hotels and casinos in Las Vegas.

He got married for a second time in 1957, but this marriage failed like the first one. Hughes eventually left the country and lived the life of a hermit. He was phobic about germs and succumbed to drug addiction.

He was the world's first billionaire, but that did him little good when he died in 1976, while being flown back to the United States for medical treatment. He died alienated and alone. And I'm sure that in his final moments, he would have gladly traded places with anyone wealthy enough to have a phone, just so he could have someone to talk to.

"Do not be deceived. Evil company corrupts good habits."

1 Corinthians 15:33

May 12

Pigeon or Statue?

Life is full of ups and downs. But most of us just want ups and ups. The reality is that we all go through tough times. Some days you get to be the pigeon, but other days you're the statue.

We can do everything in our power to avoid negative experiences, but they don't avoid us. Sometimes I try to take life one day at a time, but the days seem to gang up on me all at once. No matter who you are, where you live, what you do, or what you've experienced, life will deal you a blow from time to time.

Famed television host and author Dennis Wholey said it like this: "Expecting the world to treat you fairly just because you're a good person is like expecting the bull to not charge you because you're a vegetarian."

The question is not whether you will have bad experiences, but how you respond to them. Life is ten percent what happens to you and 90 percent how you respond.

Warren G. Lester said, "Success in life comes not from holding a good hand, but in playing a poor hand well."

Anyone can win with a winning hand. But success is reserved for those who know how to act when life treats them like the statue.

"All things work together for good to those who love God and are called according to his purpose."

Romans 8:28

May 13

Buy Ducks

There was a chicken farmer whose land was flooded every spring. He didn't want to give up his farm, but when the water backed up onto his land and flooded his chicken coops, it was always a struggle to get his chickens to higher ground. Some years he couldn't move fast enough and hundreds of his chickens drowned.

After his worst spring ever, and having lost his entire flock, he came into his farmhouse and said to his wife, "I've had it. I can't afford to buy another place. I can't sell this one. I don't know what to do."

His wife offered the obvious. "Buy ducks."

Author Neale Donald Walsh asserted, "Life begins at the end of your comfort zone."

If you're like me, you've been through a few floods in your life. But remember, Psalm 23 promises God will carry us *through* the valley, not just *into* the valley.

President Kennedy was asked how he became a war hero. "It was easy," he said. "Somebody sunk my boat."

Charles Kettering, of General Motors, said, "You never stub your toe standing still."

Sometimes, life sends you a flood. And sometimes, it is good to buy ducks.

"He is the one who goes before you. He will be with you. He will not leave you or forsake you. Do not be afraid."

Deuteronomy 31:8

May 14

Regrets

He was an American hero, a decorated veteran of World War I. He was a farmer, a rancher, a builder, and a self-made success story. But to me, he was simply "grandpa." He was young. Then he got old.

On his 99th birthday, I asked him if he was afraid of dying. He said he didn't expect to die. He reasoned, "Only one person in 10,000 dies past the age of 99."

Unfortunately, grandpa would become a statistic. But he had no regrets.

Ne regrets: two powerful words.

In a national study, senior adults admitted to four regrets. "I should have loved more fully, given more freely, laughed more often, and taken more risks." So, for those of you under 100, let's talk. The only way to avoid regrets later is to make changes now.

Lucy once told Charlie Brown, "My plan is to change the world, and I think I'll start with you."

But there is only one person you can really change, and that person is you.

Some day you will be old. There's really not much you can do about it. So prepare yourself. Love more fully, give more freely, laugh more often, and take more risks. Then, when you are 100, you can say, "no regrets."

"I have fought the good fight, I have finished the race, I have kept the faith."

2 Timothy 4:7

May 15

Getting Older

You have reached middle age when you try to find out where the action is so you can go somewhere else.

There was a guy who was really proud of his four-year-old daughter. He was convinced she was the smartest kid in the world. One day, he took her to an outdoor mall in the wintertime. She was all bundled up with coat, boots, and mittens, to stay warm. Her dad ran into an old friend.

"Ask my daughter how old she is!" he told his buddy, in hopes that his girl would impress him with her answer.

His friend said, "Okay, little girl. How old are you?"

The girl replied, "I can't tell you. I have my mittens on."

It's hard to count with your mittens on. But it's also hard to stay young.

I have only read one article that gave advice that really works, in my task to stay young. It read, "You can stay young indefinitely if you eat wisely, get plenty of sleep, work hard, get plenty of exercise, have a positive mental outlook, and lie about your age."

I don't know how old you are. I'm not sure I know how old I am. But God has numbered our days, and he wants every one of them to count.

"Whatever you do, do it to please the Lord."

Colossians 3:23

May 16

One Woman's Story

Denis Waitley said, "Personal development is the belief that you are worth the effort, time, and energy needed to develop yourself."

Let's consider one woman's story. Johnnetta McSwain was born to a single mother who didn't want her and told her so. Raised in Birmingham, living with her uncles, she was the object of constant sexual abuse. Johnnetta dropped out of high school and had her first child out of wedlock at age 19. To support herself, she turned to shoplifting.

But at age 30 she wrote, "Today I woke up and realized I had nothing to celebrate. It is time to make a change."

She earned her GED, then enrolled in Kennesaw State University. At the start of every semester, she went to the bookstore on campus and tried on a cap and gown, looking at herself in the mirror and imagining what it would be like to graduate.

She completed her bachelor's degree in three years. Then she earned a master's degree, and is now working on her doctorate.

Johnnetta said, "I got tired of hearing, 'No you can't,' and decided, 'Yes I can.'"

That's what God says when he looks at you! Yes you can! God has uniquely gifted you with the ability to serve him.

"Then Huram made the pots and the shovels and the bowls. So Huram finished the work that he was to do for King Solomon for the house of God."

2 Chronicles 4:11

May 17

Obvious Questions

A young family was touring the FBI Headquarters. They were shown pictures on the wall of the ten most wanted men. The family's young lad asked, "Why don't you just keep them when you take their pictures?"

Here's another great question, asked by a little girl of her dad, who was a pastor. "What do John the Baptist and Kermit the Frog have in common?"

The pastor/dad was clueless. "I have no idea, honey. What do John the Baptist and Kermit the Frog have in common?"

"They have the same middle name!" she said.

Kids indeed ask some wonderful questions. That's how they learn.

Questions must be a good thing, because there are a lot of them in the Bible. "What is your life?" "What shall I do with Jesus who is called Christ?" "If a man dies, shall he live again?" "What think ye of Jesus?" "What shall it profit a man if he gains the whole world but loses his own soul?"

Kids are full of questions. The Bible is full of questions. Life is full of questions. But there is good news. For every problem there is a solution, and for every question there is a God.

The best way to get in trouble is to turn somewhere else for the answers to life's most important questions.

"In those days there was no king in Israel; everyone did what was right in his own eyes."

Judges 21:25

May 18

Computers

A man had a problem with his new computer so he called the company tech help. The man on the phone started to talk in computer jargon, confusing the owner of the computer. He said, "Sir, I am struggling to understand what you are saying. Can you please talk to me as if I was four years old?"

"Okay," the technician said. "Son, could you please put your mommy on the phone?"

Someone noted how the car industry might be different if GM had developed their technology like Microsoft.

For no apparent reason, your car would crash twice a day. Every time they painted new lines on the road, you'd have to buy a new car. A simple maneuver might cause the car to shut down, at which time you'd have to re-install the engine. Macintosh would make a car that was twice as fast and more efficient, but could only be driven on five percent of the roads. Every time Ford made a new car, you'd have to learn how to drive all over again.

Now, I'm all for computers. But aren't you glad your car doesn't crash as often as your computer does? Sometimes, the most blessed life is the one lived simply.

"May we be thoroughly complete, prepared for every good work."

2 Timothy 3:17

May 19

How to Win Carnival Games

Ethan Trex has done the world a great favor. He has studied carnival games and devised a winning strategy. Follow these simple tips and you can be the king of carnivals, a prince to preschoolers.

Let's start with the "Balloon Dart Throw." The scam is that the darts are dull and much lighter than normal darts. And the balloons are under inflated, which makes them harder to pop. The strategy is to not hurl the darts hard, but to loft them up, so they can come down onto their target with the assistance of gravity.

Ever tried the "Basketball Shoot"? The rims are smaller than regulation and oval-shaped. The backboards have a harder bounce, the balls are overinflated, and the rims are higher. The trick is to toss the ball underhanded; it's all about getting a good arc on the ball.

Then there is the "Milk Bottle Pyramid." The bottoms are heavier. So if you aim for the middle, you'll never win. You must go low!

Now, let's talk about the "Game of Life." The scam is it looks like you can win by your own strength. The trick is to recognize you can't win unless you depend totally on God.

"I will go with you to Egypt, and I will bring you up again."

Genesis 46:4

May 20

I Feel Your Pain

I had a friend with a terrible toothache. I was there for him.

"So you have a toothache?" I asked him. "Have you been brushing after every meal?"

My friend said, "Yes! But I don't even want to think about brushing right now. My tooth hurts so bad!"

I pressed on. "Are you flossing? I bet you aren't flossing. You deserve to be in pain!"

"Go away," my friend pleaded. "You aren't helping!"

"I bet I know your problem," I continued. "I bet you haven't been getting regular checkups. That's why you hurt. It's your fault. You need to own up to your pain."

In this made-up story, I became more of a nuisance than a blessing. While none of us would do that to our hurting friend, how do we treat those with other problems?

"You are hurting because you aren't right with God!"

"You need to get back in church!"

"If you weren't such a terrible sinner, you wouldn't be in this mess!"

Sure, we mean well. But it's not enough to just mean well. I'm pretty sure you know someone who needs comfort. But our attitudes of judgment and condemnation make us nothing more than a nuisance.

"When they kept asking Jesus, he said to them, 'He who is without sin, let him cast the first stone.'"

John 8:7

May 21

Superman or Batman?

A little boy and his family moved often over a period of a few years. It's tough when you are in and out of different schools so often. One day when he was sitting at home in a melancholy mood, the boy asked his dad, "Who do you want to be, Superman or Batman?"

Dad replied, "Well, son, I'm busy right now."

"Come on, Dad! Who do you want to be, Superman or Batman?"

"Well, Superman, son. I want to be Superman, because he can fly."

But the boy continued, "Dad, aren't you going to ask me who I want to be?"

His dad responded, "Okay, son, who do you want to be?"

"I want to be Batman," replied the boy.

"That's good, son."

"But don't you want to know why I want to be Batman?"

"Okay, why, son?"

"I want to be Batman because Batman has a friend."

Dad said, "Son, do you need a friend?"

"Yeah, Dad. I need a friend more than I need Superman."

I suspect some of you may need a friend. Someone you know needs a friend. Superman is overrated. He looks good. But when you get in trouble, you need a friend. Take the boy's word for it. You want to be Batman.

"Two are better than one, because they have a good reward for their labor."

Ecclesiastes 4:9

May 22

Stages of a Cold

A husband's reactions to his wife's colds during the first seven years of marriage evolve. Year 1: "Sugar Dumpling, I'm really worried about my baby girl. You've got a bad sniffle and there's no telling about these things with all the strep going around. I'm putting you in the hospital. I know the food is lousy, but I'll be bringing your meals in from Landry's."

Year 2: "Listen, Darling, I don't like the sound of that cough and I've called the doctor to rush over here. Now you go to bed like a good girl."

Year 3: "Maybe you should lie down, Honey."

Year 4: "Now look, Dear, be sensible. After you feed the kids, do the dishes and mop the floor, you better get some rest."

Year 5: "Why don't you take an aspirin?"

Year 6: "If you'd just gargle or something instead of sitting around barking like a seal all evening, you might get better."

Year 7: "For Pete's sake, stop that sneezing! Are you trying to give me pneumonia?"

Does this sound familiar to anyone other than my wife? Remember the nice guy you used to be? Guess what? That was the man your wife thought she was marrying.

"For this reason a man should leave his father and mother and be joined to his wife, and the two shall become one."

Ephesians 5:31

May 23

How to Tell You're Aging

Are you getting older? If you aren't sure, let me help. You can tell you are getting older when everything hurts, and when it doesn't, it isn't working. You forget things you just said or wrote. You feel like the morning after, and you haven't been anywhere. Your little black book contains only names ending in M.D. You get winded playing chess. You decide to procrastinate, but never get around to it.

You are getting older if you look forward to a dull evening at home. Your knees buckle but your belt won't. You forget things you just said or wrote. The best part of your day is over when the alarm goes off. Your back goes out more than you do. A fortune teller offers to read your face. You forget what you just said or wrote.

The only person who says they enjoy old age is the one who is so old they forgot what young age felt like. There are only two stages in life: pimples and wrinkles.

But God said he was "I AM." That means "present tense at all times."

Whether you are pimples or wrinkles, young or old, God is there. I'm thankful I am still young, for one day I may forget what I just said or wrote.

"Jesus said to them, 'Most assuredly, I say to you, before Abraham was, I AM.'"

John 8:58

May 24

Good Knight

Movement and direction are two different things. When you are lost looking for your car in the parking lot, you have movement. But what you need is direction. You are like the blind discus thrower, keeping everyone's attention, but setting no records. You need direction. The key is to not shoot the bull or pass the buck. You need a plan.

There was a knight who went to see the king after a great battle. He rode on a limping horse, leaning to one side, bloody, bruised, and scarred. The king asked, "What has befallen you, Sir Knight?"

The knight responded, "Sire, I have been laboring in your service, robbing and burning your enemies to the west."

"You've been doing what?" asked the king. "I don't have any enemies to the west!"

The knight said, "You do now!"

You need direction. Too many approach life with a "fire, ready, and aim" mentality.

Grocery stores number their aisles because they have a plan. Every successful business has a plan. You need a plan. God has a plan. You should start there!

"I will instruct you and teach you in the way you should go; I will guide you with my eye."

Psalm 32:8

May 25

I've Got a Beef!

In a recent edition of *Reader's Digest*, Chris Woolston identified a real problem: to meat or not to meat. It seems that studies show that burgers, steaks, and hot dogs (all red meat) are part of the American dietary tradition. But our cravings may be killing us. After tracking food choices of more than 121,000 adults for up to 28 years, Harvard researchers found that people who eat three ounces of red meat every day were about 13 percent more likely to die, usually from heart disease or cancer, than those who don't eat red meat. And daily servings of processed meat such as bacon raise the risk of early death by 20 percent.

But wait! A 2012 report found that Americans who regularly eat lean beef get more protein, zinc, potassium, and B vitamins than people who don't. A 2010 report estimated that 15 percent of the nation's protein, but only four percent of her fat came from beef.

So what do you do? You listen to the words of Jesus. You'll remember the passage. Let me paraphrase. "Man shall not live by red meat alone, although some is pretty good. Rather, he must live by every word spoken by my Father who is in heaven."

"Man shall not live by bread alone, but by every word that proceeds from the mouth of God."

Matthew 4:4

May 26

Marketing

A local farmer came to the conclusion that the local car dealer had profited greatly by all the add-on options that came with each car. Then one day the car dealer informed the farmer that he was coming around to buy a cow. In a spirit of justice, the farmer attached the following price information to the cow: Basic cow - $500. Two-toned exterior - $45. Extra stomach - $75. Product storing compartment - $60. Straw chopper - $120. Four spigots at $10 each - $40. Cowhide upholstery - $125. Dual horns - $15. Automatic fly swatter - $38. Fertilizer attachment - $185. Total - $1,233.

Charles Brower said, "If Columbus had applied modern survey methods to his proposed voyage, the market test would have told him in advance that the world was flat and that sea monsters would swallow him. Ferdinand and Isabella would have cancelled their appropriation. America would never have been discovered, and all of us would be Indians."

We can learn valuable lessons in marketing from the farmer and from Columbus. But as believers, we have a product so wonderful, it almost sells itself.

"Let the words of my mouth and the meditation of my heart be acceptable in your sight, Lord."

Psalm 19:14

May 27

Making Coffee

Sam Rayburn was Speaker of the United States House of Representative longer than any other man in our history. His character is revealed in the story of his friend, whose teenage daughter suddenly died one night. Early the next morning, the friend heard a knock on his door. When he opened the door, Mr. Rayburn, the most powerful man in Congress, was standing there. He said he'd come by to see what he could do to help in his friend's time of need.

The father said, "I don't know of anything you can do."

Rayburn replied, "Have you had coffee yet, today?"

His friend said he had not taken time for breakfast, in the midst of his enormous grief. So the Speaker made him some coffee. Just then, his friend remembered where Rayburn was supposed to be that morning. "Aren't you supposed to be having breakfast at the White House with President Kennedy this morning?"

Rayburn responded, "Well, I was. But I called the President and told him I had a friend in trouble, so I couldn't come."

Sometimes, all your friend needs is a cup of coffee. The President of the United States can wait.

"A man who has friends must show himself to be friendly, but there is a friend who sticks closer than a brother."

Proverbs 18:24

May 28

Bubble Gum Return

A department store manager noticed a boy staring at the handrail of an escalator. He walked over to him and asked, "Son, are you all right?"

The boy nodded yes without looking up.

"Can I help you?" he asked.

The boy shook his head no and continued to look at the handrail.

"Well, young man, do you want me to explain to you how escalators work?"

The lad replied, "No, Mister. I'm just waiting for my bubble gum to come back!"

Things are not always as they appear. The boy appeared to care about the escalator, when all he really cared about was his gum.

That translates to church. One day, a guest walked in. The usher asked him if it was his first time at that particular church. "Yes," the man replied.

"Would you like to see our bulletin?"

"No," he said.

"Would you like to see our sanctuary?"

"No," he repeated.

"Then perhaps you'd like to see our pastor."

"No, not really."

The usher asked, "Then what would you like to see?"

The guest said, "The first thing I'd like to see is your bathroom."

You can't read a man's heart by his face. He may want your brilliance. Or he may just want his bubble gum back.

> *"For now we see in a mirror, dimly, but then*
> *face to face. Now I know in part, but then I*
> *shall know as I am known."*

1 Corinthians 13:12

May 29

Stuck in Time

In 1957 there was a famous neuropsychology case that has been studied for years. The patient was called Henry M. He was born is Hartford, Connecticut in 1926. He suffered from a case of epilepsy that was so severe and debilitating that he couldn't function. At age 27, he underwent an experimental surgery in which parts of his brain were removed to try to treat his epilepsy.

The good news was that after the surgery, he no longer suffered constant debilitating seizures. And there was no negative impact on his intelligence, personality, or social abilities. There was just one side effect. He had no short-term memory.

Henry M. couldn't remember anything that happened after his surgery. He couldn't recognize his doctors. Once home, he'd do the same jigsaw puzzles over and over, and read and re-read the same magazines.

When interviewed 30 minutes after lunch, he couldn't remember a single thing he had just eaten. Henry M. was stuck in time, unable to learn, grow, or change.

As sad as that is, I know a lot of people who are the same way. For them, all change is bad. So they never grow. It's sad. Really sad.

"As you have therefore received Christ Jesus the Lord, now grow up in him."

Colossians 2:6

May 30

Advice

A grandmother who was concerned about her granddaughter's vocabulary frequently advised the child concerning her words. On one such occasion, Grandma said, "Dear child, I would like you to do something for me. Would you please promise not to use two words? One is crummy and the other is lousy."

The girl replied, "Sure, Grandma. What are the two words?"

The woman tried to give advice. But most advice is like getting kissed on the forehead. It doesn't hurt, but it doesn't help much, either.

I've learned there are two kinds of people in the world: those who want my advice and the other 99 percent. Most of us only want to learn what we already know.

I know a man who is often wrong, but never in doubt. If people want your advice, they will ask for it. But not everyone who asks for it really wants it.

I love the story of the pious old gentleman. He used to get up regularly at prayer meeting in his church and pray, "Use me, Lord, in some advisory capacity!"

Here's my advice. Don't give much advice. You'll probably accomplish more by kissing your friends on their foreheads.

"Listen to counsel and receive instruction, that you may be wise in your latter days."

Proverbs 19:20

May 31

The Speeding Ticket

A man was pulled over for speeding. The officer asked for his license. The driver said, "I lost it after four convictions for drunk driving."

The officer asked for his vehicle registration papers. The driver said he didn't have that, as he had stolen the car, killed the owner and put him in the trunk.

The officer called for back-up. Five other police cars arrived on the scene. The driver was asked to step out of his car.

"Is there a problem?" he asked.

The senior officer said to open the trunk of the car. The man complied, and the trunk was empty.

Then the senior officer said, "One of my men says you killed a person and put them in the trunk. He said you don't have registration papers because you stole the vehicle. And he tells me you don't have a license."

At that, the man produced his license and papers. They ran his record and found it to be clean.

Then the driver said, "I bet the same liar who claimed I killed someone and stole his car also told you I was speeding!"

Now, I am not condoning his action, but you have to give the man credit. He's got that "be wise as a serpent" thing down!

> *"Behold, I send you out as sheep in the midst of wolves. Therefore, be as wise as serpents and harmless as doves."*

Matthew 10:16

June 1

Fishing with Dad

Dad took us fishing a lot. One weekend, we went to Lake Somerville. It was the greatest weekend the three of us ever shared, and it provided the greatest memory I have of my dad, 34 years after his death. It was late night, and we weren't catching any fish. My brother was asleep, but dad and I enjoyed our conversation for hours, as we continued to fish.

Every few minutes, dad said to check my bait. I'd reel in the line, and the worm would be gone.

"I guess the fish got your bait," dad would say, then he'd put on another worm.

This routine was repeated dozens of times. Then dad got up to stretch. As he walked several feet away, I reeled in my line, only to find the bait was gone once again. Since dad wasn't there, I decided to put a fresh worm on my hook, myself. But when I looked into the box of worms, there were none left. I assumed dad had put the last one on before my last cast. I said nothing as dad returned.

A few minutes later, he said to reel it in again. I did, and he again pretended to put another worm on my hook. You see, dad didn't care about his time with the fish. He wanted time with his boys.

"Fathers, do not embitter your children, or they will become discouraged."

Colossians 3:21

June 2

Do What Hack Did

Okay, baseball trivia fans, who holds the record for the most RBI in one season? It's not Ruth, Gehrig, Foxx, DiMaggio, Williams, Maris, Mantle, Mays, Aaron, Bonds, Sosa, or McGuire. It's Wilson. As in Hack Wilson.

He played from 1923 until 1934. He was a good hitter, a good fielder, and a good guy. But he did nothing over his career that made him really stand out. That's why you probably never heard of him. Yet, Hack Wilson is enshrined in baseball's Hall of Fame, right next to fellows like Cy Young, Ty Cobb, and Babe Ruth. How can this be?

It all goes back to one immortal season. The year was 1930. He was named baseball's greatest player that year, as he set the all-time record with 190 runs batted in. For our non-sports readers, that means he helped others score.

He helped others be successful. And for that he is in the Hall of Fame.

You can spend your "career" trying to get noticed and to be a personal success. But instead, why don't you do what Hack did? Spend your time making others successful. And one day, you will find yourself in heaven's Hall of Fame.

"Each of you should look not only to your own interests, but also to the interests of others."

Philippians 2:4

June 3

Muskrats

A handyman named Sam was offered a full-time job by a mill owner who was having problems with muskrats at the mill's dam. The owner asked Sam to rid the mill of the pests and even provided a rifle for him to do the job. Sam was ecstatic because it was the first steady work with a regular paycheck that he'd ever had.

One day, several months later, a friend came to visit Sam. He found him sitting on a grassy bank, the gun across his knees.

"Hey, Sam. Whatcha doin?" he asked.

"My job, guarding the dam."

"From what?"

"Muskrats."

Sam's buddy looked over at the dam, and just at that moment a muskrat appeared. "There's one!" he exclaimed.

"Shoot him!" Sam didn't move.

Meanwhile, the muskrat scurried away.

"Why didn't you shoot him?" asked the friend.

"Are you crazy?" replied Sam. "Do you think I want to lose my job?"

Sam was like most of us. We like to hold onto our job.

But the ultimate sign of a leader is called legacy. Think about the greatest leader who ever lived. Jesus spent three years training a small group. Then he left. And they changed the world.

"We will not hide them from their children; we will tell the next generation the praiseworthy deeds of the Lord, his power and the wonders he has done."

Psalm 78:4

June 4

Heritage Stew

Jack Snider tells the story of the French farmers who were nearly starving early in the 1800s. They were kept alive by what came to be called "the 100-year-old soup."

Each week, to a pot which always simmered on the back of the kitchen stove, the farmer's wife would add whatever was available: a carrot, an onion, or just dandelions. But each week, something would be added with a little more water. The soup never stopped simmering. It was always there.

When the oldest daughter left, included in her dowry was a little pot of that soup.

When French immigrants arrived, those from the southeast rural area of France carried their little pot of "100-year-old soup." Some soup eaten today in South Carolina among those of French descent derives from that 100-year-old soup.

The church of Jesus Christ has been boiling for 2,000 years. Many ingredients have been added and many people have been fed. It is ever old, yet ever new. It is a constant, life-giving gift from those generations that have preceded us, but it needs constant replenishing in order that those who follow may also be fed.

"Jesus answered, 'It is written: man does not live on bread alone, but on every word that comes from the mouth of God.'"

Matthew 4:4

June 5

Drink This!

Robert Cade was a physiology professor at the University of Florida. He was also a big fan of Florida football. Dr. Cade was determined to create a liquid that could quickly replace body fluids lost due to physical exertion and hot weather. Thus, he developed a sports drink and tested it on ten of his school's football players. And for the first time in a long time, the Florida Gators posted a winning record.

Because his drink was credited for much of their success, it was tabbed "Gator Aid." Within a year or two, they shortened the name to "Gatorade."

We all need to be replenished from time to time. I used to play a little tennis. I could run all day, in the summer heat. (Then I got old.) But the highlight was always what happened after the match. We'd go to the local store and get some Gatorade.

People need the physical refreshment Gatorade provides, in times of physical exertion.

But we also need God's replenishment in times of emotional and spiritual draught. And that comes from only one source, time with God. So when you are hot, try Gatorade. When your soul is thirsty, try God.

"And afterward, I will pour out my Spirit on all people. Your sons and daughters will prophesy, your old men will dream dreams, and your young men will see visions."

Joel 2:28

June 6

Black and White

Attending a wedding for the first time, a little girl whispered to her mother, "Why is the bride dressed in white?"

"Because white is the color of happiness, and today is the happiest day of her life," said her mother.

The child thought about this for a minute, then asked, "Then why is the groom wearing black?"

Marriage is a sacred thing. It was the first institution of God, and many who have been married end up in an institution.

I heard about a woman who decided to have her portrait painted. She told the artist, "Paint me with diamond rings, a diamond necklace, emerald bracelets, a ruby broach, and a gold Rolex."

"But you aren't wearing any of those things," he replied.

"I know," she said. "It's in case I should die before my husband. I'm sure he will remarry right away, and I want his new wife to go crazy looking for the jewelry."

Some of us don't wait to drive our spouse crazy. That's what makes marriage fun. The last thing I want in my marriage is predictability. It is fun being married. Marrying Beth was the best decision I ever made. And for the record, my tux was white.

"However, each one of you also must love his wife as he loves himself, and the wife must respect her husband."

Ephesians 5:33

June 7

Patting Birds

Linus, of Peanuts' fame, was taking a lot of heat because of his newly found "calling." He liked to pat birds on their heads. Distressed little birds would approach Linus, lower their feathered pates to be patted, sigh deeply, and then walk away satisfied. This brought Linus indescribable fulfillment.

It brought Charlie Brown and Lucy embarrassment and chagrin. Charlie Brown and Linus dialogued about all this patting. Linus wanted to know, "What's wrong with patting birds on the head?"

It made sense to Linus, for this made the birds feel better and it made him feel happy all over.

"So what's wrong with it?" Charlie stared thoughtfully, and then declared rather frankly, "I'll tell you what's wrong with it. No one else does it!"

There is a great lesson here. Every one of us is uniquely gifted to be a blessing, if not to birds, then to other people. But too many of us suffer from "paralysis by analysis." If no one else is "doing it" we won't either. But true fulfillment in life will only come when you figure out your unique role.

So step out. Be yourself. Pat a bird on his head.

"Let the wise listen and add to their learning,
and let the discerning get guidance, for
understanding proverbs and parables, the
saying and riddles of the wise."

Proverbs 1:5-6

June 8

Proverbs

You can follow Billy Graham's example and read a chapter of Proverbs every day. Or you can listen to the proverbs of man. Let me offer you a few.

Dan Quayle said, "You can give a person a fish, and they'll fish for a day. But if you train a person to fish, they'll fish for a lifetime."

Coach Jack Craft once lamented, "That was the nail that broke the coffin's back."

Milwaukee Braves shortstop Johnny Logan reminded, "Rome wasn't born in a day."

Calgary City Councilman John Kushner said, "I'm speaking off the cuff of my head."

Stuart Pearce said, "I can see the carrot at the end of the tunnel."

Canadian Prime Minister Lester Pearson promised, "We'll cross that bridge when we fall off it."

And Toronto mayor Allen Lamport mused, "Let's jump off that bridge when we come to it."

This proverbial exercise teaches us two things. First, Canadians aren't good with proverbs. Second, you should read a chapter of Proverbs today. As for tomorrow, we'll jump off that bridge when we come to it.

"Above all, you must understand that no prophecy of Scripture came about by the prophet's own interpretation."

2 Peter 1:20

June 9

Sears Catalogue

The local pastor was visiting his people on the eve of the annual revival. He arrived at Mrs. Jones' home without notice. She gladly welcomed him into her home, and asked him to be seated in the living room, with her three children surrounding him with laughter and love.

Then, wanting to impress her pastor, Mrs. Jones instructed one of her kids, "Johnny, go bring me the book that mama loves so much."

She expected Johnny to return with the Family Bible. Instead, he brought in the Sears and Roebuck Catalogue.

Which book do you "love so much"? Which book would those closest to you say you "love so much"?

I'm all for reading magazines, how-to books, self-improvement books, and *Archie Comics*. (I recommend the special *2003 Jughead Double Bonus Issue*.) But there is no substitute for time in God's Word. Why not make a new commitment to spend time in the Word?

The question is not, which book does mama love so much? The question is, which book does God love so much?

David said "God's Word is a light for our path and a lamp for our soul."

Put away the catalogue for a moment. Pick up the Bible.

"From infancy you have known the holy Scriptures, which are able to make you wise."

2 Timothy 3:15

June 10

A Lot of Bull

Two sisters, one blonde and one brunette, inherited the family ranch. But after a few years they were in financial trouble. In order to keep the bank from repossessing the ranch, they needed to purchase a bull from the stockyard in a far town so they could breed their own stock. They had just $600 left.

Upon leaving, the brunette told her sister, "When I get there, if I decide to buy the bull, I'll contact you to drive out after me and haul it home."

The brunette arrived at the stockyard and decided she wanted to buy the bull. The man said it would cost $599. She paid the money, then drove to the next town to send her sister a telegram. She told the man in the office she needed to tell her sister to hitch the trailer to their pickup truck and drive out to get her so they could haul it home.

The telegraph operator explained that it cost $1 per word. Realizing she could only send one word, she said, "Send my sister the word 'comfortable.'"

The operator said, "Why the word 'comfortable?'"

The brunette explained, "My sister is blonde. She'll read it slowly: com-for-ta-bull."

Come for the bull. Give her credit for knowing how to communicate with her sister. Communication is huge in any relationship. Nothing is more important than the words we use.

"Set a guard over my mouth, O Lord; keep watch over the door of my lips."

Psalm 141:3

June 11

Knee-Mail

I have just heard about a new form of communication. I'm sure you are familiar with texting, facebook, text blasting, and twitter. You old timers may remember something called a yellow pad. You may recall an ancient device known as a "typewriter."

Then there used to be another form of communication between the era of carving in stones and facebook. It was called "mail." People would write letters or send cards through something called the United States Postal Service. They would put stamps on the envelopes, representing the cost of delivering the "mail" in rain, hail, snow, or meteor showers.

Actually, they still use "mail" today. Last year, 166,875,000,000 items were sent through the mail. That is 166 billion pieces! I know what you're thinking. "Who are these people who still use 'snail mail?'"

We like our communication to be done fast. That's why we use email.

I've got a form of communication that is even quicker than that. I call it "knee-mail." Here's how it works. Go to your knee, talk to God, and he will hear you right now! Then send me a telegraph, and let me know how it works.

"Pray continuously."

1 Thessalonians 5:17

June 12

Dead Dog

A man ran into the vet's office carrying his dog, screaming for help. The vet rushed his dog to the examination table. The vet examined the dog, then said, "I'm sorry, but your dog is dead."

The dog's owner demanded a second opinion, so the vet went to the back room and came out with a cat and put the cat down next to the dog. The cat sniffed the dog's body, looked at the vet, and meowed. The vet turned and said, "I'm sorry, but the cat thinks your dog is dead, too."

The man wanted a third opinion, so the vet went to the back again, and brought out a black Labrador retriever. The Lab sniffed the dog and barked twice. The vet said, "I'm sorry, but the Lab thinks your dog is dead, also."

The man was finally resigned to the fate of his dog and asked for a bill. It was $650.

"You are charging me $650 to tell me my dog is dead?" screamed the man.

"Well," the vet replied, "I would have charged you just $50 for my initial diagnoses. The additional $600 was for the cat scan and lab tests."

I know, that's a really bad joke! But here's something serious. One day, you will also die. No cat scan or lab test will be able to save you. And then comes the judgment. Are you ready?

"Do not be afraid of those who kill the body but cannot kill the soul. Rather, be afraid of the One who can destroy both the body and the soul in hell."

Matthew 10:28

June 13

Mad Max

They called him "Mad" because he was nuts. They called him "Max" because that was his name. "Mad Max" Jukes had 13 children. None of them were raised in a strong moral home or in church. Max trained them to put themselves first in life.

History records 1,026 descendents of Max Jukes. How did his parenting strategy work out? 300 of his descendents ended up in prison, 190 became prostitutes, and 509 became alcoholics.

Living in the same state as Max Jukes was a man named Jonathan Edwards, who also had 13 kids. They turned out differently. Of Edwards' 929 offspring, 430 became ministers, 86 were professors, 13 became university presidents, 75 were authors, seven served in the U.S. Congress, three were elected governors, and one became Vice President of the United States.

Two men and 1,955 descendents. Jonathan Edwards was a godly, educated, family man. "Mad Max" was not a godly, educated, family man.

You can be a "Mad Max" or a Jonathan Edwards. It's up to you. But keep in mind, your decision will affect generations to come.

"Listen, my son, to your father's instruction and do not forsake your mother's teaching."

Proverbs 1:8

June 14

Just Like Mom's

A couple returned from their honeymoon and set up house. On the first morning, the wife made her husband breakfast as a special treat. She fried eggs, made toast, and poured him a big cup of coffee.

To her disappointment, he responded, "It's just not like Mom used to make."

She tried to hide her hurt feelings. The next morning, she was at it again. And once again, her young husband said, "Thanks, dear, but it's just not like Mom used to make."

Two more times she made him breakfast. Each time, she got the same sorry response. So the next morning, she cooked the eggs until they were as hard as rubber. She incinerated some bacon. She kept putting the bread back in the toaster until it was crispy. And she brewed the coffee until it was like mud. When her husband came to the table, she put his breakfast in front of him. He sniffed the coffee, took one look at his plate, and explained, "Hey! It's just like Mom used to make!"

What the young bride needed to understand was that great childhood memories trump a good breakfast anytime. So today, even if you don't make breakfast, make a memory!

"I thank my God every time I remember you."

Philippians 1:3

June 15

Trash and Dreams

Tom Fatjo was into garbage. He was a graduate of Rice University and a respected member of the Willowbrook Country Club in Houston. Then his life was forever changed by a garbage strike. Yes, a garbage strike.

Fatjo began to dream. He dreamed of owning his own garbage truck and starting his own business. Within ten years Tom was the "guru of garbage." Together, Tom's trash team turned the trash trade totally around. His dream evolved into the largest solid waste disposal company in the world, Browning-Ferris Industries, with annual sales of over $1 billion.

Tom had a dream. He went on to build ten other large, successful companies. When asked the key to his success, Fatjo said, "I'd lay awake at night, thinking about owning a garbage truck. I'd daydream about it at the office. I knew that this was my destiny. I had to do what I wanted to do."

What do you want to do? You will never be happy chasing someone else's dreams. Chase your own dreams.

This week, ask yourself what you really want to do. And next week, think of old Tom when you take out the trash.

"The plans of the diligent lead to profit as surely as haste leads to poverty."

Proverbs 21:5

June 16

Fighting Failure

Thomas Edison. The name is synonymous with brilliance. The man invented hundreds of things. But he is best known, of course, for the light bulb. While we take the light bulb for granted, they never dreamed of such a thing before Edison. But did you know that he failed in his first attempt to make the light bulb? Then he tried again. Again he failed. 1,000 times, Edison failed.

Can't you imagine his friends asking old Tom what he was doing?

He'd say, "I'm inventing the light bulb."

They'd say, "What's a light bulb?"

On and on he kept at it.

Then one day the light came on, in his head, then in the bulb. I would explain the working of a light bulb to you, but my space is limited! Suffice it to say that if not for the persistence of old Tom, we'd all be in the dark today.

Here's the lesson. Don't ever give up on your dreams. Find something you're good at. Then go for it. Sure, you'll fail. Muhammad Ali once said, "My goal when I step into the ring is to get up more than I go down."

So chase your dreams. One day the light will come on. You may never be as famous as Tom, but the world will be a brighter place.

"I was afraid and went out and hid your talent in the ground."

Matthew 25:25

June 17

In a Box

Do you ever play *Monopoly*? I love that game. Give me Boardwalk and a hotel and I'm happy. You can have Mediterranean, Water Works, and Baltic Avenue. Keep your railroads and "Get Out of Jail" card. Give me Boardwalk.

I love the power that comes from owning real estate and watching my opponent stop one space short of "Go." That's my property they landed on, and they will pay . . . dearly!

But when the game is over, it all goes back in the box. That's a lot like life. The "stuff" doesn't last. Boardwalk is fine, for awhile. But eventually, the only things that matter are the things that last.

Did you ever meet the fellow who was on his death bed, complaining that he spent too much time with his family, too much time with friends, and not enough time at work? He doesn't exist.

This world offers a lot of toys. Go buy your BMW, boat, big house, and new golf clubs. Buy a summer home and a winter home, a lake house and a penthouse. There's nothing wrong with that. Just remember, when the game is over, it all goes back in the box.

"If we live, we live to the Lord; and if we die, we die to the Lord. So, whether we live or die, we belong to the Lord."

Romans 14:8

June 18

I'm Quitting Sports

I have been a huge sports fan my whole life. But no more! I am never going back to another live sports event, for several reasons. Every time I go, they want my money. The people I sat with last time didn't even know my name. The seats were not comfortable. The coach never came to visit me in my home. I never even got a call. The referee made a decision with which I could not agree. I was sitting with some hypocrites who were only there to see what others were wearing. Some of the games went into overtime, which made me late getting home.

The band played songs I didn't know. They scheduled the games at times when I had other things to do. My parents made me go to games when I was young, which I've always resented. I read a book on sports, so I know more than the coaches do, anyway.

As for my kids, I'll let them decide if they want to go to sporting events when they are old enough to make that decision for themselves.

So, I am done with sports. I've decided to spend my time in a place where none of these things can ever happen. Sunday, I'm going to start going to church.

"He is the head of the body, the church; he is the beginning and the firstborn from among the dead, so that in everything he might have the supremacy."

Colossians 1:18

June 19

The Show Must Go On!

Minnie believed in her four sons: Harpo, Groucho, Chico, and Zeppo. She taught them, "The show must go on!"

Minnie served as the Marx Brothers' agent, manager, and critic. She got a neighbor to teach Chico the piano. She got Groucho his first job in Gus Edwards' vaudeville act. When the boys did their first motion picture, Minnie saw it 51 times.

So on September 14, 1929, it was no surprise that Minnie would plan to attend their show, *Animal Crackers*, right after she had dinner with her husband, Sam Marx.

As they were leaving the restaurant, Minnie gasped, "I'm having a stroke."

She would never speak again.

The boys were notified just minutes before the start of the play. They knew what Mama would say. "The show must go on!" So they performed in her honor.

They laughed and danced. And when the show was over, they rushed to her hospital bedside. They were too late. But they upheld the family motto. "The show must go on!"

None of us knows the day or hour that our curtain will fall for the last time. So live each day to its fullest. "The show must go on!"

*"Glorify the Lord with me; let us exalt
his name together."*

Psalm 34:3

June 20

The End Is Near!

Famers Fred and Luke were fishing on the side of the road. They made a sign that said, "The end is near! Turn yourself around now before it's too late!"

They held the sign up for all motorists to see as they drove down that street. Many drivers honked their appreciation for the sign. But one driver was not so happy. He pulled over and shouted, "Leave us alone, you religious nuts!"

Suddenly, Fred and Luke heard a big splash.

Fred grinned at Luke then said, "Do you think we should change the sign to say 'Bridge Is Out' instead?"

Billy Graham was asked how close we are to the end. He said, "If we could put the entire timeline of the human race on a 24-hour clock, beginning with creation and concluding with the end times, it is currently 11:59 p.m."

For those of us who are believers, our task is to hold up the sign. We are to be about the business of warning others that the end is closer than it has ever been. For those of us who are not yet believers, our task is to come to faith in Christ while there is still time. If you don't, you may make a big splash, but then you'll have a huge sinking feeling.

"You also must be ready, because the Son of Man will come at an hour when you do not expect him."

Matthew 24:44

June 21

All That Matters

Nineteenth century preacher Charles Spurgeon said, "By perseverance the snail reached the ark."

Emerson commented, "A man is a hero, not because he is braver than anyone else, but because he is brave ten minutes longer."

What is the quality that matters most in life? How about perseverance? Someone said, "Failure is the path of least persistence."

Consider the honey bee. To produce one pound of honey, he must visit 56,000 clover heads. Since each head has 60 flower tubes, he must make 3.36 million visits to produce one pound of honey. He flies enough to circle the earth three times.

Winston Churchill said the key to victory, in WWII or in life, was to "never, ever, ever, ever give up."

Learn from the Little League boys. Down by 21 runs in the top of the first inning, one boy remained optimistic.

"Why are you still cheering?" they wanted to know.

"It's simple," said the boy. "We haven't batted yet."

It doesn't matter what the score is. Persevere. Never, ever, ever give up. Remember, by the grace of God, you will get the last at bat. Perseverance. It's all that matters.

"As for you, brothers, never tire of doing what is right."

2 Thessalonians 3:13

June 22

Sincere, but Wrong

Sincerity is overrated! That's a strong statement, isn't it? We want people to be sincere, even if we disagree with them. But is sincerity all it's cracked up to be?

I mean, Charles Whitman was sincere when he shot and killed 16 people from the tower at the University of Texas. The young Arab terrorist was sincere when he drove his carload of explosives into the Marine barracks in Beirut, killing 241 American peacekeepers. Sirhan Sirhan was sincere when he killed Robert Kennedy. Adolf Hitler was sincere when he wrote *Mein-Kampf*. Benedict Arnold was sincere when he betrayed his county on the banks of the Hudson. And Judas was sincere when he sold his soul for 30 silver coins.

I can drive west on Interstate 10 out of Houston in a sincere search for Dallas. I can swallow arsenic in a sincere attempt to ease a headache. I can eat more ice cream in a sincere effort to lose weight. I can lay on the couch in a sincere attempt to get in shape.

Here's another one for you. I can follow a man-made religion in a sincere effort to find God. I'd be sincere. But I'd also be wrong.

"For the commands are a lamp, this teaching is a light, and the corrections of discipline are the way to life."

Proverbs 6:23

June 23

The Pitching Horse

Years ago, legendary baseball manager Leo Durocher was accosted by a large horse who said, "I'd like to join the Dodgers if you've got a place for me."

"What can you do?" Durocher asked.

"Well, I can bat," said the horse.

"Pick out a bat and show me," said Durocher.

The horse looked over the pile of bats, selected one and stepped out to the plate with the bat between his teeth. The pitcher threw his best fastball. The horse hit it over the fence.

"That's pretty good," said Durocher. "What else can you do?"

"I'm a mighty good first baseman," said the horse.

"Get over there," said Durocher.

The horse then took throws from other fielders and successfully caught several pop ups.

"I'm also a good shortstop," the horse volunteered, and he took a few grounders, fielding each with grace.

"All right," said Durocher, finally convinced. "We'll make a place for you on our team! But tell me, can you pitch?"

The horse sneered and replied, "Are you kidding me? Who ever heard of a horse who could pitch?"

You may not be able to pitch, but God, as your manager, has a place for you on his team!

"You are no longer foreigners and aliens, but fellow citizens with God's people and members of God's household."

Ephesians 2:19

June 24

Dress Rehearsal

Charles Shultz, of Peanuts fame, captured the feeling many of us have had in a comic strip in which Charlie Brown says to Linus, "Life is just too much for me. I've been confused from the day I was born. I think the whole trouble is that we're thrown into life too fast. We aren't prepared."

Linus responds, "What do you want, a chance to warm up first?"

Unfortunately, there is no warm-up in life. There is no dress rehearsal. If you are like most people, you have taken some time and effort to design your career, and probably, your retirement. But have you taken the time to design your life?

If you don't design your own life plan, chances are you will fall into someone else's plan. And guess what they likely have planned for you? Not much!

Greg Matte says, "You wouldn't care what others thought of you if you knew how little they did."

I have conducted hundreds of weddings. The good ones had a dress rehearsal, because the couple (mostly the bride) wants to get it right.

What about your life? What are you aiming at? If the answer is "nothing," I guarantee you will hit it!

"We are confident, I say, and would prefer to be away from the body and at home with the Lord."

2 Corinthians 5:8

June 25

Flying First Class

A blonde got on an airplane and sat in the first class section. The flight attendant rushed over and told her she must move to the coach section because she didn't have a first class ticket. The blonde responded, "I'm blonde, I'm smart, and I have a good job. I'm staying in first class until we reach Jamaica."

The flight attendant was irritated and went for the head flight attendant, who went to the blonde and asked her to move to coach. She repeated, "I'm blonde, have a good job, and I'm staying in first class."

The head flight attendant then went to the co-pilot, who went to the lady, with the same results.

Finally, the pilot was called in. He walked over to her and whispered in her ear. She immediately got up and moved to coach. They asked the pilot what he had whispered. He said, "I just told her the first class section doesn't go to Jamaica."

I have never flown first class. I've never had the pleasure of paying hundreds of dollars for an upgrade in peanuts. I'm fine with coach. And I know where I'm going.

I'd rather reach my promised eternal destination in coach than ride first class and end up in the wrong place.

"If a man dies, will he live again? All the days of my hard service I will wait for my renewal to come."

Job 14:14

June 26

Churchill's Funeral

Winston Churchill arranged his own funeral. There were stately hymns in St. Paul's Cathedral and an impressive liturgy. When they said the benediction, he had arranged for a bugler high in the dome of St. Paul's Cathedral on one side to play *Taps*, the universal signal that the day is over.

But when that was finished, there was a long pause and then a bugler on the other side played *Reveille*, the signal of a new day beginning. It was Churchill's way of communicating that while we say "Good night" here, it's "Good morning" up there.

Jesus said, "I am the resurrection and the life; he who believes in me, though he were dead, yet shall he live."

When a man steps out of his own grave, he is anything that he says that he is and he can do anything he says he can do!

I have conducted somewhere between 1,200 and 1,500 funeral services. One thing was true of each of them. The body stayed put.

But Jesus' body was raised from the dead. Because he lives, we can live forever. Replace *Taps* with *Reveille*. When night falls, that merely opens the door for a "Good morning" that will never end.

"In a flash, in the twinkling of an eye, at the last trumpet, the dead will be raised imperishable, and we will be changed."

1 Corinthians 15:52

June 27

It Will Never Happen

Man has a history of saying, "It will never happen," and then it does.

Consider this, from *The Quarterly Review*, in 1925. "What can be more palpably absurd than the prospect held out of locomotives traveling twice as fast as stagecoaches?"

Then there was Lee Deforest, scientist and inventor. In 1926 he said this. "While theoretically and technically television may be feasible, commercially and financially, I consider it an impossibility, a development of which we need not waste our time dreaming."

And in 1901, William Baxter, Jr. wrote in *Popular Science*, "As a means of rapid transit, aerial navigation (airplanes) could not begin to compete with the railroad."

I save the best for last. *The Literary Digest* made this ironclad prediction in 1889. "The ordinary 'horseless carriage' is at present a luxury for the wealthy; and although its price will probably fall in the near future, it will never, of course, come into as common use as the bicycle."

Yes, we have a history of being often wrong, but never in doubt. And here's a line I hear a lot today. "Jesus can't possibly return during my lifetime!"

"Men of Galilee, why do you stand here looking into the sky? This same Jesus, who has been taken from you into heaven, will come back in the same way you have seen him go into heaven."

Acts 1:11

June 28

Best Question Ever

Life is full of questions. Most of us ask over 50 questions a day. Someone made a fortune off the statement, "Don't ask why."

My response is "Why not?"

We ask when, where, how, who, and what, dozens of times each day. We ask for help when we are in need. Fifty percent of the adult population asks for directions when they are lost. (The other 50 percent are called "men.")

Life is full of statements. "Why is grass green? What makes rainbows? Why does Grandpa have more hair growing from his ear than from his head? Why do clocks run clockwise? Why is a fly ball ruled a fair ball when it hits the foul pole? Why do we have to stay out of the pool for 30 minutes after we eat lunch?"

I have a question of my own. What is the greatest question ever asked? What is the one question we should ask ourselves several times each day?

Here's my suggestion. Ask yourself this, every time you face an important decision. "What is the wise thing to do?"

That's it! "What is the wise thing to do?"

If you're like me, the answer will usually be obvious. Try it. It makes life a lot simpler. Don't ask me why!

"You desired faithfulness even in the womb; you taught me wisdom in the secret place."

Psalm 51:6

June 29

Thirty-Three Percent Have This Problem

It afflicts 100 million Americans and causes 38,000 deaths each year, including 1,500 on the road. It costs the U.S. a whopping $70 billion worth of productivity. Sixty-four percent of teens suffer from it. It hits hardest between ages 30 and 40. Fifty percent of seniors suffer from it. Treatments range from mouth guards to herbal teas to medication.

I am talking about insomnia. America can't get to sleep. To fight back, Americans consume 30 tons of sleeping pills, aspirin, and tranquilizers every day!

Thomas Edison lived off 15-minute naps. But Albert Einstein averaged 11 hours of sleep each night. In 1910 we slept an average of nine hours; now we are down to seven.

It's funny. We are the only creatures who struggle with sleep. Dogs doze, bears hibernate, and my cat sleeps 23 hours a day.

So what makes us (people) different? We worry. We worry a lot. Psychologists say that 90 percent of what we worry about never even happens. But we worry anyway.

I'm reminded of a Carpenter who lived 2,000 years ago. He said, "Give me your burdens. Do not worry."

The dog, bear, and cat get it. What about you?

"Cast all your anxiety on him because he cares for you."

1 Peter 5:7

June 30

Dirty Looks

A mother and her adult daughter were out shopping one day, trying to make the most of a big sales weekend before Christmas. As they went from store to store in the mall, the older woman complained about everything: the crowds, the poor quality of the merchandise, the prices, and her sore feet.

After the mother experienced a particularly difficult interaction with a clerk in one department store, she turned to her daughter and said, "I'm never going back to that store again. Did you see that dirty look she gave me?"

The daughter answered, "She didn't give it to you, Mom. You had it when you went in!"

There was a man who had been married for 45 years. Someone asked him if he ever woke up grumpy. He responded, "No, I usually let her sleep in."

Whether you are Grumpy, Dopey, or another of the cast of characters, you are who you are by choice. The woman in the store probably had a dirty look on her face because she had something dirty in her heart.

Jesus said that what is in a person comes out. So don't worry about your dirty look. Do something about your heart.

"He will yet fill your mouth with laughter and your lips with shouts of joy."

Job 8:21

July 1

Dive In!

The story is told of a wealthy Texas oil man. He owned a large company and lived on a large ranch. One day, he hosted an outdoor BBQ for hundreds of his employees. After dinner, they all went out back to see his new, huge swimming pool. The pool was built in the shape of Texas.

The eccentric tycoon then suggested a little game. All the men present would jump in the pool at one side, and swim to the other side. The winner could have anything he wanted.

There was one problem. The pool was full of alligators. When the man fired the gun to start the race, only one young man jumped in. He swam furiously, battling alligators all the way. He heroically made it to the other side.

When he got out, with holes in his clothes and scratches on his body, the tycoon congratulated him.

"Wow! That was great! You won. What do you want?"

The young man responded, "I want one thing. I want the name of the fellow who pushed me into the pool!"

Life is like that pool. It offers great rewards to those willing to take a chance.

But be like Jesus. Don't jump in for yourself, but to please your Father. Don't be too timid. Dive in to the abundant life! Don't wait to be pushed.

> *"I seek not to please myself but the one who sent me."*

John 5:30

July 2

Ticks and Dinosaurs

We all have wrestled with life's most important question. What killed all the dinosaurs? Some say it was an asteroid. Others say global warming did it. My theory is that King Kong was somehow involved. But a new hypothesis has emerged.

Some scientists believe that the real culprit was ticks and mosquitoes. Perhaps they spread disease to the dinosaurs or poisoned the plants that the dinosaurs ate. The huge dinosaurs were "bugged" until they were "ticked" off. Eventually, the giant mammals were driven to extinction.

What bugs you? I bet it's the little stuff. It's always the little stuff. We can handle the big stuff, like money problems, difficulties at work, and our favorite team missing the Super Bowl. It's the little stuff that bugs us.

I'm okay with the idea of losing my mind. It's losing my keys that I can't stand. One day my car was stolen. Boy, was I mad! I had left my phone in the car, so I had no way of calling the police. Yes, it's the little bugs flying around our heads that irritate us to the point of lunacy.

Nehemiah did a great work for God, building the walls around Jerusalem. But Tobiah, who did nothing to contribute, criticized from the sideline. He nearly "bugged" Nehemiah to death. But Nehemiah never lost his focus on what God wanted him to do. Do what Nehemiah did. Learn from the dinosaur. Watch out for the ticks.

"Tobiah the Ammonite, who was at his side, said, 'What they are building, even a fox climbing up on it would break down their wall of stones!'"

Nehemiah 4:3

July 3

80-Year-Old Jogger

I love the story about the 80-year-old man who went jogging. One day he was seen running with a woman who was 25. His cardiologist spotted him. The doctor pulled him aside and asked, "What do you think you're doing?"

"I'm following your advice," the jogger replied.

"What advice was that?"

"Don't you remember, doc? After my physical last week, you said, 'Get a hot mama and be cheerful!'"

His physician responded, "That's not what I said! I didn't say, 'Get a hot mama and be cheerful.' I said, 'You've got a heart murmur. Be careful!'"

Most of us are like my uncle who died a few years ago. He didn't hear too well. You had to scream at the man. But we screamed at him for 40 years. The problem was that he, like most of us, heard what he wanted to hear.

Now, I'm all for encouragement. But we also need daily reality checks. There is a verse in the Bible that says, "Listen." In fact there are several verses that say that. But I can't seem to find one verse that simply says, "Talk."

So, before you do something goofy, learn to listen. Listen to your heart. Listen to the Good Doctor. And be careful!

> *"Sin is not ended by multiplying words, but the prudent hold their tongues."*

Proverbs 10:19

July 4

The Window

G.W. Target tells a great story, which I will shorten for our purposes today. It is called *The Window*. It is the story of two men, both critically ill, who shared a hospital room. One man was in the bed next to the window, where he had a clear view beyond the confines of their room. The other man had no view of the window from his bed.

The man without the view asked his new friend to describe the view outside the window. His friend told him of the park across the street, the children playing, the river through the woods in the distance, and the beauty of the sunset each day. One day, he described the parade that passed by, with jugglers, a band, and a giant float.

Then one night, the man near the window died in his sleep. The other man pled to be moved to the window bed. The nurses were happy to oblige. He was so excited to finally see the beauty he had been hearing about from his friend.

Then he pulled himself up so he could peer outside, and he saw it. A blank wall. That was it.

Here's the lesson. The pursuit of happiness is a choice. It is an attitude. It is all about what you choose to focus on.

"Be made new in the attitudes of your mind."

Ephesians 4:23

July 5

World's Greatest Pitcher

I love the story of the boy who stepped onto the ball field and announced, "I am the greatest hitter of all time."

He then tossed the ball into the air and swung his bat. He missed. Strike one. Undeterred, he announced a second time, "I am the greatest hitter of all time."

He tossed the ball up and swung again. Again he missed. Strike two.

Even louder, he shouted, "I am the greatest hitter of all time."

A third time, he tossed the ball into the air. A third time, he swung his bat. And a third time, he missed.

Unfazed, the boy bragged, "I am the greatest pitcher of all time!"

That is the definition of confidence. When Babe Ruth retired, his 714 home runs ranked first all-time. But he also set the record for strikeouts. Ty Cobb had the highest career batting average ever. But he made an out five out of eight at-bats. Nolan Ryan is the all-time strikeout king, who pitched a record seven no-hitters. But he also lost close to 300 games.

Here's the lesson. Confidence is a big thing. It is the gift of God. So go ahead. Step onto the field. Toss the ball into the air. Do your best. Believe in yourself. And never quit swinging.

"Let us then approach the throne of grace with confidence, so that we may receive mercy and find grace to help us in our time of need."

Hebrews 4:16

July 6

I'm Tired

I'm tired. I'm worn out. My get-up-and-go has got-up-and-went. What is the problem?

At first, I blamed it on middle age, wax build up, or not watching enough TV. But I've done my homework, and now know why I'm tired. It's simple. I am overworked.

Let me explain. The population of this country is 300 million. One hundred and twenty-six million are retired. That leaves 174 million to do the work. There are 113 million in school, which leaves 61 million to do the work. Of this total, 33 million work for the government. That leaves 28 million to do the work.

Six million are in the armed forces, which leaves 22 million. Take away the 21,800,000 who work for state and local governments, and that leaves 200,000 to do the work. There are 188,000 in hospitals, so that leaves 12,000 to do the work. Now, there are 11,998 people in prisons.

That leaves just two people to do the work. You and me. And I'm not sure about you, because you're sitting there reading this book. No wonder I'm tired. It's a good thing God created the Sabbath Day. I need it. I can't wait. Because I'm tired.

"The Lord replied, 'I will go with you, and I will give you rest.'"

Exodus 33:14

July 7

Deck Chairs

Life can be complicated. It used to be that I had all the answers. Then something happened. The questions got harder.

I am jealous of those who live in a black-and-white world where there are two distinct views: their view and the wrong view. I find myself living life more in the gray these days.

I can relate to my favorite historical figure, Charlie Brown. One day, Lucy is philosophizing and Charlie is listening. As usual, Lucy has the floor, delivering one of her dogmatic lectures.

"Charlie Brown," she begins, "life is a lot like a deck chair. Some place it so they can see where they're going. Others place it to see where they've been. And some place it so they can see where they are in the present. Where do you place your chair, Charlie Brown?"

Charlie sighs, then responds, "I can't even get my chair unfolded!"

Perhaps you are a visionary. Your chair faces forward. Perhaps you like to reminisce. You face backward. Perhaps you live in the "now." Your chair reflects that. Or perhaps your life is unsettled right now.

That's okay. There's hope. Let God help you unfold your chair.

"Therefore, since we are surrounded by such a great cloud of witnesses, let us throw off everything that hinders and the sin that so easily entangles, and let us run with perseverance the race marked out for us."

Hebrews 12:1

July 8

Humility? It's Tough!

Humility is hard to come by. I think I may be the only person I know who is truly humble. And I say that will all humility.

The opposite of humility is pride. The two can't co-exist.

I love the old eighteenth century hymn by Isaac Watts. He wrote, "When I survey the wondrous cross, on which the Prince of glory died, my richest gain I count but loss, and pour contempt on all my pride."

How are you doing in the "pride" category? You will probably never be as humble as I am, but you can still try. Consider the options before you.

Greece said, "Be wise and know yourself."

Rome said, "Be strong and discipline yourself."

Religion says, "Be good and conform yourself."

Epicureanism says, "Be resourceful and expand yourself."

Psychology says, "Be confident and assert yourself."

Materialism says, "Be possessive and please yourself."

Ascetism says, "Be lowly and suppress yourself."

Humanism says, "Be capable and believe in yourself."

Pride says, "Be superior and promote yourself."

But Jesus says, "Be unselfish and humble yourself." So do what I did. Become incredibly humble.

"When the Lord saw that they humbled themselves, this word of the Lord came to Shemaiah: 'Since they have humbled themselves, I will not destroy them but will soon give them deliverance.'"

2 Chronicles 12:7

July 9

Happiness and Money

Christina Onassis said, "Happiness is not based on money. And the best proof of that is our family."

A man explained why he bought his new car. "I was faced with the choice of buying a $50 battery for my old car or a new car for $50,000. And they wanted cash for the battery."

The Bible says more about money than just about any other subject. Jesus' parables were dominated with the theme of money. Interestingly, the Bible does not condemn money. It condemns the love of money. There is nothing wrong with having money so long as your money doesn't have you.

It is natural to look for happiness where we can find it the easiest. For many of us, that involves money. We are like the drunk who was seen crawling along the ground under a streetlight late one night.

"What are you looking for?" he was asked.

"I'm looking for my wallet."

His friend responded, "Are you sure you lost it here?"

"No," said the drunk. "I dropped it a half a block from here."

"Then why are you looking for it here?"

"Because there's no streetlight over there!"

Time Magazine did a survey. They found that people are seeking happiness more than anything else. The problem is we are looking in the wrong place.

"Keep your lives free from the love of money and be content with what you have."

Hebrews 13:5

July 10

Finding a Good Man

Recent surveys indicate that 52 percent of those over the age of 25 are single. I am not naïve enough to believe these single saints are all interested in getting married. Some of them are too smart for that!

But if you are a single woman, and you opened today's devotional in hopes of finding dating advice, you came to the right place. I am here to help. The answer to finding the right guy is prayer. You must pray, asking the Lord to direct you to the right man, the man who will make you happy all the days of your life.

And for those of you who don't know how to pray, I can help you with that, as well.

Here, I offer a prayer. Use it as your own. Don't even feel obligated to tell God where you got it. He probably already knows, anyway. So ladies, if you are looking for a guy, here's your prayer: "Father in heaven, hear my prayer, and grant it if you can. I've hung a pair of trousers here; please fill them with a man."

If you pray that prayer from your heart, it's just a matter of time till you meet that special man. Perhaps you'd like to come up with your own prayer. The point isn't the words anyway. God listens to your heart.

"Then when the king's edict is proclaimed throughout all his vast realm, all the women will respect their husbands, from the least to the greatest."

Esther 1:20

July 11

One Person

Why don't you do more?

"I'm just one person," you say.

To that, I quote the Hebrew word. "Bologna."

One person can do a lot! Let's consider an example. One man invented the bifocals most of you are using to read this print right now. He did it at the age of 79. The same fellow was the first to harness the electricity needed for you to turn on your coffee pot this morning. He founded an Ivy League school and fathered the U.S. Mail. He invented the lightning rod and designed the heating stove. This fellow spoke and wrote in five languages, despite just two years of formal education.

Who was this man? Most of you guessed it: Ben Franklin. One might call him a bit of an over-achiever. Do you know people like that?

Mark Twain said, "Few things are harder to put up with than the annoyance of a good example."

At the risk of annoying you with the example of Mr. Franklin, I challenge you to look into your own life. You are just one person. Correction: you are one person. (Leave out the "just.")

But did you know the Bible says, "I can do everything through him who gives me strength"? Don't trust me. Ask Ben.

"I can do everything through him who
gives me strength."

Philippians 4:13

July 12

Paul Newman

One day, a tourist was standing in line to buy an ice cream cone at a Thrifty Drug Store in Beverly Hills. To her utter shock and amazement, who should walk in and stand right behind her but Paul Newman! Well the lady, even though she was rattled, determined to maintain her composure. She purchased her ice cream cone and turned confidently and exited the store. However, to her horror, she realized that she had left the counter without her ice cream cone. She waited a few minutes untill she felt all was clear, and then went back into the store to claim her cone.

As she approached the counter, the cone was not in the little circular receptacle, and for a moment she stood there pondering what might have happened to it. Then she felt a polite tap on her shoulder, and turning around, was confronted by, you guessed it, Paul Newman. The famous actor then told the lady that if she was looking for her ice cream cone, she had put it into her purse.

People are funny. We act crazy when we meet someone famous. Here's a solution. Meet God and embrace him. Then nobody else will seem so impressive.

"Then Moses said to God, 'Who am I,
that I should go to Pharaoh and bring the
Israelites out of Egypt?'"

Exodus 3:11

July 13

The Right Book

There is one thing that we all have in common. It doesn't matter if you are liberal or conservative, tall or short, young or old. We all want to be successful.

Admittedly, we define "success" in a myriad of ways. But however you define it, you want it. We all do, and that's okay.

I love to visit bookstores. I often find myself gravitating to the self-help section. On a recent perusal of a local store, I came across the following titles: *Passport to Prosperity, Winning Moves, Good Greed, Leadership Secrets of Attila the Hun, Winning Through Intimidation, Cashing In On the American Dream, The Art of Selfishness, How to Retire at 35, Techniques that Take You to the Top, How to Get What You Really Want,* and *Secrets to Quick Success.*

Who are we kidding? Even if these books worked, is there really anything to be gained by being selfish or rich?

Jesus said the dumbest thing anyone can do is to get lots of worldly goods, but lose his own soul. I found that in another book. It's called the Bible.

> *"All Scripture is God-breathed and is useful for teaching, rebuking, correcting, and training in righteousness, so that the man of God may be thoroughly equipped for every good work."*

2 Timothy 3:16

July 14

I Am

Do you ever find yourself living in the past, or maybe in the future? I am a planner. I live by lists. I am constantly planning my next move.

Whether you tend to live in the past (nostalgic) or in the future (fantasy), neither really works. That is because God is the God of right now.

Helen Mallicoat has offered a timeless piece of literature that reminds us that God is the great "I AM." She writes: "I was regretting the past and fearing the future. Suddenly my Lord was speaking. 'My name is I AM,' he said. Then he paused. I waited, and he continued. 'When you live in the past, with its mistakes and regrets, it is hard. I am not there. My name is not I WAS. When you live in the future, with its problems and fears, it is hard. I am not there. My name is not I WILL BE. When you live in this moment, it is not hard. I am here. My name is I AM."

Where are you living today? Focus on the past and you will be bitter. Let go of the past and you will be better. Forget the future. Live for today.

Walk your dog, watch a sunrise, call a friend, say a prayer. Remember, you will be talking to the great "I AM."

"Moses said to God, 'Suppose I go to the Israelites and say to them, the God of your fathers has sent me to you, and they ask me, what is his name? Then what shall I tell them?' God said to Moses, 'I AM WHO I AM. This is what you are to say to the Israelites. I AM has sent me to you.'"

Exodus 3:13-14

July 15

Titanic

Robert Ballard was a man on a quest. He wanted to find the *Titanic*. And on September 1, 1985, he discovered the sunken ship in the North Atlantic, more than 350 miles off the coast of Newfoundland.

I got chills when I read his account for the first time. He sent down that bright probe light and saw that sight more than two miles below the surface of those icy waters. "My first direct view of *Titanic* lasted less than two minutes, but the stark sight of her immense black hull towering above the ocean floor will remain forever ingrained in my memory. My lifelong dream was to find this great ship and during the past 13 years the quest for her has dominated my life."

What quest is dominating your life today? What do you dream about when you are laying in bed late at night? What would you do if you could do anything? What is the carrot that keeps you going?

God created us with passion. Ask him to give you a passion worth committing your life to.

"Therefore, my dear brothers, strand firm. Give yourselves fully to the work of the Lord."

1 Corinthians 15:58

July 16

Get Out of Bed!

"Get out of bed!" said the mother to her son . . . who was 38.

"I don't want to," he groaned, as he pulled the covers over his head.

"But you have to get up," she insisted. "It's Sunday, and church starts in an hour."

"But I don't want to go to church," he complained. "Why do I have to go?"

Trying to maintain her patience, his mother suggested, "You need to go to church for three reasons. First, you need to go because I am your mother, and I said so. Second, church will do you good. And third, you're the pastor!"

There are times all of us would rather stay in bed. I heard about a minister who told his church, "I'm here because I have to be. I'm paid to be good. But most of you are good for nothing." Now, that's honesty.

So what do you do this Sunday, when you'd rather sleep in? You deserve the extra rest. The church will be there on Easter. Get up anyway. Here's an idea. Don't go to church for yourself. Do it for everyone else. Whether you're paid to be good, or "good for nothing," your church will be a better place if you listen to your mom and get out of bed!

"Praise the Lord. Praise God in his sanctuary."

Psalm 150:1

July 17

Unity

In a parable she calls "A Brawling Bride," Karen Mains paints a vivid scene, describing a suspenseful moment in a wedding ceremony. Down front stands the groom in a spotless tuxedo, handsome, smiling, full of anticipation, shoes shined, every hair in place, anxiously awaiting the presence of his bride. All attendants are in place, looking joyful and attractive. The magical moment finally arrives as the pipe organ reaches full crescendo and the stately wedding march begins.

Everyone rises and looks toward the door for their first glimpse of the bride. Suddenly there is a horrified gasp. The wedding party is shocked. The groom stares in embarrassed disbelief.

Instead of a lovely woman dressed in elegant white, smiling behind a lace veil, the bride is limping down the aisle. Her dress is soiled and torn. Her leg seems twisted. Ugly cuts and bruises cover her bare arms. Her nose is bleeding, one eye is purple and swollen, and her hair is disheveled.

"Does not this handsome groom deserve better than this?" asks the author.

And then comes the clincher. "Alas, his bride, the church, has been fighting again!"

> *"I appeal to you, brothers, in the name of our Lord Jesus Christ, that all of you agree with one another so that there may be no divisions among you and that you may be perfectly unified."*

1 Corinthians 1:10

July 18

Golf and God

I am to golf what rap is to music. Technically, I am a golfer, as I have hacked at the ball an average of once a year over the past ten years.

One day, I was playing out of the rough. There was a tree directly between me and the green. God knew my ball would be right there, but he stuck a tree in my path anyway. I never hit my target, so I aimed right for the tree. Then it hit me – the ball, that is. It didn't hit the trunk of the tree, just a small branch. But the ball came right back at me. It is amazing what big damage a small branch can cause. One tree limb turned a promising double bogey into something much worse.

What are you aiming at? Standing between every man and his target is a small branch. Remember, not all branches are made of wood. Some are made of bad habits or attitudes. What is your target?

An old philosopher once said, "If you aim at nothing, you will hit it every time." The best way to miss the branch is by not swinging the club. But if you do that, you will never hit the green.

So keep swinging, and keep your eye on the ball, or the ball may keep an eye on you. And watch out for small branches.

"Delight yourself in the Lord and he will give you the desires of your heart."

Psalm 37:4

July 19

The Grocery List

Nothing matters more in marriage than communication. I love the story about the lady who sent her husband to the grocery store to buy the necessary ingredients to make a cake. He came home with one carton of eggs, two sacks of flour, three boxes of cake mix, four sacks of sugar, and five cans of frosting. His wife looked at his bag of groceries and lamented, "I never should have numbered the list."

My wife sent me to the store for bread one time. I came home with a hundred other things, but forgot the bread.

Communication is critical. We receive 35,000 messages each day. We speak 16,000 words. Communication is made up of three things: what we say (seven percent), how we say it (38 percent), and what others see (55 percent).

As for retention, we remember 15 percent of what we hear, but 85 percent of what we see. Communication is critical, especially in marriage.

Archie Bunker once complained to Edith, "I speak in English, but you hear in Dingbat."

So guys, before you go to the store for your wife, make sure you understand what she wants. And ladies, before you send your husband to the store, ask yourself, "Is this really a good idea?"

"Then the Lord reached out his hand and touched my mouth and said to me, 'Now I have put my words in your mouth.'"

Jeremiah 1:9

July 20

Gettysburg

Things weren't going particularly well for the North. That was when President Lincoln exercised one of his greatest assets, his ability to empower others. After the failed leadership of Ambrose Burnside and Joseph Hooker, Lincoln placed the command of the Army of the Potomac into the hands of General George G. Meade. It was June, 1863. Within hours of Meade's appointment, Lincoln sent a courier to him. The courier bore this message from the President.

"Considering the circumstances, no one ever received a more important command; and I cannot doubt that you will fully justify the confidence which the Government has reposed in you. You will not be hampered by any minute instructions from these headquarters. Your army is free to act as you may deem proper. All forces within the sphere of your operations will be held subject to your orders."

Meade's first challenge would confront him at a small Pennsylvania town named Gettysburg. Meade stopped Lee.

The war turned because Lincoln understood the power of expressing total trust in another person. It worked then, and it works today. Find God's servant, then empower him and follow him.

"For he is God's servant to do you good."

Romans 13:4

July 21

Coca-Cola

In 1997, one of the finest business leaders in the world died. His name was Roberto Goizueta, and he was the chairman and chief executive of the Coca-Cola Company. A few months before he died, he said, "A billion hours ago, human life appeared on Earth. A billion minutes ago, Christianity emerged. A billion seconds ago, the Beatles performed on The Ed Sullivan Show. A billion Coca-Colas ago . . . was yesterday morning."

He told the Atlanta newspaper he had no plans for retirement. Six weeks later he was dead. And so was Coca-Cola. Or was it?

Normally, when the CEO suddenly goes away, the company goes in the tank. But not Coke. Goizueta had grown Coke from a $4 billion company to a $150 billion company. But he did something more important than that. He groomed Douglas Ivester to take his place, if and when the need would arise. Goizueta taught Ivester everything he knew, just in case. And "in case" happened. It always does.

You see, the key to your success in any venture is not what you do, but what you prepare others to do. Paul mastered this concept, and he told Titus to do the same. He understood the importance of finding good men and training them to lead the next generation.

"An elder must be blameless, entrusted with God's work."

Titus 1:6

July 22

Over a Hundred Years Ago

The year was 1911. The South Pole was not the vacation paradise it is today. But a Norwegian explorer named Roald Amundsen set out to change that. His goal was to be the first man to reach the South Pole.

He studied the methods of the Eskimos and other experienced Arctic travelers and determined that his team's best course of action would be to transport all their equipment and supplies by dogsled.

When assembling his team, Amundsen chose expert skiers and dog handlers. His strategy was simple. The dogs would do most of the work as the group traveled 15 to 20 miles a day. Rather than rely on his own strength, and that of the other men, they would rely on the strength of the dogs.

At the same time, a British explorer named Robert Falcon Scott led a group toward the same goal. But his men did all the work, instead of the dogs.

He eventually made it, all right. But he was exhausted from doing all the work himself, when he didn't have to. And when he arrived at the South Pole, Scott and his weary explorers were greeted by a Norwegian flag flapping in the wind.

"The righteous cry out, and the Lord hears them; he delivers them from all their troubles."

Psalm 24:17

July 23

Dealing with Opposition

There once lived a man named Nehemiah. He built a wall of Biblical proportions. In fact, you can read about it in the Bible in the book that bears his name. In 52 days, Nehemiah built a massive wall to protect Jerusalem against attack.

But he built more than a wall. Nehemiah built the nation's self-esteem, beauty, and pride. But at every step, he faced opposition. And from his experience, we learn two valuable truths that apply only to people who try to do something bigger than themselves.

First, we learn to expect opposition. The only person who faces no opposition is the person sitting still. Expect criticism, but don't take it personally. Remember, you will be criticized for doing anything, so make sure you are doing the right thing.

The second truth is that you must keep on track. Keep working as though it all depends on you. And keep praying as though it all depends on God. Don't give up, and don't get discouraged.

Jerry Falwell was right when he said, "You can define the greatness of a man by what it takes to discourage him."

"No weapon forged against you will prevail, and you will refute every tongue that accuses you."

Isaiah 54:17

July 24

Save One Child

Nicholas Winton was a young stockbroker in London. The year was 1939. Hitler's armies were ravaging Czechoslovakia, tearing families apart. Parents were marched to concentration camps, and the children were abandoned.

Winton got wind of their plight and resolved to help them. He used his vacation to travel to Prague where he met parents who were willing to give their children over to his care. Over the next five months, Winton took five trips, transporting 669 children to safety.

After the war, Winton didn't tell anyone what he had done, not even his wife. But in 1988 she discovered an old scrapbook in the attic, which told the whole story, listing every name.

She got Winton to tell her the story, and then Mrs. Winton went to work. Unknown to her husband, she contacted the rescued children, now in their 70s and 80s. And on a fall morning of 2009, she gave her husband the biggest surprise any 100-year-old man has received since the days of Sarah and Abraham.

The 22 survivors showed up at his house to say "Thank you." And they presented him with cards from their 7,000 descendents.

"It is good to give thanks."

Psalm 92:1

July 25

Dying Slave Owner

John Newton is best known for writing *Amazing Grace*. This former slave trader served as a minister from 1764 until his death in 1807. He was a confidant of well-known leaders such as Hannah More and William Wilberforce. His hundreds of hymns fill churches with music.

Yet on his deathbed he said to a young minister, "I'm going on before you, but you'll soon come after me. When you arrive, our friendship will no doubt cause you to inquire for me. But I can tell you already where you'll most likely find me. I'll be sitting at the feet of the thief whom Jesus saved in his dying moments on the cross."

That is a fascinating statement. Of all the places Newton could go in heaven, he wanted to go see the repentant thief. That is actually a statement of great humility.

What Newton was saying was that he recognized his own failings, and could identify with the worst sinner saved by grace.

I'm sure you're perfect! But I'm really not. I find comfort in gentle reminders that God's amazing grace is extended to everybody, including John Newton, the thief on the cross, and even me.

"With great power the apostles continued to testify to the resurrection of the Lord Jesus, and much grace was upon them all."

Acts 4:33

July 26

Don't Quit!

I recently read *The Six Phases of a Project*, which lists a step-by-step progression (or regression) of any initiative. In order, the six phases are 1) enthusiasm, 2) disillusionment, 3) panic, 4) search of the guilty, 5) punishment of the innocent, and 6) praise for the nonparticipants.

When things aren't going well, we are encouraged to quit. Let's consider how one man made a difference, simply by refusing to let a young boy go down this road.

Ignace Jan Paderewski was the greatest composer/pianist of his day. He was scheduled to perform in a great concert hall one evening. In the crowd was a nine-year-old boy. Before the concert began, the boy ran to the stage, sat at the piano and played *Chopsticks*. The crowd shouted in disapproval. Paderewski heard this from backstage, rushed out, sat by the boy, and began to play a harmony that went with his *Chopsticks*. And he whispered into the boy's ears, "Keep going. Don't quit."

When you are ready to quit, just remember there is Someone by your side, who can make a great song of your feeble efforts. And he is whispering in your ear, "Keep going. Don't quit."

"I will make an everlasting covenant with them:
I will never stop doing good to them, and I will
inspire them to fear me, so that they will never turn
away from me."

Jeremiah 32:40

July 27

Hysterical Laws

In Alabama, it is against the law to buy peanuts after sundown.

Pennsylvania law books record a case in 1971, when a man sued Satan for his own bad luck. The case was thrown out on the grounds that Satan did not live in Pennsylvania.

In Vermont, it is illegal to whistle underwater.

In Lake Charles, the law forbids allowing a rain puddle to remain in one's front yard for more than 12 hours.

And Kentucky has several wise laws. You must bathe at least once a year. If you throw an egg at a public speaker, you will spend a year in jail. And females in bathing suits are not allowed on any highway, unless they are escorted by two officers armed with a club. This law does not apply to females who weigh less than 90 pounds or more than 200 pounds. Nor does the law apply to female horses.

Did you know the ancient Jews had hundreds of laws? They had one for every day of the year, and another for every bone in the body.

Then a man named Jesus arrived on the scene. He said, "I have come to fulfill the law." Translation: "Just follow me."

And don't visit Kentucky this year unless you took a bath last year.

"Christ is the end of the law so that there may be righteousness for everyone who believes."

Romans 10:4

July 28

Swallowing Goldfish

Though most fads seem to spring up from no-where, goldfish swallowing can be traced back to one individual and one specific date. On March 3, 1939, Harvard student Lothrop Withington, Jr. swallowed a live fish to win a $10 bet. Days later, not to be outdone, a college student in Pennsylvania downed three fish seasoned with salt and pepper. When a fellow classmate upped the ante to six goldfish, the gauntlet had been thrown down and the fad spread like wildfire on campuses across the country. Before the goldfish craze faded a few months later, thousands of goldfish had met their gruesome ends and even coeds had taken up the challenge.

Now, I love seafood as much as anyone. I love shrimp, catfish, scallops, trout, oysters, and crabmeat. I even like the "fish" they sell out of the chain restaurant named after a pirate. But I draw the line at goldfish.

But Lothrop was like a lot of us. He was willing to swallow anything, whether it was good for him or not. You hear a lot of "stuff." But you don't have to swallow it all.

"All of us have become like one who is unclean, and all our righteous acts are like filthy rags; we all shrivel up like a leaf, and like the wind our sins sweep us away."

Isaiah 64:6

July 29

Holy Huddles

I was insecure as a child. I think it goes back to my infant years. When mom used to rock me, she used really big rocks. My insecurities carried over into my teen years. When I watched football games on television, I hated it when the players got into huddles. I assumed they were talking about me.

Actually, there was a day when they didn't huddle up at all. The quarterback would tell each player what to do. Then it all changed at the powerhouse of college football: Gallaudet University. Located in Washington, D.C., Gallaudet is a school for the deaf. The quarterback calls the plays by sign language.

In the old days, one of their quarterbacks noticed the defense was watching him call the plays. So he asked the players to "huddle up," so he could call the plays without being seen by the opposition.

The custom continues today, on the football field and in the church. Yes, in the church! In most churches, we are more concerned with "holy huddles" (meetings, gatherings in our buildings) than we are with putting points on the board (ministry, service).

Church, it's time to break the huddle!

"My dear children, I write this to you so that you will not sin. But if anybody does sin, we have one who speaks to the Father in our defense – Jesus Christ, the Righteous One."

1 John 2:1

July 30

Praying Lions

The man was an experienced mountain climber, hiker, and outdoorsman. But this day would be unlike any other in his entire life. Lost, searching for a way down, he spotted a lion nearby. Worse yet, the lion spotted him. The lion started his approach. The man had no chance to escape. So he prayed.

He said, "God, you can see I'm in trouble here. I'm lost and I'm stuck. There is a lion coming, and he looks really hungry. If you get me out of this mess, I'll do anything you want me to do. I'll give to the poor, I'll be a better husband, I'll be a good father, and I'll even go to church this Easter. Just get me out of this mess."

When he finished his prayer, he looked up. It was a miracle! Just as he prayed, the lion stopped. The lion sat. Then the lion prayed.

"Wow! A praying lion!" the man thought to himself. "This lion must be a Christian!"

Then he heard the lion's prayer. "Lord, thank you for this meal you have prepared for me."

Don't worry. No animals (or people) were hurt in the telling of this joke. But you can get hurt, really badly. How! By waiting until you are in trouble before you pray.

"Call upon me in the day of trouble; I will deliver you, and you will honor me."

Psalm 50:15

July 31

New Math

I was not a math major, so I could be wrong. But it seems some of the following could be a bit off. Tony Blair said, "The single most important two things we can do are . . ."

Tennis legend Pat Cash described player Lleyton Hewitt. (Yes, "Lleyton" spells his name that way.) Said Cash, "His two greatest strengths are his legs, his speed, his agility, and his competitiveness."

Kevin Keegan announced a soccer game. He said, "Three things can happen: Chile can win or they can lose."

Jerry Coleman said of a baseball hitter, "That is his nineteenth homer. One more, and he will hit double figures."

Larry Bowa said, "We talked five times. He called me twice and I called him twice."

Running back George Rogers said, "I will gain 1,500 yards or 2,000 yards, whichever comes first."

And a game show host asked the contestant to name a prime number between ten and 20. The response was "seven."

But here's another crazy mathematical fact. One plus one equals a majority. That works, if the "one plus one" are you and God.

"You, dear children, are from God and have overcome them, because the one who is in you is greater than the one who is in the world."

1 John 4:4

August 1

Unanswered Prayers

We often concern ourselves with things we cannot control. A nervous passenger on an ocean liner asked the captain what would happen if the ship hit an iceberg.

"Nothing," said the captain. "The iceberg would keep on floating as if nothing happened."

That great theologian Garth Brooks understood this when he wrote the song, Thank God for Unanswered Prayers. I can identify with that.

I remember the girl I had a crush on in high school. I prayed that she would marry me some day. It didn't work out, and I was devastated. Then, a few years later, I saw her at a psych hospital. (No, I wasn't a patient.) I barely recognized her, as 50 percent of her wasn't there when I had seen her last. I bowed and prayed, "Thank you, Jesus, for unanswered prayers!"

Life is like a parade. We see what is in front of us. But God sees the whole parade.

Even the best head football coach wears a headset. That is so the other coaches up high in the press box, with a much better view of the whole field, can tell him what is really happening on the field.

So thank God for one of his greatest gifts: unanswered prayers.

*"This is the confidence we have in
approaching God: that if we ask anything
according to his will, he hears us."*

1 John 5:14

August 2

Highest Paid Judge

I love the quote from Babe Ruth. When he was awarded baseball's first $100,000 contract, he was asked, "How do you justify making more money than the President of the United States?"

"It's simple," said the Bambino. "I had a better year than he did."

Salaries do not always reflect the importance of one's job. There are jobs that pay minimum wage, that I wouldn't (and couldn't) do for a million dollars.

But I don't know of a more obvious disparity in salary than in the legal profession. Consider the tale of two judges. Who do you think makes more money, Supreme Court Judge Ruth Bader Ginsberg or Judge Scheindlin? One makes $190,100 and the other earns $25 million per year. One decides cases that affect millions of Americans, while the other decides cases that affect a handful of people. One does her work quietly, behind the scenes. The other does her work in front of ten million people every day. Got it, yet?

The $25 million judge is better known by her first name, Judy. So what's the point? Some of the most profound work we do goes unnoticed and unappreciated. But that's where lives are changed.

World-changers work quietly, and they influence those closest to them.

"Jonathan took off the robe he was wearing and gave it to David, along with his tunic, and even his sword, his bow, and his belt."

1 Samuel 18:4

August 3

Failed Bank Robbery

A guy decided to rob the bank because he really needed the money. He didn't know anything about robbing banks. So he practiced what he would say over and over. He got the sack to put the money in, and a revolver, and then practiced sticking the sack over a counter and pointing the gun in someone's face while saying, "Don't mess with me. This is a stick up."

When it came time for the real thing, he was really nervous, but also confident that he had it down pat.

However, when he got into the bank, fear took over and he handed the lady the revolver, raised the sack, and said, "Don't stick with me. This is a mess up."

The bank robber was crippled by his own fear.

Remember the children's story, *Chicken Little*? Chicken Little thought the sky was falling. She told Henny Penny the sky was falling, and the animals stampeded. At last, they met Mr. Fox, who offered them refuge in his den. Because of their panic, they accepted, and Mr. Fox had a feast.

The cure for fear is faith. An old Scottish proverb says, "Fear knocked on the door. Faith answered, and there was no one there."

"For you did not receive a spirit that makes you a slave again to fear, but you received the Spirit of sonship, and by him we cry, 'Abba, Father.'"

Romans 8:15

August 4

Elizabeth Taylor

Contrast Allota Warmheart with Elizabeth Taylor. They are both famous women. Warmheart is not her real name, of course. As for Taylor, she appeared on the cover of *Life Magazine* more than anyone in history. I've never met Warmheart, but I did see Taylor one night, up close.

Beth and I were visiting the Fairmont Hotel in San Francisco nearly thirty years ago. When we came off the elevator, the media was there, taking pictures, anxious for Elizabeth Taylor's arrival in the lobby. She was expected at any moment, and she did not disappoint.

Sure, she was married 148 times. But she was arguably the most famous American woman of the last century. And we got to see her. Looking back, I find it curious that everyone knew she was there. But it wasn't hard to figure out. You see, Elizabeth Taylor always stayed in hotels under the name of Elizabeth Taylor.

Contrast that to a star of today, who checks in under the name of Allota Warmheart. You probably know her better as Britney Spears. I prefer, and learn from, the humility of Elizabeth Taylor. Jesus said to be who you are, not some "Allota Warmheart."

*"Let them see the purity and reverence
of your lives."*

1 Peter 3:2

August 5

Larry Bird

I am a chaplain for the Houston Rockets. I usually do about a dozen games, meeting with any coaches and players who feel they need prayer. And for the record, some of their biggest wins have come in games following my chapel services. But I must admit it has more to do with what the players do on the court. And that has to do with what they do before the game.

As chaplain, I am on the court for thirty minutes before each game, while the players are doing their "shoot-around." Some of the players spend countless minutes running through their shooting drills, taking as many as 300 shots before the game.

The best example of pre-game preparation may be Larry Bird, known as "Larry Legend" because of his incredible exploits on the court. Bird's greatness is illustrated by a key playoff game when Coach K.C. Jones called a timeout. Jones diagrammed a play. Then, as the players broke the huddle, Bird stepped up and said, "Get the ball to me and get out of the way."

Jones responded, "I'm the coach, and I call the plays!"

Then he turned to the players and said, "Get the ball to Larry, and get out of his way."

Basketball is like life. It depends on great leaders who understand the need for preparation and leadership.

"Be always on the watch, and pray that you may be able to escape all that is about to happen, and that you may be able to stand before the Son of Man."

Luke 21:36

August 6

Walk Like a Pigeon

Do you live your life too fast? Does cleaning up your dining area consist of throwing fast food bags out of the back of your SUV? Do you carry a blow-up passenger in your car so you can drive in the HOV lane? Did your last anniversary dinner involve a microwave? Do you go through the "Under 20 Items" line at Walmart with 150 items in your two carts? Do you ask how much something costs at the Dollar Store? Did you forget your twin's birthday? When you text, do you use abbreviations like "lol" and "btw"?

There's a verse in the Bible that says, "Be like the pigeon; see how he walks."

You may have noticed that pigeons walk funny. They walk that way so they can see where they are going. A pigeon has difficulty focusing its eyes, so it must bring its head to a complete stop before each step to refocus.

But here's a verse that is really there. "Be still and know that I am God."

Stay focused on God and what he has for you. Don't let anything, or anyone get you sidetracked.

And if you don't know what "lol" and "btw" stand for, you're probably on the right track.

> *"I sent messengers to them with this reply: I am carrying on a great project and cannot go down. Why should the work stop while I leave it and go down to you?"*

Nehemiah 6:3

August 7

Princess Diana

In 1981, Diana became the most talked about person on the globe when she married Prince Charles. Nearly one billion people watched Diana's wedding ceremony televised from St. Paul's Cathedral. This "commoner," who had once been a kindergarten teacher, would rally people to causes such as AIDS research, leprosy, and a ban on land mines.

In the beginning, Diana's title had given her a platform to address others, but she became a person of influence in her own right. In 1996, when she was divorced from Prince Charles, she lost her title, but that didn't diminish her impact on others. When her funeral was broadcast on television, it was translated into 44 languages. The total audience was 2.5 billion people, which was more than twice the number who watched her wedding.

What made Diana special was not that she was influential. It was what she did with that influence.

Colin Powell said it well. "You have achieved excellence as a leader when people will follow you, if only out of curiosity."

Leadership is influence. We all have some. What are you doing with yours?

*"Live such good lives among the pagans
that, though they accuse you of doing
wrong, they may see your good deeds and
glorify God on the day he visits."*

1 Peter 2:12

August 8

Power of Prayer

There has never been a time when we knew more about prayer, but prayed so little. Let's review the messages of several churches, advertising the need for prayer on their church signs.

The Berean Baptist Church in Foley, AL announced, "Preaching moves men. Prayer moves God."

The Immanuel Lutheran Church in Osmond, NE announced, "No matter how far you've run away from God, he's only a prayer away."

Glendora, CA has a church called The Church of the Brethren. They recently posted, "God answers knee-mail."

There's more. Another church announced, "Don't pray for a lighter load. Pray for a stronger back."

Here are some more. "Life is fragile. Handle with prayer."

"This church is prayer conditioned."

"When troubles call on you, call on God."

But my favorite is the sign in front of the Diamond Hill United Methodist Church in Berkeley Heights, NJ. It read, "Seven days without prayer make one weak."

I have two questions for you. The first is not real important. Do you believe in prayer? The second question is huge: Do you pray?

"The disciples said, 'Lord, teach us to pray.'"

Luke 11:1

August 9

Billy the Kid

On his last day in office, Governor Bill Richardson of New Mexico did what every other governor had done for the past 130 years. He refused to issue an official pardon for notorious outlaw Billy the Kid.

Also known as Henry McCarty, William Bonney, and William Antrim, "The Kid" was responsible for anywhere from eight to 22 deaths. Historical documents show that in 1879, Billy was promised a pardon by the governor of New Mexico, Lew Wallace, in exchange for testimony against three men accused of killing a one-armed lawyer during the Lincoln County Wars. But Governor Wallace reneged for some reason. Knowing the legal system would keep him behind bars for life, Billy the Kid broke out of prison.

In his escape he killed four guards. He would soon be ambushed and killed on July 14, 1881. But this didn't help the families of the four men. Richardson said this fact weighed heavily in his decision to not grant the pardon.

There are two lessons here. First, choices have consequences. Second, seek your pardon from God, not man.

"For every living soul belongs to me, the father as well as the son. Both alike belong to me. The soul who sins is the one who will die."

Ezekiel 18:4

August 10

The Dress

The poor country farmer was livid when he confronted his wife with the receipt for a $250 dress she had bought.

"How could you do this?" he exclaimed.

"I don't know," she wailed. "I was standing in the store looking at the dress. Then I found myself trying it on. It was like the devil was whispering to me, 'Gee, you look great in that dress. You should buy it.'"

"Well," the farmer persisted, "you know how to deal with the devil? Just tell him, 'Get behind me, Satan!'"

"I did," replied his wife, "but then he said, 'It looks great from back here, too!'"

I don't want to get in the middle of things between the farmer and his wife. I've never met them. But I have had my share of run-ins with the devil. I have learned one thing. Don't negotiate with the devil.

The Bible says to "resist the devil and he will flee from you."

But the key is what it says just before that verse: "Submit yourself to God."

So, before you do something crazy like buying a $250 dress, submit yourself to God. Sure, the devil will say you look good in that dress. But remember, anytime you do what he wants, you look really good to him.

"Satan disguises himself as an angel of light."

2 Corinthians 11:14

August 11

Napoleon and Lee

Okay, history buffs, what did Napoleon and Robert E. Lee have in common? It has to do with influence. The answer is that they both exhibited personal concern for the men under their command.

Napoleon made it a practice to know every one of his officers by name and to remember where they lived and which battles they had fought with him.

Lee was known to visit the men in their campsites the night before any major battle. Often, he met the next day's challenges without having slept.

Norman Schwarzkopf often found ways of connecting with his troops. On Christmas in 1990, during the Persian Gulf War, he spent the day among the men and women who were so far away from their families. He wished each one a blessed Christmas.

There are two things you need to know about leadership. First, leadership is influence. Second, influence is done up close. You impress people from a distance, but you influence them up close.

That is what your coach did. That is what your teacher did. That is what your parents did. That is what your pastor did. And that is what your Savior did.

"As iron sharpens iron, so one man sharpens another."

Proverbs 27:17

August 12

Happy Endings

A preacher was trying to establish rapport with an inmate who was about to be executed by the electric chair. The day of his execution came and the pastor was anxious to say the right words. He thought "good-bye" seemed trite and "see you later" a little inappropriate.

As the inmate started to leave, the pastor said, "More power to you!"

The fact is, when our time comes to die, we need "more power."

A man had a trusty old pickup truck. He told the undertaker he wanted to be buried with his old truck.

The undertaker said, "Why would you want that?"

The man replied, "I've never seen a hole yet, that this pickup couldn't get me out of."

There is one hole your truck won't get you out of. It's called death.

I'm reminded of the little boy whose mother took him to the kennel to pick out a new dog. He chose a rather homely puppy whose tail was wagging briskly. His mom asked why he chose that particular dog, to which the lad replied, "I wanted the dog with the happy ending."

Nothing matters during this life as much as the end of life. Put your faith in Christ, and you will have a happy ending.

"I eagerly expect and hope that I will in no way be ashamed, but will have sufficient courage so that now as always Christ will be exalted in my body, whether by life or by death."

Philippians 1:20

August 13

The First TV

It goes back to 1883, when Paul Nipko invented a scanning device that could break down an image into a sequence of tiny pictorial elements. Experiments continued into the 1920s. In 1928 GE presented the first dramatic production on television. NBC began telecasts from New York in 1932. In 1939 America saw its first televised baseball game. The first official network broadcast came on February 1, 1940, on NBC. Rumor has it that Mickey Rooney was the anchor.

Early milestones included the coverage of Pearl Harbor in 1941, The *Jackie Gleason Show*, and wrestling. By 1948 there were 36 stations on the air. New York and Los Angeles each had seven stations. Houston had one. I believe Dave Ward anchored the local news.

From such humble beginnings, television has exploded to what we have now. I was pondering this the other day as I watched the water polo match between Riverdale High School and the local YMCA, on ESPN 27.

Isn't it amazing how much progress we have made as a nation? We are no longer burdened with reading books and talking about the things of God as a family, to pass the time.

> *"You must teach what is in accord*
> *with sound doctrine."*

Titus 2:1

August 14

Flotation Device

On an airplane one day, I had forgotten to put my tray table up in its "upright and locked position." The flight attendant gave me "the look." I immediately put it up.

Then I wondered why putting up the tray table is such a big deal. I have never heard of a plane crash where the only ones who died were the ones who forgot to put their tray tables in the upright and locked position.

Then the flight attendant gave her speech, pointing to the exit doors. "The white lights lead to the red lights that lead to the exit doors," she instructed. Now, I'm thinking, "At 30,000 feet, why do I need exit doors?"

Then I'm told, "You have a flotation device under your seat." Now, I'm worried that I'm on the wrong plane, because my flight over the desert southwest doesn't cross any bodies of water larger than a whirlpool.

But I am comforted to hear about the "black box" that can survive any crash. "Why don't they just make the plane out of the same material they use to make the black box?" I wonder.

Now I'm really worried. On the plane, and in life, what I really need isn't a flotation device. I need a parachute.

"Remain in me, and I will remain in you."

John 15:4

August 15

Colin Powell

Colin Powell served under President Reagan. During a critical juncture in military planning, Powell argued for a particular strategy. Reagan disagreed, but went along with his General.

The plan failed, and dozens of American lives were lost as a result. When Reagan faced the media, he was asked why he followed the failed strategy, and whose idea it was. He looked to Powell, standing off to the side, winked at him, then answered the media. "It was my plan, and I take full responsibility for it," said the President.

Colin Powell was seen shedding a tear, moved by the loyalty of his Commander-in-Chief. An aide standing nearby saw the General motion toward the President, and heard him whisper. "I will do anything for that man."

It is amazing what effect loyalty has on people. Anyone can root for us when we are up. It's the ones who stand with us when we fall that make the difference.

Follow the Reagan example. Think of someone you know who has made a really big mistake. Then go to them. Stand with them, by them, and for them. And you will have a friend for life.

"Do not seek revenge or bear a grudge against one of your people, but love your neighbor as yourself. I am the Lord."

Leviticus 19:18

August 16

Church Signs

I love church marquees. Some churches use their signs to advertise a coming speaker or message. But I like the sign at Friendship Baptist Church in Midway, GA. It read, "Soul Food Served Here."

New Life Fellowship in Statesboro, GA posted, "Come Inside for a Free Faith Lift."

Nashville has the Blakemore Church of the Nazarene, which recently advertised, "Visitors Welcome. Members Expected."

Then there was the sign in front of Nashville's Natchez Trace Church of Christ. It said, "Trade God Your Pieces for His Peace."

But my favorite sign stood in front of a small Assembly of God Church in South Houston years ago. It proclaimed, "Try One of Our Delicious Sundays."

Did you know that the average church has 75 signs? That may sound high, but it's true. You see, the average church in America has 75 people in attendance on Sunday morning. And when those people leave, they become the best (or worst) advertising the church has.

If you don't have a church home, find a church near you this week, and try one of their delicious Sundays. But remember, it's how you live on Monday that matters most.

"Consider it pure joy, my brothers, whenever you face trials of many kinds, because you know that the testing of your faith develops perseverance."

James 1:2

August 17

Father Benjamin

Winds blow the ship off course, and the sailors spot a surprisingly well-developed unchartered island. The people are well fed, irrigation systems are complete, and roads connect the villages. The captain asks the chief for an explanation. "How has this island progressed like this?"

He received a quick response. "Father Benjamin. He educated us, built schools, dug wells, and built clinics."

The captain asks to meet Father Benjamin. He is taken to two medical clinics.

"Is this where Father Benjamin lives?"

The native guides look puzzled, then take him to the canals. The captain protests. "I don't see Father Benjamin here. Please take me to where he lives."

They take him to a chapel where Benjamin taught them about God. "Is this where he lives?"

"Yes," they affirm.

"May I talk to him?"

The natives say, "No, that would be impossible, for he died many years ago."

The captain replies, "I asked to see where he lives, and you showed me a clinic, canals, and a chapel. You said nothing of his death."

"You didn't ask about his death." The chief explains. "You asked to see where he lives. We showed you."

"God vindicates the generation who seeks him, those who seek his face."

Psalm 24:6

August 18

Too Much Caffeine

If you get a tax refund of $2,000, you can do one of two things with that money. First, you can use it to make a good down payment on a new car. Or you can do what millions do every day, and buy one cup of coffee at Starbucks.

If you have $10,000, you can get five cups. But take it easy on the caffeine. I'm not a coffee drinker, but I can recognize one anywhere. They are the ones bouncing off the walls. The other day, I saw a man who was so high on caffeine that he was duck hunting with a rake. Too much caffeine.

You know you've had too much coffee when you find yourself answering the door before the doorbell rings or you have converted your car's radiator to brew a pot on the way to work.

You've had too much coffee if Juan Valdez names his donkey after you, or you can play ping-pong without a partner. Your coffee filters are monogrammed. You chew on other people's fingernails. Your eyes stay open even when you sneeze.

And you know you've had too much coffee when you can jump start your car without cables or you can photograph yourself ten feet away without a timer. Or maybe you ski uphill.

Perhaps it's time to lay off the coffee and start your day the way Jesus did.

"While it was early in the morning, Jesus went into a mountain by himself, and there he prayed."

Mark 1:35

August 19

Allah Is God!

On April 18, 2007, three Christians in Turkey were killed for their beliefs. Necati Aydin was one of them. He was a 35-year-old pastor in the city of Malatya. In a country of 76 million people, Christians number 153,000. And the persecution from Muslims is severe.

It seems Necati came to his office that morning with two friends. They were ambushed by a group of Muslims, captured, and told to shout, "Allah is God!" They were ordered to recite, "There is no God except Allah, and Muhammad is his prophet."

When Necati refused, the torture began. For an agonizing hour, they were cut, beaten, and terrorized. Finally, when they refused to say "Allah is God," their throats were sliced.

Their dying words were, "Christ is Messiah. Christ is Messiah."

This leads me to a question. These men gave up their lives for Christ. What have you given up lately?

God may not be asking you to give up your life. But could you at least give up your parking spot, your place in line, or your pew on Sunday morning? Could you at least give up a little time to feed the hungry?

And say it with me: "Christ is Messiah."

"Then he said to them, 'Whoever wants to be my disciple must deny himself, take up his cross, and follow me.'"

Luke 9:23

August 20

Helping the Wrong Way

Two men in a restaurant noticed that another man kept falling off his stool. Apparently he was so drunk that he couldn't sit on his stool. Being good Samaritans, they offered to take him home. They dragged him to the door, and placed him in the car. He fell down three times on the way to the car.

When they got him to his house, he fell down four times on the way to the door. They finally made it to the porch and rang the doorbell. When his wife answered the door, they told her they had brought her husband home.

She said, "Great, but where's his wheelchair?"

Sometimes, we try to be helpful, but only make things worse.

This disease especially afflicts the species known as "men." We try to fix things, and sometimes they don't need fixing. Remember, husbands, your wife rarely wants your sage advice. She wants your hug.

And the next time you see someone who has fallen, before you try to pick him up, determine why he fell in the first place.

Before you speak, listen. Before you act, pray. Before you "help" someone, determine that your solution is better than their problem.

"A perverse man stirs up dissension, and a gossip separates close friends."

Proverbs 16:28

August 21

Praying Sisters

Peggy Smith was 84. Her sister, Christine, was 82. Peggy could barely see and Christine could hardly walk. But together, they changed Scotland. It happened in 1849 on the Scottish Island of Lewis, in the tiny village of Barvas.

Their pastor longed for revival. He preached for revival. But nothing happened. Nothing, that is, until he visited Peggy and Christine, and asked them to pray. Unable to attend church, they figured that was the least they could do. So Peggy and Christine began to pray for a movement of God.

They invited a few friends to join them. They extended their prayer gatherings to six hours, starting at 10 p.m. They prayed that evangelist Duncan Campbell would come to their little church for a one-night meeting.

Campbell came for five weeks. He led four services every day, at 7 p.m., 10 p.m., midnight, and 3 a.m. The move of God was undeniable. Hundreds were converted. Saloons went out of business. Gambling ceased. Marriages were restored. And all of Scotland was changed.

It is amazing to see what happens when two sisters decide to really pray.

"If you remain in me and my words remain in you, ask whatever you wish, and it will be given you."

John 15:7

August 22

Dog Lessons

I have the best dog in the world. Heidi is a West Highland terrier, better known as a Westie. I would be perfectly satisfied never having any other dog.

But I notice that others prefer different kinds of dogs. But let's stay within the "terrier" family. The word terrier comes from the Latin *terra*, meaning "earth." They come in many shapes and sizes. There is the Scottish terrier, the Dandie, Dinmont, Skye, Bedlington, and Fox terrier. The American Kennel Club recognizes more than 20 terriers, including the Boston terrier, Lhasa Apso, and Yorkshire terrier. They range from ten to 23 inches, and from 11 to 50 pounds. Most have small eyes, large teeth, and strong feet.

My Westie is more fun than a hundred people. She runs, chases, retrieves, catches, and most importantly, she adores her master.

The lesson from the terrier is diversity.

God made dogs that way, and he made people that way. But unlike people, dogs aren't judgmental. They like everyone and are willing to utilize anyone's front yard without discrimination. And unlike people, they adore their master, and love to hear his voice after a hard day.

"No one has ever spoken like this man does."

John 6:46

August 23

George Szell

He was born in Budapest in 1897. George Szell was one of the most gifted pianists in the world. He debuted with the Vienna Symphony at the age of ten. But no one remembers George the pianist. They remember George the conductor. You see, George made a critical decision early in his life. More on that in a bit.

By age 20, George was conducting the Strasbourg Opera. By age 27, he was the principal conductor of the Berlin State Opera.

Szell made his American debut in St. Louis in 1930. He conducted at the Metropolitan Opera House in New York. Then, he built the Cleveland Orchestra into the world's finest. He became a U.S. citizen there, where he led world-class musicians until his death in 1970.

For 25 years, George Szell led the finest orchestra in the world.

So what was the "critical decision" George made early in life? He decided to not focus on his own skills as a solo pianist, but rather on the ability to lead others. That is what made him famous.

And like George, when you and I learn to be a conductor in life, rather than a solo act, we will make great music.

"As they were walking along and talking together, suddenly a chariot of fire and horses of fire appeared and separated the two of them, and Elijah went up to heaven in a whirlwind."

2 Kings 2:11

August 24

Time Zones

In a meeting in St. Louis in 1872, U.S. railroads proposed a system of four time zones for their own use, but it was October of 1883 before the plan was finally approved. Until then, we were all on the same clock.

In August, 1884 the U.S. Congress authorized President Chester A. Arthur to convene an International Meridian Conference, to consider a proposal for a system of world time zones. The conference was held in Washington, D.C. in October, 1884. The world accepted the proposals, which railroads were already utilizing.

There was just one problem. They agreed, in 1884, to have four time zones, but it wasn't until 1918 that Congress instructed the Interstate Commerce Commission to establish actual boundaries between the different zones.

Now, we have eight time zones in America, to accommodate Alaska and Hawaii. But think about it. For 34 years (1884-1918) we had four time zones, but nobody knew what was going on since there were no boundaries.

Life is like that. We all have good intentions, but until we establish boundaries, morally and relationally, we are in trouble.

"Make no friendship with a man given to anger."

Proverbs 22:24

August 25

Gripers

A grandmother took her little grandson to the beach. She put a sun hat on him, and he brought his little bucket and shovel. After they were settled, Grandma went to sleep. All of a sudden she woke up and realized the boy was gone.

"What happened?" she thought.

She looked out and saw the boy had drifted far out into the ocean. People were in a panic, screaming and hollering. She got on her knees and prayed desperately for God to save him. Just then a huge wave came roaring in and the little fellow was dumped right in front of her. She looked at the boy, then looked up toward heaven. She put her hands on her hips in protest, and shouted, "Lord, he had a hat on when I lost him!"

Gripers just look for a reason to be mad. You try to help, and they become more angry. They don't want solutions; they want misery. And they want you to be miserable.

They are like the man who hadn't kissed his wife in 30 years, and then shot the first man who did. You can gripe if you want. Write your congressman, your pastor, and your editor. But think about it. Does being miserable really make you happy?

"Godliness with contentment is a great gain."

1 Timothy 6:6

August 26

It's the Small Stuff

Small changes lead to big things. Addition comes before multiplication, crawling before walking, and high school before college. No one starts at the top except a gravedigger. If you want to do great things in your life, start doing small things in a great way. If you want to have a great marriage, do the small things.

You may say, "I would die for my wife." She doesn't want you to die for her; she just wants you to take out the trash. Whisper three magical words in her ear like "I love you," or better yet, "Let's eat out." Try giving her a small thing, like the remote control.

Yes, it's the small stuff that lasts. Go for a walk in the park. You may notice that while rabbits abound, you won't find many dinosaurs. Do something small for a friend today.

If you can't afford a gift (that they won't keep anyway), give them a card (that they may keep forever). Don't buy your kid a car; take him for a drive. Don't give someone $1,000; give them a smile. I'll say it again. It's the small stuff that matters.

Small things are powerful. Maybe that's why God used a baby to change the world.

"For unto you is born this day in the
City of David a Savior."

Luke 2:11

August 27

Squirrels and Beetles

On September 11, 1995, a squirrel climbed onto the Metro-North Railroad power lines near New York City. He set off an electrical surge which weakened an overhead bracket which let a wire dangle toward the tracks, which tangled in a train which tore down all the lines. As a result, 47,000 commuters were stuck in Manhattan for hours that evening.

An enormous pine tree growing in the mountains of Colorado was only half grown when the Pilgrims landed at Plymouth Rock. A close study revealed that it had been struck by lightning 14 times and survived centuries of Colorado's hard winters. Age didn't destroy it. Avalanches didn't move it. Fires didn't kill it.

Many came to believe the old tree was indestructible. But, in the end, a beetle destroyed that huge tree. There is a lesson to be learned from the stories of the squirrel and the beetle. It's usually not the big stuff that kills us. It's that one secret sin, seemingly harmless, that eats away at us until it brings us down.

> *"He said to me, 'Son of man, have you seen what the elders of the house of Israel are doing in the darkness, each at the shrine of his own idol?' They say, 'The Lord does not see us; the Lord has forsaken the land.'"*

Ezekiel 8:12

August 28

It Happened Today

It happened on August 28, 1938. Max Factor, founder of modern cosmetics, died. Traveling in Paris, he was kidnapped. They used a decoy to capture the kidnapper, but he never showed up to collect the ransom. The man was never caught.

But Max would never recover from the trauma. His doctor ordered him to come home to Beverly Hills. It was there that Max Factor died on this day in 1938.

But something else happened that very same day. While the death of Max Factor filled the headlines, the other event, taking place in Houston, Texas, went mostly unnoticed.

A carpenter and his wife gave birth to their fourth child, Kenneth. Kenneth would graduate from Jefferson Davis High School in Houston. Oh, he did something else. He was voted the "favorite singer of all time" in a USA Today poll, in 1986.

But "Kenneth" was too formal for the young man. Now they just call him Kenny. Kenny Rogers. On one day, a man died and a man was born. But going back a little further than August 28, 1938, another Man died, so you could be born. Born again.

"Before I formed you in the womb I knew you.
Before you were born, I set you apart."

Jeremiah 1:5

August 29

Home Run King

When Mark McGwire hit 70 home runs in 1998, he broke Roger Maris' record of 61, set in 1961. Maris had broken Babe Ruth's record of 60 home runs, hit in 1927. But whose record did Babe Ruth break?

It was the great Ned Williamson, who hit 27 homers in 1884. Back in 1876, the original home run king was the immortal George Hall, who hammered five home runs.

I did the math. At the rate of five home runs per season, George would have had to play form 1876 until 2029 to catch Barry Bonds' career mark. George would have to play 153 years without injury to do it. Rumor is, George is contemplating a comeback.

No, five home runs doesn't sound like much. But keep in mind, they only played 154 games back then. Who knows what George would have done with today's schedule of 162 games?

But you can't take this away from George. He was an original. In 1876, when nobody cared, he did what nobody had ever done before.

Now, think about your life. God created you as an original. What is it that you want to do, that nobody has done before? God made you uniquely. He has a plan for your life. He knows you intimately and loves you completely.

"O Lord, you have searched me, and you know me."

Psalm 139:1

August 30

A Blade of Grass

Dirt carpeted the floor. Rats scurried beneath the grated vent. Roaches roamed the walls and crawled over sleeping prisoners. The cell offered no bunk, no chair, no table, and no way out for American General Robbie Risner.

For seven years, North Vietnamese soldiers held him and dozens of others in the Zoo, a POW camp in Hanoi. Solitary confinement, starvation, torture, and beatings were routine. Interrogators twisted broken legs, sliced skin with bayonets, and crammed paper into their mouths.

How did General Risner survive this? He stared at a blade of grass. Several days into his incarceration, he wrestled the grate off a floor vent, stretched out on his belly, lowered his head into the opening, and peered through a pencil-sized hole in the brick and mortar at a singular blade of grass. Aside from this stem, his world had no color. So he began his days with head in vent, heart in prayer, staring at the green blade of grass.

Is your world sometimes dark and colorless? Do what Risner did. Stick your head outside the darkness and find some color.

What you see defines who you become. Take Jeremiah, for example. Actually, don't. Read his words of self-perpetuating misery, and run the opposite direction.

"Cursed is the day I was born! May the day my mother bore me not be blessed."

Jeremiah 20:14

August 31

It Never Works

Let's do a fun exercise. Think of someone who has made a mistake. Now, let's figure out the best way to point out their error, because pointing out their error is your responsibility. Your advanced level of perfection gives you that right.

But how do you do it? It will do no good to point out their shortcomings if they don't receive it well. So before you share your criticism, follow these time proven steps. First, never offer them praise. People hate that. Sure, God made that person in his image, and that person has a lot of positive traits. But don't ever go positive.

Second, approach them with an attitude of judgment. Don't ask questions; only accuse.

And third, never forget your own lofty level. When Jesus said, "Get the log out of your eye first," he wasn't talking to you. He was only speaking to sinners.

Psychologists tell us that we need to hear 17 positive statements in order to be able to take one criticism. But what do they know? You found someone who made a mistake. Your job is to tell them!

"Encourage one another daily."

Hebrews 3:13

September 1

Marian Anderson

She was the first black American contralto, who won international acclaim as a concert soloist. She was once asked, "What has been the greatest moment of your life?"

She had many great moments, such as 1955, when she became the first black to sing with the Metropolitan Opera in New York. Then there was the publishing of her autobiography, an instant best seller. In 1958 she became a delegate to the United Nations. She gave a private concert at the White House, for the Roosevelts and the King and Queen of England. There was her 1963 Presidential Medal of Freedom. And then there was Easter Sunday in Washington D.C. when she stood beneath the Lincoln statue and sang for a crowd of 75,000.

But none of these were the greatest moments for Marian Anderson. She said, "My greatest moment was the day when I went home and told my mother that she wouldn't have to take in washing anymore to make a living."

Humble beginnings make for a great story. And sometimes, they make for a great life. But what really matters isn't where you started, but where you end.

"Let your eyes look straight ahead. Fix your gaze directly before you. Give careful thought to the paths for your feet and be steadfast in all your ways."

Proverbs 4:25-27

September 2

Overcoming Your Past

We all have a past. We all have issues. We all have something to overcome. A quick survey of Scripture reveals several great men who had much to overcome, sometimes because of bad choices, and sometimes because of unavoidable circumstances. But in each case, they got up off the mat and rose to greatness.

With Moses it was murder. With Elijah it was severe depression. With Peter it was public denial. With Samson it was recurring lust. With Thomas it was cynical doubting. With Jacob it was deception. With Rahab it was prostitution. With Jephthah it was his illegitimate birth.

I love the words of Isaiah, who said, "Look to the rock of your salvation, and to the pit from which you were dug."

Moses, Elijah, Peter, Samson, Thomas, Jacob, Rahab, and Jephthah all came out of "the pit." But you will never find a single complaint from any of these eight. Not one complaint.

Why is this? They learned that what doesn't kill us shapes us. God uses "the pit" to humble us, mold us, and grow us. Are you in "the pit"? You will come to see this as one of God's greatest gifts.

"Look to the rock of your salvation, and to the pit from which you were dug."

Isaiah 51:1

September 3

Mired in the Weeds

It was October 13, 1960. Andy Jerke was just like every other boy growing up in Pittsburgh. He loved baseball, and especially his hometown Pirates. On this day, the Pirates were hosting the vaunted New York Yankees for Game 7 of the World Series. The game came down to the bottom of the ninth inning. The score was tied. And Andy was there, at Forbes Field.

Then he remembered he had promised his mother to be home by 4:30 to help with dinner. So he left the game in the bottom of the ninth, to walk home.

As he was walking across the lot beyond the outfield wall, a baseball landed near his feet. Andy picked up the ball, and a security man informed him that Bill Mazeroski had just hit that ball for a game-winning home run. And now the ball belonged to Andy.

Today's value of that ball, which Mazeroski signed for the youngster, is set at $100,000. But you may want to close your eyes for the end of the story.

Andy played with the ball a year later and lost it in a field. He looked ten minutes, but never found it. Today, over 50 years later, he still has that glorious memory. But he wishes he also still had the ball.

What happened? It's simple. The ball, like many of us, got mired in the weeds.

"Just as the weeds are pulled up and burned in the fire, so it will be at the end of the age."

Matthew 13:40

September 4

Gimpers

You won't find one in the National Wildlife Federation's *Manual of Rare Species*, but rare it is. Like the bald eagle, the prairie bison, and the whooping crane, gimpers are seldom seen on our landscapes. They are occasionally spotted on college campuses, in the business world, and even in churches.

So what is a gimper, anyway? Plug in these clues. In the 1976 Summer Olympics, Bruce Jenner was a gimper. In the six-day war, Moshe Dayan was a gimper. So was Vince Lombardi, as a football strategist. A gimper of motherhood was Susanna Wesley. Donald Barnhouse was a gimper preacher. As a creative thinker, Leonardo da Vinci was a gimper. One of our gimper presidents was Abraham Lincoln. Thomas Edison was a gimper inventor.

So what, exactly, is a gimper? You can look it up. A gimper is defined as a person who is "committed to the core, thoroughly and unequivocally." They make commitments, then stick to their commitments.

Gimpers change the world. Jesus Christ was the greatest gimper who ever lived. Listen to his famous words, with a slight interpretation. "Follow me, and I will make you gimpers."

Yes, you can be a gimper, too.

"When a man makes a vow to the Lord, he must do everything he says he will do."

Numbers 30:2

September 5

Grandmas and Stamp Machines

There was a long line at the post office. A man stood in the line, noticing the lady in front of him was there to buy stamps. After 30 minutes he said, "Excuse me, but there is a stamp machine over there. That would be a lot quicker than waiting in this long line."

She replied, "That's okay. We're almost to the desk."

A few minutes later, he said, "But the stamp machine would be so much quicker."

She responded, "Oh, I know, but that old stamp machine would never ask me how my grandchildren are doing!"

Some of you are screaming to grandma, "Learn to adapt! Use the stamp machine!"

Adaptability is good for some things. Fifty one million watched the final episode of the *Survivor* series that had 16 men and women "stranded" on an island near Borneo. The survivor became an instant millionaire. When asked how he won, he said, "I learned to adapt."

So, if you want to make money, learn to adapt. Use the stamp machine.

But if you want to be happy, stay in line. Be patient. Nothing is better than having someone ask, "How are your grandchildren doing?"

There is no substitute for the personal touch. Consider the woman with the issue of blood. She was so desperate to touch God that she was willing to stand in line.

"If I touch his clothes, I will be healed."

Mark 5:28

September 6

A Muzzle

Let's talk about "talk." We all do it. It's hard to communicate without talking (though men try this often with their wives, rarely with good results). Most of us probably talk too much.

The Bible says the tongue is hard to tame. It says that we sin more with our tongue than with the rest of our body. We can tame Flipper and Trigger and Shamu and Lassie. We can train falcons to land on our wrists, pigeons to carry our message, dogs to fetch the paper, elephants to stand on rolling balls, tigers to sit on stools, and alligators to turn over and get their bellies rubbed. But the tongue? Impossible to train!

William Norris, the American journalist, was a master of communicating truth with rhymes. He once wrote, "If your lips would keep from slips, five things observe with care: to whom you speak, of whom you speak, and how, when, and where."

Publius, the Greek philosopher, offered this. "I have often regretted my speech, but never my silence."

King David said it like this: "I will guard my ways, that I may not sin with my tongue; I will guard my mouth as with a muzzle."

Okay, enough talk. Now I will follow Publius' advice.

"The tongue of the wise adorns knowledge, but the mouth of the fool gushes folly."

Proverbs 15:2

September 7

Driving Fast for Jesus

A preacher was pulled over for speeding. The officer asked him why he was going so fast.

"I'm trying to obey Scripture," was the preacher's response.

"Please explain that to me," asked the kind officer.

"It's simple," he said. "Jesus said, 'Whatever you do, do it quickly.'"

The officer said, "I know the Bible a little bit myself. I believe Jesus was talking to Judas when he said that. And I believe Judas was guilty of a greater crime. Here is your ticket."

If you must speed, sing along with me. At 45 mph, sing, *God Will Take Care of You*. At 55 mph, the song is *Guide Me, O Thou Great Jehovah*. At 65 mph, sing *Nearer, My God to Thee!* At 75, sing *Nearer, Still Nearer!* When you hit 85, it's *This World Is Not My Home*. When the speedometer gets to 95, sing *Lord, I'm Coming Home*. And anything over 100 mph warrants *Precious Memories*.

If you are like me, you live life in the fast lane. That doesn't make it right, but that's how it is for most of us. I suggest you pull over. At least, slow down. Driving fast can be fun. But you miss the scenery. And you may miss your next birthday.

Driving fast may make sense to you. But I suggest you do things that make sense to God instead.

"As the heavens are higher than the earth, so are my ways higher than your ways and my thoughts than your thoughts."

Isaiah 55:9

September 8

One Word for God

We were in high school. Mary was completely normal in every way but one. Mary was blind. She often asked me to describe what things looked like: clouds, flowers, and the sunset. I could never do it in less than ten minutes. Clouds, flowers, and the sunset are too awesome to describe with just a few words, to someone who has never seen them.

So how would you describe God for someone who has never seen him? The old prophet Isaiah took on this task. Read his words. "Holy, holy, holy is the Lord of hosts. The whole earth is full of his glory."

In the Hebrew language, repetition performed the role of our modern highlighter. Repetition stood for emphasis. No verse ever describes God as "strong, strong, strong" or as "wise, wise, wise." The only description given three times was "holy."

The Hebrew word is *qadosh*, meaning "cut off, separate." In other words, Isaiah is saying that God is unique. He is like no other. And he calls us to holiness, as well.

Sure, you're smart, beautiful, and funny. But are you holy?

"Be holy because I am holy."

1 Peter 1:16

September 9

In One Year

If Brian Williams had been alive in 1809, his evening news broadcasts would have concentrated on Austria, not Britain or America. The attention of the entire world was focused on Napoleon as he swept across helpless hamlets like fire across a Kansas wheat field. From Trafalgar to Waterloo, his name was synonymous with superiority. But at that time of invasions and battles, babies were being born in Britain and America. But who cared about babies when Napoleon was such a monster? Well, someone should have noticed!

You see, in 1809, the following took their first breaths: William Gladstone, Alfred Tennyson, Oliver Wendell Holmes, Edgar Alan Poe, Charles Darwin, and Robert Charles Winthrop. And in 1809, a rugged log cabin in Hardin County, Kentucky, owned by an illiterate wandering laborer was filled with the infant screams of a newborn boy named Abraham Lincoln.

They were all born in the same year, but nobody seemed to notice.

So as you plan your next year or two, keep in mind, what will make the biggest difference may be that which goes unnoticed. Follow the example of King David. He had killed giants, which was noticed by the world. But he said the key to real joy was in simply fearing the Lord.

"Blessed are those who fear the Lord, who find great delight in his commands."

Psalm 112:1

September 10

Pray

According to a recent report by *Newsweek*, 91 percent of women pray, as do 85 percent of men. That number rises to 95 percent for the sick and 100 percent for golfers once they are on the green.

So what is prayer, anyway? A little girl said prayers are messages sent up at night and on Sundays when the rates are low.

For most of us, prayer is what we do when we need God to bail us out of some mess we created ourselves. We are like the boy who prayed, "God, either make Boston the capital of Vermont or lose my test paper by tomorrow morning."

When we pray, God answers in different ways. Sometimes, he says "no" because you don't need what you want. Sometimes, he says "no" because you have the wrong motive. Sometimes the timing is wrong, so God says "slow." Other times, you just aren't ready, so God says "grow." Then there are times when everything is just right, so God says "go."

Our problem is we get confused between what is a good idea and what is a God idea.

Life is like climbing mountains. When the wind comes against you, it is always a good idea to get on your knees. Spend a few moments with the God of the universe.

"Remember Jesus Christ, raised from the dead, descended from David."

2 Timothy 2:8

September 11

Surviving 9/11

Cheryl McGuiness kissed her husband, Tom, goodbye, and took her teenage kids to school that Tuesday morning. Awhile later, she got a call from a friend asking if Tom was at home. It was September 11, 2001.

Cheryl's friend asked about Tom because she knew he was a pilot for American Airlines. And her friend had just heard that a plane had been hijacked and crashed into the World Trade Center.

Then things got worse. After an hour or so, a car pulled up in front of Cheryl's house. Out stepped an executive for the Airlines. It was his task to tell Cheryl that Tom was the pilot on that plane. Everyone on board had perished.

Three years later, Cheryl wrote a book, *Beauty Beyond the Ashes*.

She wrote, "As unfair, unreasonable, and impossible as it seems, we still have work to do after tragedy strikes. Life may pause, but it doesn't stop."

Now, Cheryl asks every day, "What does God have for me? What can I do for him?" Her kids are now grown, and Cheryl has remarried. She survived by seeing God's new plan.

You can do the same thing. Move forward, but never move alone. You can experience beauty beyond the ashes.

"Jacob replied, 'I will not go unless you bless me.'"

Genesis 32:26

September 12

Four Gods

Did you know there are four Gods? In a study conducted by two sociologists at Baylor University in 2011, it was found that Americans basically believe in four different Gods.

The survey of 1,648 adults found an amazing 95 percent believe in God, with the other five percent being self-identified atheists or agnostics. The most popular God, according to the survey, is the authoritative God, accepted by 28 percent. The other three are the distant God (24 percent), benevolent God (22 percent), and critical God (21 percent).

Which God do you believe in? Is it the authoritarian God, who comes down hard on sin, the distant God who started creation, then backed off, the benevolent God who is caring, or the critical God who judges us at the end of the day? The answer may surprise you.

We find all four in the Bible. The authoritarian God is found in 1 Samuel 3. The distant God is found in Ecclesiastes and Esther (which has no mention of God). The benevolent God is found in John 3:16. And the critical God is in Matthew 25.

You see, God is bigger than a single label. So avoid the counsel of those who offer flippant, simple answers about the character of God. He is big. He doesn't fit the boxes we often try to put him into.

Spend time with the wise who understand this.

"Whoever walks with the wise becomes wise."

Proverbs 13:20

September 13

Brothers

Guess how many sets of brothers have played Major League Baseball? If you get it right, without cheating, you win! Let me help. There were the Waner brothers, Paul and Lloyd. They combined for 5,611 hits, and are the only brothers in the Hall of Fame. Of more recent vintage are the Alomar brothers, Roberto and Sandy. The sons of a former player, they combined for eighteen All-Star appearances and eleven Gold Gloves.

Phil and Joe Niekro perfected the knuckleball, and won a combined 539 games. The three Alou brothers (Jesus, Matty, and Felipe) had over 5,000 hits, and once batted back-to-back-to-back in the same line-up, in 1963.

The greatest brother combo would have to be the DiMaggios: Vince, Dom, and a fellow named Joe. They combined for 22 All-Star appearances. Sure, each of these players was great in his own right. But as Dom once said, "Nothing is as sweet as doing it with your brother."

He spoke for 350 sets of baseball brothers! And he spoke for all of us who have brothers with whom we can serve and for whom we can pray.

"Pray for one another, that you may be healed."

James 5:16

September 14

Roughrider

Teddy Roosevelt was my kind of man: smart, humorous, and a great outdoorsman. Come to think of it, we share nothing in common. But I can still appreciate him for who he was.

He was President of the United States, but he was so much more. He was a cowboy in the Wild West, an explorer, and a big game hunter. He rode as a cavalry officer in the Spanish-American War. As the vice presidential candidate in 1900, he gave 673 speeches and traveled 20,000 miles while campaigning for President McKinley. And years after his presidency, while preparing to deliver a speech in Milwaukee, Roosevelt was shot in the chest by a would-be assassin. With a broken rib and a bullet in his chest, Roosevelt insisted on delivering his one-hour speech before allowing himself to be taken to the hospital.

Late in life, Teddy was asked the key to success. He offered a simple answer. And his answer applies to you today. Said the ultimate Roughrider: "Spend yourself in a worthy cause."

That's it.

So you need to do three things with your life. First, find your "worthy cause." Second, commit everything you are to that dream. And third, find someone to chase your dreams with.

"Do two walk together, unless they be agreed?"

Amos 3:3

September 15

Is It Love?

Bill and Steve were discussing the possibility of love. "I thought I was in love three times," Bill said.

"You thought it was love?" Steve asked. "What do you mean?"

"Three years ago, I cared very deeply for a woman who wanted nothing to do with me," Bill said.

"Wasn't that love?" Steve asked.

"No, that was obsession. Then two years ago, I cared very deeply for an attractive young woman who didn't understand me."

"Wasn't that love?" asked Steve.

"No, that was lust." Bill continued, "And just last year, I met a woman while I was on a cruise. She was gorgeous, intelligent, a great conversationalist, and had a super sense of humor. Everywhere I followed her on that ship, I would get a very strange sensation in the pit of my stomach."

"Well, surely that was love, wasn't it?" asked Steve.

"No," answered Bill. "That was motion sickness."

A young boy complained to his dad that he was rejected by the girl whom he loved. His dad said, "Oh, it's just puppy love, son."

The boy responded, "Maybe so, but it's real to the puppy."

Some kinds of love feel like motion sickness. But God's love is unmistakably clear.

"Whoever does not love does not know God,
for God is love."

1 John 4:8

September 16

Useless Weapons

The prize for the most useless weapon of all time goes to the Russians. They invented the "dog mine." The plan was to train the dogs to associate food with the undersides of tanks, in the hope that they would run hungrily beneath advancing Panzer divisions. Bombs were then strapped to the dogs' backs, which endangered the dogs to the point where no insurance company would look at them.

Unfortunately, the dogs associated food solely with Russian tanks. The plan was begun the first day of the Russian involvement in World War II, and abandoned on day two.

The dogs with bombs on their backs forced an entire Soviet division to retreat.

This brings me to two brief and simple points. First, no matter how sincere we may be, some days are best forgotten. And second, some things that seem important at the time become hilarious after a little time passes.

Perhaps that is why Psalm 90:12 encourages us to "number our days."

Let's learn a lesson from those dogs with bombs on their backs. Some of the best-laid plans blow up in our faces. When the smoke clears, try smiling instead of crying.

"Through wisdom your days will be many, and years will be added to your life."

Proverbs 9:11

September 17

Another Doctor

I'm sure you've heard about the man who went in for a physical. His doctor said he was fat. The man said he wanted a second opinion, so the doctor gave him one. "Okay, you're ugly, too."

I heard about a doctor who was making the rounds in a ward of terminally ill patients. He asked each of them whether they had any final requests. To one older lady, he said, "Is there anything you especially want before you pass on?"

She replied, "Yes, I'd like to see my immediate family one more time."

"Of course," said the doctor. "We'll arrange it."

He asked a second patient for his final wish. "I'm a Catholic," murmured the man. "I'd like to see a priest for confession and last rites."

"Certainly," replied the doctor.

Then he approached the third patient. "Have you any last wish, sir?" he inquired.

"Yes," gasped the old man. "My last wish is to see another doctor."

Actually, research suggests this man may get well. Studies confirm that when a patient focuses on living instead of dying, he does much better. Perhaps you are struggling right now. You have two choices: act better or act bitter.

"Get rid of all bitterness, rage and anger."

Ephesians 4:31

September 18

Titanic's Sister

I learned five things yesterday. I learned that the top reason students go to college is to prepare to make more money. I learned that the first person named *Time Magazine's* Man of the Year was Charles Lindberg. I learned that the first drive-in service station was opened by *Gulf Oil Company* in Pittsburgh, on December 1, 1913. I learned that the first city with a million people was Rome. And I learned that the *Titanic* had an identical twin.

Whoa, say that again! That's right, the *Titanic* had an identical twin.

The builders of the *Titanic* made two ships one hundred years ago, not just one. And they were identical in every way.

The name of the other ship was the *Olympic*. Both ships were thought to be indestructible. Then, on a cold night in April, 1912, it happened. The *Titanic* hit an iceberg and sunk. Fifteen hundred lives perished in the icy waters of the North Atlantic. But the *Olympic* enjoyed a 25-year career without incident.

These twin ships offer a metaphor on life. God has made us all equal in his sight. But some make bad choices and sink. Others make wise choices and prosper. The ships were the same. The difference was one of choices.

"Many are the plans in a person's heart, but it is the Lord's purpose that prevails."

Proverbs 19:21

September 19

Straighten Them Out!

A chicken and an elephant were locked in a cage together. The chicken turned to the elephant and said, "We need to set a few ground rules. First, let's not step on each other."

The chicken was looking at it from his point of view. Our chicken point of view affects our relationships with others. Our tendency is to want to straighten people out for our own benefit.

If you think straightening people out is your job, I suggest you become a funeral director. That way, when you straighten them out, they will stay straightened out.

Remember, God is the construction manager. Have you ever seen a sign that read, "Slow! Men at Work?"

These signs are usually accompanied by a dozen guys sitting around eating sandwiches. I have a suggestion for you. The next time you see someone who needs fixing, imagine a sign posted beside them: "Slow! God at Work."

And there may be another sign: "Keep Out!"

You see, you don't always see. God is at work, whether you see it or not. Those people who need to be straightened out aren't what they ought to be. But they aren't what they're gonna be either!

"Bear with each other and forgive one another.
Forgive one another as the Lord has forgiven you."

Colossians 3:13

September 20

A Good Idea?

Do you know a good idea when you see it? Let's go back in time and revisit some really good ideas. I'm talking about the VW Beetle, liquid paper, the Remington typewriter, Scrabble, and Coca Cola. Surely, these were all instant hits, right?

Judge for yourself! The first year, VW sold just 330 Beetles. In its first year, Americans bought 1,100 bottles of liquid paper. Remington sold eight typewriters. Five hundred and thirty-seven Americans bought the new game called Scrabble. And Coca Cola sold all of 25 bottles the first year.

They say first impressions are everything. I think VW, Remington, and the people who make liquid paper, Scrabble, and Coke would disagree.

Now think about your life.

In recent years, you probably made a few resolutions. And some of them may have had a bad first year. But that is why we have a God of a second chance.

Don't give up on your dreams. Don't give up on yourself. But most of all, don't ever give up on your God.

As Mohammed Ali said, "What matters is not how many times you go down, but how many times you get up." The God of a second chance has given you a new start to life today. Make it count.

"Blessed is the one who perseveres under trial because, having stood the test, that person will receive the crown of life that the Lord has promised to those who love him."

James 1:12

September 21

Last Meal

Three men, an Italian, a Frenchman, and a Spaniard, were condemned to be executed. Their captors told them that they had the right to have a final meal before their execution. They started with the Frenchman. "Give me some French wine and French bread," he requested.

So they gave it to him, he ate it, and then he was put to death.

Next, it was the Italian's turn. "Give me a plate of pasta," said the Italian.

So they brought it to him, he ate it, and then he was executed.

Now it was the Spaniard's turn. "I want a big bowl of strawberries," he said.

"Strawberries? Are you serious?"

"Yes, I want strawberries," he repeated.

His executioners replied, "But strawberries aren't even in season!"

"I know," said the Spaniard. "I'm willing to wait."

The Bible says, "It is appointed for a man to die, and then the judgment."

You can be certain of both. Eating strawberries may put things off a bit, as in our story. But nothing can change the facts. You are going to die.

The question is not whether you will die, but whether you will be ready. That's something only you can answer. And God.

"The dust returns to the ground it came from, and the spirit returns to the God who gave it."

Ecclesiastes 12:7

September 22

Dear Dad

A college student sent a letter to his dad, and his dad was happy to respond with a letter of his own.

Let's start with the son. "Dear Dad, $chool is really great. I am making lot$ of friend$ and $tudying very hard. With all my $tuff, I $imply can't think of anything I need, $o if you would like, you can ju$t $end me a card, a$ I would love to hear from you. Love, your $on."

The reply came quickly. "Dear Son, I kNOw that astroNOmy, ecoNOmics, and oceaNOgraphy are eNOugh to keep even an hoNOr student busy. Do NOt forget that the pursuit of kNOwledge is a NOble task, and you can never study eNOugh. Love, Dad."

I recently led our church through a study of prayer. We discovered, from the actual prayers of Jesus, that the point of prayer is not to change circumstances as much as it is to change hearts. Prayer is not about bending God's will toward us, but bending our hearts toward God.

Sometimes, we are like the college student who wanted money from his dad. We treat God like Santa Claus. But the mature believer doesn't just bring God his "ask." He brings God his heart.

"Then Jesus told his disciples a parable to show them that they should always pray and not give up."

Luke 18:1

September 23

Revival

Three churches worked together to sponsor a community-wide revival. It was a rare demonstration of cooperation for the Baptists, Methodists, and Presbyterians. When the revival was over, the three pastors got together to evaluate the revival's success. The Methodist minister was pleased. "We gained four families," he said.

The Baptist preacher chimed in. "We did even better than that! We gained six new families!"

Reluctantly, the Presbyterian said, "This was the best revival our church has ever had. We got rid of the ten families that were our biggest trouble makers!"

I once had a denominational leader ask me if our church would start a new church.

"What do you want from us?" I asked.

He said, "We need families to leave your church to be a part of the new congregation. How many families are you willing to send us?"

I responded, "It depends. If you pick the families, I'll give you five. If I get to pick the families, I'll give you 15."

Of course, real revival isn't about numbers of people joining a church. But when revival comes to your life, you will never be the inspiration for a column like this!

> *"If my people, who are called by my name, will
> humble themselves and pray and seek my face
> and turn from their wicked ways, then I will
> hear from heaven, and I will forgive their sins
> and heal their land."*

2 Chronicles 7:14

September 24

Legalistic Sundays

God created Sundays for four things: worship, family, rest, and televised NFL games in the fall.

Never content to leave well enough alone, state legislatures have provided more detail for how we are to honor the Lord's Day. All across the fruited plain, we have great laws that make Sunday the sacred event God intended.

Let's review. In Vermont, it is illegal to deny the existence of God. In Alabama, it is against the law to spit on the floor of a church. In Georgia, you can't carry an ice cream cone in your back pocket on a Sunday. It is a crime to ride a merry-go-round on Sundays in Idaho. In Indiana, if you use the Lord's name in vain on a Sunday, the fine is $3 for each offense, with a maximum fine of $10 per Sunday. In California, animals cannot mate within 1,500 feet of a church on a Sunday. In Virginia, it is unlawful to conduct business on a Sunday, with the exception of almost every industry. And you cannot hunt any animal except raccoons, which may be hunted until 2:00 a.m.

But I am proud to be a Texan, where the law simply states that one must acknowledge a supreme being to hold public office.

"Remember the Sabbath Day by keeping it holy."

Exodus 20:8

September 25

Who Killed Warren Harding?

How did President Harding die? Is it possible that his wife killed him? Florence Harding accused the sitting President of infidelity, amid rumors that he had fathered a child with a much younger woman. She put the FBI onto him. Their evidence proved him to be guilty of her accusation. Then Mrs. Harding was known to have asked a few friends about poison and powder. "Just curious," she said.

Then, in 1923, the President got sick. It happened after a dinner with family and friends, a dinner prepared by his wife. He died a week later. At first, it was ruled a heart attack, then a stroke. But he had been very sick since the dinner "party."

So they suggested an autopsy, but that had to be approved by Mrs. Harding. She refused.

Looking back, doctors surmise that his symptoms reflected those of poisoning. We may never know for sure. But we do know this. Choices have consequences. And when Warren Harding chose to live outside of the bounds of marriage, things would never be the same.

Did he die of a heart attack? Was it a stroke? Or was it poisoning? If it was poisoning, who's to blame?

"Do not be deceived; God cannot be mocked.
A man reaps what he sows."

Galatians 6:7

September 26

Rise and Whine

There have always been two groups of people. Do you remember the First Church of the Promised Land Relocation Committee? The committee split. Some of them came back from their field trip full of grapes. The others came back full of gripes. Gripers have a pained expression on their faces.

One day, Charles Spurgeon was talking to some young preachers about the importance of maintaining a proper facial expression when they preach. He said, "When you preach on heaven, you ought to smile, and joy should be evident on your face."

A young, antagonistic preacher asked Spurgeon, "What is our face supposed to look like when we preach on hell?"

Spurgeon replied, "In your case, young man, just look normal."

Somewhere, many of us got the idea that to be religious is to look painful.

One guy was asked if he was a minister. He said, "No, I've just been sick for a few days."

Chuck Swindoll had it right. Life is ten percent what happens to you and 90 percent how you respond. It is our response that brings us the most trouble.

Each day, you have a choice: rise and whine or rejoice that this is the day the Lord has made.

"Why should the living complain when punished for their sins?"

Lamentations 3:39

September 27

Having a Bad Day?

When you woke up this morning, was the bird that was singing outside your window a buzzard? Did you put your pants on backward, only to discover they fit better that way? Did you wake up and discover that your waterbed had leaked, but then you remembered you don't have a waterbed? Have you ever had a pity party, but got no pity and no one came to the party?

If you are having a bad day, you need to choose to be thankful. If you don't know where to start, read the headlines in the paper and be glad it didn't happen to you. If you can't pay your bills, be thankful you aren't your creditor.

Be like the boy who was thankful for his glasses. He reasoned, "My glasses keep the other boys from hitting me and they keep the girls from kissing me."

If you still can't find anything to be thankful for, thank God for your nose. Thank God for putting it on right side up. If he had put it on upside down, when it rains, you would drown. And when you sneeze, you would blow your head off.

No, God "nose" what he is doing. He made you just right. You have much to be thankful for.

"God saw all that he had made, and it
was very good."

Genesis 1:31

September 28

What's Your IQ?

In the 1960s, a teacher was given a roster showing the actual IQ test scores of the students of one class, and for another class a roster in which the IQ column had been mistakenly filled in with the students' locker numbers. The teacher assumed that the locker numbers were the actual IQs of the students when the rosters were posted at the beginning of the semester.

After a year it was discovered that in the first class the students with high actual IQ scores had performed better than those with lower locker numbers.

I love what Ruth Graham once said about Billy Graham. "It's my job to love Billy. It's God's job to make him good."

Now replace the name Billy with the name of your husband, wife, child, friend, pastor, or boss. Don't try to change people. Try to encourage them.

The only person you can change is yourself. As the story with the IQs demonstrates, most of us become what others tell us we are. So find someone you want to become special and tell them they are special already.

> *"Therefore encourage one another*
> *with these words."*

1 Thessalonians 4:18

September 29

101-Year-Old Saint

Anne Scheiber was 101 when she died in 1995. She lived in a tiny, run-down apartment in Manhattan. She had been there since 1943. Anne paid $400 a month. She lived on Social Security. When she retired due to health reasons, in 1945, her annual salary was $3,150. But Anne got by settling for used furniture, used clothes, and no car. She didn't subscribe to a newspaper. It was simply too expensive.

So imagine the surprise of Norman Lamm, president of Yeshiva University in New York City, when he learned that Anne had left the school in her will. The old lady whom Lamm had never met left the school $22 million.

It seems Anne was quite a student of stocks. Upon her retirement in 1945, she invested her $5,000 life's savings in Schering-Plough Corporation stock. Those stock holdings grew to $22 million.

But Anne never spent the money on herself. She was committed to making a difference for the next generation.

You know, you can do even more than Anne! You have more money now than she had then. How do I know? Because you could at least afford this devotional book.

"Let the word of God dwell in you richly, teaching and admonishing one another."

Colossians 3:16

September 30

Play for Pay

A man came home from work every day, sat in his recliner, and enjoyed a little peace and quiet. But one day the neighborhood boys discovered that the man's backyard was a natural ball field. So they started playing ball there every afternoon, making lots of noise and disturbing our friend.

He would go outside and holler at them, but the next day, they'd be back. Then he had an idea. He went outside and called the kids. They eventually came. He apologized and said he was sorry he had run them off.

He said he'd learned to really enjoy the noise they made and asked if they'd come and make the noise again. He said that if they'd come back, he'd pay each one of them a quarter.

The kids were excited and showed up the next day. Each day, he asked them to return the next day, but for a reduced pay. He lowered his offer each day until they were each receiving five cents per day. Then he offered them a penny.

They refused to play for just a penny, so they quit. What happened? The boys became like us. What we did for fun yesterday, we do for pay today, and will quit if we lose our pay tomorrow.

"But Jehu took no heed to walk in the law of the Lord God of Israel with all his heart, for he did not depart from the sins of Jeroboam."

2 Kings 10:31

October 1

The Love of a Wife

Nothing will make a man more successful than a wife who believes in him. This was the story of Nathaniel and Sophia. One day, Nathaniel came home from work for the last time. "What is wrong?" asked Sophia.

"I've been fired," admitted her husband.

His job in a customhouse was over, as was his confidence.

But Sophia shocked Nathaniel with her response. "Praise God!" she exclaimed. "Now you have time to write your book!"

"Yes," said Nathaniel. "I've always wanted to write a book. But what shall we live on while I am writing it?"

To his amazement, Sophia opened a drawer and pulled out a large sum of money. "Where on earth did you get that?" Nathaniel asked her.

"I have always known you were a man of genius," she said. "I knew that someday you would write a masterpiece. So every week, I have set aside a little money from the allowance you gave me for housekeeping. And now I have enough money to last us for a whole year."

From her trust and confidence came one of the greatest novels in American literature, written by Nathaniel Hawthorn, *The Scarlet Letter*.

"Marriage should be honored by all."

Hebrews 13:4

October 2

Time for Leftovers

Do you remember something we used to eat, called "leftovers?" You see, there once was a period in American life when we did something we called "cooking." On Sundays, everyone went to something called "church." Then we went home and had pot roast, while sitting around something we called a "dining room table," later replaced by the much more practical TV tray.

Before the meal, we all bowed our heads while dad led something called a "prayer." At this thing called "dinner" ("supper" if you were from the South), the family had something called "conversation."

Then, one Monday, as the family gathered around the table at 6:00 sharp, mom served up something we used to call "leftovers." Sunday's roast became Monday's roast beef sandwiches. Sunday's gravy for the potatoes became Monday's gravy over the bread. And no one complained, because we were happy to have something called "family time."

But today, we have microwaved food, microwaved talk, and microwaved lives. As a kid, I never thought I'd say it, but here goes. I really miss the leftovers!

"Your wife will be like a fruitful vine within your house; your children will be like olive shoots around your table."

Psalm 128:3

October 3

Scars

A single guy arrived at work with scars on both of his ears. A friend asked what happened. He said, "It was terrible. I was ironing my shirt, the phone rang, and I picked up the iron instead of the phone."

"That's awful," said his friend.

"But what happened to the other ear?"

The man replied, "The guy called back."

We need to learn from our scars and not do the same dumb things over and over.

If you look closely at the bridge of my nose, one finger on my left hand, my right thumb, and my left forearm, you will see scars. It goes back to August 27, 1968, when I ran into the sliding glass door of our apartment, thinking the door was open. I stood in a brief moment of shock, as the glass shattered and cut me in a dozen places. That was over 45 years ago, but I learned from my scars. I haven't run into a glass door since.

Thomas asked if Jesus was really risen. When told that he was, Thomas said he'd only believe it if he saw the scars from the nails on the cross.

You'll carry your scars for the rest of your life, but they can be used for good. Since Jesus had scars, he knows how to handle yours.

"This is how we know what love is: Jesus Christ laid down his life for us. And we ought to lay down our lives for our brothers."

1 John 3:16

October 4

The House You Build

A wealthy man's foreman had been a great worker. One day, the man told his foreman that he was going on a lengthy vacation. He said, "Build a great house while I am gone. Spare no expense on materials and construction. I will be back in six months, and when I return, I'll want the keys to the house."

The foreman started building the house, but soon realized that if he used substandard materials he could pocket the extra money. So that is what he did. The house was second rate because it was built with second rate materials.

When the wealthy man returned, he asked for the keys to the house.

"Did you build me a great house?" he asked.

"Yes," replied the foreman.

"Did you use the finest materials?"

"Yes," he said.

Then his boss said, "Great, because this house is for you," and he handed him the keys.

Think about the house you are building. And remember, the house you build today is the house you'll have to live in tomorrow.

Your house is built on character, daily choices, and discipline. If you build with the wrong materials, your dream house will become your worst nightmare.

"Desire without knowledge is not good; how much more will hasty feet miss the way!"

Proverbs 19:2

October 5

No Fear

The Bible says it 365 times, once for every day in the year: Fear not.

There are three reasons for that. First, fear makes you frail. Doctors report that almost all chronic patients have one problem: fear. Second, fear makes you frantic. It will paralyze you into inactivity. The only thing worse than wrong action is inaction. Third, fear makes you foolish.

I heard about a high school football player who intercepted a pass. He ran down the sideline, toward the opponent's end zone. Glancing back, he saw the shadow of someone chasing him. So he cut across the field, but when he glanced back, the shadow was still there. As he neared the end zone, he dove for the goal line, to avoid the tackle. What he didn't know was that the shadow was his. There were no players with 20 yards of him.

His fear made him look foolish before 5,000 fans. I know the feeling.

When I was in second grade, a bully tormented me every day, knocking me down and tearing up my homework. It was only when I finally confronted her that my fear went away.

Don't run from your fears. Confront them in the power of God.

> *"So do not fear, for I am with you; do not*
> *be dismayed, for I am your God. I will*
> *strengthen you and help you."*

Isaiah 41:10

October 6

Horse in the Trash

An angry owner took his frustration out on his hard-working horse by throwing it in the trash dump to die. He had his crew pour trash on him every hour to bury the horse alive. But each time, the horse shook off the trash and stomped on it. Each time he did this he rose a little higher. After the third day he was free.

I'm not saying that you won't ever have trash dumped on you, but that God is able to take it and turn it into treasure.

The issue is not whether you get dumped on in life, but how you respond.

A mailman with a new route came to a house with a mean-looking dog on the porch. When he approached the mailbox, the dog jumped 20 feet in the air, and then sat down. The owner walked out to check on the commotion.

The mailman asked in amazement, "Why did he do that?"

The owner replied, "We took his chain off yesterday, and he hasn't realized it."

The dog was living in the past. We all live in the past from time to time.

But Jesus came to help you overcome your trash and to overcome your past. He died to set you free. It's time for you to live your life off the chain.

"If any man is in Christ, the new creation has come. The old has gone, the new is here!"

2 Corinthians 5:17

October 7

Leaping Frogs

Think of five frogs sitting on a log. One decides to jump off. How many are left? Five. Thinking of jumping and jumping are two different things.

Lots of people "decide" to do things, but they never do them.

Finding Forrester is a great movie. Sean Connery plays the part of a legendary writer who mentors a young man who has great potential as a writer. Connery tells Forrester to begin typing. He said, "Just type what comes to mind."

The key to success is not planning, but doing.

A construction crew was putting a drain line in a building. A power cable was directly in the path of their work. Construction stopped while an electrician was called who declared that there was no electrical power to the cable.

The foreman asked, "Are you sure the power is dead to the cable and there is no danger?"

"Absolutely," replied the electrician.

"Well then, you cut the line."

After a pause, the electrician said, "I'm not that sure."

Most of us don't take action because we aren't that sure. But there comes a time when you need to start typing, a time to cut the cable.

There comes a time when you need to jump off the log.

> *"Forget the old things. Behold, I am*
> *doing a new thing."*

Isaiah 43:18

October 8

Excuses

An old proverb says, "Excuses are like armpits. We each have two of them, and they both stink."

I love kids. They are great with excuses. When a kid comes home late, he never says, "I stopped at Jimmy's, started playing, and forgot to come home."

Instead, he claims he had to stop on the way home to rescue a cat or help an old lady. Have you ever heard a child say, "I didn't finish my homework because I'm lazy and played video games instead"?

Have you ever heard them say, "Sorry, I just decided I'd rather watch television than memorize prepositions"?

Clubhouse Magazine held a contest for kids. They asked for the best excuse they could come up with for not doing their homework.

The winner said, "I went on a hot air balloon ride, and we were going to crash because there was too much weight in the basket. I threw my homework out, and it saved our lives."

Where do our kids come up with these crazy stories? I mean, who are their role models? We, as their parents, need to find out who is raising our kids to be this way. We need to hold them accountable. No more excuses.

"Start children off on the way they should go, and even when they are old they will not turn from it."

Proverbs 22:6

October 9

You Can Do It!

This is what the head of MGM said after watching Fred Astaire's first screen test. "Can't act! Can't dance!"

It was said of Vince Lombardi, "He possesses minimal football knowledge."

Socrates was called "an immoral corrupter of youth."

Beethoven was called "hopeless as a composer" by his own conductor.

Walt Disney was fired by a newspaper editor for lack of creativity.

Thomas Edison's teachers said he was "too stupid to learn anything."

Albert Einstein did not speak until he was four or read until he was seven.

Louis Pasteur was a mediocre student, ranking 15th out of 22 students in his chemistry class.

Leo Tolstoy, author of *War and Peace*, flunked out of college.

Henry Ford went broke five times before he finally succeeded.

Winston Churchill failed the sixth grade.

And 18 publishers turned down Richard Bach's 10,000-word story about a "soaring" bird, until Macmillan finally agreed to publish *Jonathan Livingston Seagull*.

Don't listen to man. Listen to God. When you have a legitimate dream, God says four words: You can do it! Stay pure. Stay strong. Stay focused.

"But Daniel resolved not to defile himself with the royal food and wine, and he asked the chief official for permission not to defile himself."

Daniel 1:8

October 10

Your Hair

Here are some things you may not know about hair. If you are blonde (coloring doesn't count), you were given about 150,000 hairs to work with. Brunettes must get by with 100,000 and redheads with just 60,000. So, if you're a frustrated redhead, it's okay to express your frustration in many ways, but don't pull your hair out; you can't afford to.

The average eyebrow has 550 hairs. (As an aside to all men, feel free to trim your eyebrows before they cover your eyes like a poodle.)

Ten percent of men shave only with an electric razor, while 30 percent of women do. The average beard has 15,500 hairs. Half of Caucasian men go bald, compared with 18 percent of African Americans and almost no American Indians.

Fifty percent have gray hair by age 50 (more if you have more than two kids). Cutting your hair does not make it grow. The life span of one hair is five years.

And here's one more truth. God has your hairs numbered. While that isn't hard for the follicly challenged, it says something about how intimately you are known by your God. So get to know him. Life is short.

You are hair today, and gone tomorrow.

"Indeed, the very hairs of your head are all numbered. Don't be afraid; you are worth more than many sparrows."

Luke 12:7

October 11

Note to the Pastor

The local minister wanted to do a better job of connecting with his congregation. One Sunday, he preached on the need for the people to spend more time together. In the sermon, he announced that he would take the lead in this new initiative. He asked every person in the congregation who wanted a personal visit in their home from the pastor, to simply indicate that on a sheet of paper, to be placed in the offering plate.

After the offering had been received and the service had ended, the pastor made his way to the room where the deacons count the money.

He announced, "I'm not here to check out today's offering. I want to collect all the notes from the people wanting me to visit them in their homes."

He was dismayed to discover that only one such request was submitted. It read, "We appreciate the pastor's desire to visit his flock, and respectfully ask that he visit us in our home someday this month."

It was signed by the pastor's wife and kids. Someone has written a paraphrase of a well-known verse in the Bible. "What does it profit a man to gain the whole world if he loses his own family?"

> *"Rejoice in the good the Lord has*
> *done in your house."*

Deuteronomy 26:11

October 12

Battle of the Sexes

I have this theory, tested over 30 years of marriage, that men and women are somewhat different. Studies show that men are more likely than women to run stoplights, while women are more likely to change lanes without notice. Fifty-one percent of men say TV remote controls have "significantly changed" their lives, compared with just 39 percent of women. (The other 61 percent of women are married, and have therefore never been able to touch the remote.) Men leave their hotel rooms cleaner than women do.

If you're an average man, you'll spend 81 minutes in your car today, compared to 64 minutes for a woman. Men laugh 69 times per day, compared to just 55 times for women.

Marriage makes a woman more likely to be depressed, while having the opposite effect on men.

When snow skiing, men tend to fall on their faces. Women fall the other way.

Yes, we are different. Did you know the same Bible that tells men to "love" their wives tells women to "respect" their husbands?

Indeed, we are different. Women are shopping for Christmas presents by July, while men have the good sense to wait until the last possible moment.

God made us different. And then he said, "It is good."

> *"God created mankind in his own image, in the image of God he created them; male and female he created them."*

Genesis 1:27

October 13

The Wall

A journalist was assigned to the Jerusalem bureau of his newspaper. He got an apartment overlooking the Wailing Wall. Whenever he looked at the wall he saw an old Jewish man praying and wondered whether there was a story here.

He went to the wall and said, "You come to this wall every day. What are you praying for?"

The old man replied, "I pray for world peace, then I pray for the brotherhood of man. I go home, have a glass of tea, and I come back to the wall to pray for the eradication of illness and disease."

The journalist was taken by the old man's sincerity and persistence. "You mean you have been coming to the wall to pray every day for these things?"

The old man nodded.

"How long have you been doing this?" The man replied,

"About 25 years."

The amazed journalist asked, "How does it feel to come and pray every day for 25 years for the same things?"

The old man said, "It feels like I'm talking to a wall."

Here's the good news. Whether you feel like you are talking to the wall, the ceiling, or the hand, Someone is always listening. And he is glad to hear your voice.

> *"The prayer offered in faith will make the sick person well; the Lord will raise them up."*

James 5:15

October 14

Dog at the Hotel

A man wrote a letter to a small hotel in a Midwest town he planned to visit on his vacation. He wrote, "I would very much like to bring my dog with me. He is well-groomed and very well behaved. Would you be willing to permit me to keep him in my room with me at night?"

An immediate reply came from the owner of the hotel. "I've been operating this hotel for 25 years. In all that time, I've never had a dog steal towels, bed clothes, or silverware. I've never had a dog remove a picture from the wall. I've never had to evict a dog in the middle of the night for being drunk and disorderly. And I've never had a dog run out on paying his bill. Yes, indeed, your dog is welcome at my hotel. And, if your dog will vouch for you, you are welcome to stay here, as well."

I have traveled with my dog many times. We've stayed in hotels together. All she needs to be happy is to walk with her master at night, sleep with her master, and awaken to her master the next day.

It's really too bad that people aren't as smart as dogs. Learn to find joy by walking with your Master throughout today.

"Enoch walked faithfully with God; then he was no more, because God took him away."

Genesis 5:24

October 15

Dumb Flies

The other day I was in a room listening to the desperate sounds of a life-or-death struggle going on a few feet away. There was a small fly burning out the last of its short life's energies in a futile attempt to fly through the glass of the windowpane. The whining wings tell the poignant story of the fly's strategy: try harder. But it's not working. The frenzied effort offers no hope for survival.

Ironically, the struggle is part of the trap. It is impossible for the fly to try hard enough to succeed at breaking through the glass.

Across the room, ten steps away, the door is open. Five seconds of flying time and this small creature could reach the outside world it seeks. With only a fraction of the effort now being wasted, it could be free of this self-imposed trap.

The breakthrough possibility is there. It would be so easy. How did it get so locked in on the idea that this particular route and determined effort offer the most promise for success? There was no doubt this approach would ultimately kill the little fly.

And it will kill you and me. With God, the answer is not trying harder. The answer is trusting more.

"For we maintain that a person is justified by faith apart from the works of the law."

Romans 3:28

October 16

Abe Didn't Quit

Abraham Lincoln said, "The sense of obligation to continue is present in all of us. A duty to strive is the duty of us all. I felt a call to that duty."

Abe didn't quit, despite all the failures he had known in life. In 1816 his family was forced out of their home. In 1818 his mother died. In 1831 he failed in business. In 1832 he ran for the state legislature and lost. That same year, he lost his job. In 1833 he borrowed money to live on, and took 17 years to pay it back. In 1835 his fiancé died. In 1836 he had a nervous breakdown and was in bed for six months.

In 1838 Lincoln made it to the state legislature, but lost in his race to become speaker. In 1843 Lincoln ran for Congress and lost. In 1846 he ran again, and won. He ran for re-election in 1848 and lost. In 1849 he sought a job as land officer and was rejected. In 1854 he ran for Senate and lost. Two years later he sought the Vice-Presidential nomination and lost. In 1858 he ran for Senate and lost again. And in 1860 he was elected President of the United States.

Lincoln said, after one defeat, "The path was worn and slippery. My foot slipped from under me, but I said, 'It's only a slip, not a fall.'"

"So we rebuilt the wall till all of it reached half its height, for the people worked with all their heart."

Nehemiah 4:6

October 17

Feeding the Dead

I have a friend who worked as a nutritionist at a hospital. She told patients what to eat. One day, she went into a room, ready to feed the patient. There was just one small problem. When she approached the patient, she noticed that he was dead. He had died four hours earlier. Her assignment was to feed the man, but she made an executive decision. She decided that it really wouldn't be worth the trouble. Dead people don't need food, they need life.

One day, an old man was wondering if his wife had a hearing problem. He was standing behind here while she was sitting in her chair. He asked her, "Honey, can you hear me?"

There was no response. He moved closer and repeated the question, "Honey, can you hear me?"

Still, he got no response. This time, he got right behind her and yelled, "Honey, can you hear me?"

She replied, "For the third time, yes!"

We all need to hear God's voice. We all need to be spiritually fed. But unfortunately, some of us have had our ears clogged by the things of this world. Or worse yet, we are spiritually dead.

We don't need food; we need a resurrection.

"Whoever has ears, let them hear."

Matthew 11:15

October 18

Check on the Patient

A woman called St. Matthews Hospital. She asked for patient information. Then she asked for information on Sarah Finkel.

The operator said, "Let me see. Oh yes, it says here that Mrs. Finkel is in Room 332. She is doing very well. The doctor will visit her this afternoon, and expects to release her at that time. She should be home by tomorrow morning."

The woman calling the hospital said, "That's wonderful! Praise God! I'm so glad to hear the good news!"

At that, the operator said, "You must be close to Mrs. Finkel!"

The woman responded, "No, I *am* Mrs. Finkel. I called you on my cell phone, because I can't get a nurse in here to tell me what is going on!"

A lot of us are like poor Mrs. Finkel. We don't know how we're doing. Others know how we're doing, but they aren't talking. And sometimes we can't tell how we're doing on our own. We need people to be honest with us.

I bet you can think of a dozen people who are a mess right now. But you will likely leave yourself off the list, though you may be the biggest mess of all. So do what Mrs. Finkel did. Ask for outside help.

"The way of fools seems right to them, but the wise listen to advice."

Proverbs 12:15

October 19

Paying the Fine

Once, when Mr. LaGuardia, the famous ex-mayor of New York, was presiding at a police court, they brought a trembling old man before him, charged with stealing a loaf of bread. He said his family was starving.

"Well, I've got to punish you," said Mr. LaGuardia. "The law makes no exception, and I can do nothing but sentence you to a fine of ten dollars."

Then he added, after reaching into his pocket, "and here's the ten dollars to pay your fine. And now I remit the fine."

Then, tossing the ten dollar bill into his famous outsized hat, he said, "Furthermore, I'm going to fine everybody in this courtroom 50 cents, for living in a town where a man has to steal bread in order to eat. Mr. Bailiff, collect the fines, and give them to this defendant."

The hat was passed, and the incredulous old man, with a light of heaven in his eyes, left the court room with $47.50.

We are all like that old man. We have made mistakes. It's called "sin." We are all guilty. A fine has been assigned. But a loving Judge has already paid the penalty, and blessed us with far more than $47.50.

"Like newborn babies, crave pure spiritual milk, so that by it you may grow up in your salvation."

1 Peter 2:2

October 20

Legally Dead

This really happened. A journal of the Massachusetts Bar recorded the following exchange between an anonymous attorney and a pathologist in a recent murder trial.

"Doctor, before you performed the autopsy, did you check for a pulse?"

"No."

"Did you check for breathing?"

"No."

"So then, is it possible that the patient was alive when you began the autopsy"

"No."

"How can you be so sure?"

"Because his brain was sitting on my desk in a jar."

Even then, the attorney would not back down. He continued, "Is it possible the patient could be alive, nevertheless?"

The pathologist responded, "Yes, it is possible that he could have been alive, and practicing law."

Vice President Dan Quayle once commented, while speaking at the National Negro College annual event, "A mind is a terrible thing to waste, or to never have."

Whether you've lost your mind, never had a mind, or your mind is in a jar, there is hope. With whatever you have left, the Bible says to "love the Lord with all your mind."

What you think today, you do tomorrow. Don't worry about changing the world. Just mind your own business.

"Jesus replied, 'Love the Lord your God
with all your heart, and with all your soul,
and with all your mind.'"

Matthew 22:37

October 21

A Little Girl's Pennies

Hattie Wiatt, a little girl, came to a small Sunday School and asked to be taken in, but it was explained that there was no room for her. In less than two years she fell ill and died with a secret. No one knew her secret until they discovered something beneath her pillow. They found a torn pocketbook with 57 pennies in it, wrapped in a scrap of paper on which was written, "To help build the little temple bigger, so that more children can go to Sunday School."

For two years she had saved her pennies for the cause which was nearest her heart.

The pastor told the incident to his congregation, and the people began making donations for the enlargement. The papers told it far and wide, and within five years those 57 pennies had grown to $250,000, and today in Philadelphia stands the historic Baptist Temple, which seats 3,500 every Sunday morning.

Beside the church, they have constructed a college for 1,400 and a hospital. And it was all made possible because of a little girl and her 57 pennies.

Think about that the next time you see a little girl with a big smile and a bigger heart.

"Who dares despise the day of small things?"

Zechariah 4:10

October 22

Be Creative!

When kids are five, they all think they can draw. By age ten, almost none of them still believe they can draw. What happens? Goofballs like you and me tell them they can't do it.

God was a Creator before he was anything else. We serve a creative God. And since we are made "in his image," we must be a creative people.

So be creative! Go ahead! Create! Oh, I know what you're thinking. "I'd be more creative, but I'm waiting for inspiration, permission, reassurance, or someone to smooth the way. I'm waiting for the rest of the rules, someone to change, or wider fairways."

You would be creative, but you figure, "I am waiting until I have more time, mutual consent, a better time, a more favorable horoscope, tomorrow, or four Aces. I am waiting for the absence of risk, someone to discover me, better instructions, Chicken Little to return, the pot to boil or a signal from heaven. I'm waiting for shorter lines, my ship to come in, a better deodorant, the check to clear, the rates to go down, or the Iceman to cometh."

I have a suggestion. Quit waiting and start walking. Quit thinking so much. Start creating!

"You foolish person, do you want evidence that faith without deeds is useless?"

James 2:20

October 23

Chasing Jim Brown

Jim Brown was a football player with no equal. The year was 1957. A 10-year-old boy in California idolized Brown and set a goal to be like him. But this tall, skinny lad had much to overcome. He grew up in the ghetto where he never got enough to eat. Malnutrition took its toll, and a disease called rickets forced him to wear steel splints to support his bowed-out legs. He had no money to buy a ticket to get into the game, so he waited patiently outside the locker room until the game ended, so he could try to get Jim Brown's autograph.

When Brown approached, the boy said, "I have your picture on my wall. I know you hold all the records. You're my idol."

Brown signed his autograph, then began to walk away. But then, the boy proclaimed, "Mr. Brown, one day, I'm going to break every record you hold!"

Brown was impressed and asked, "What's your name, son?"

The boy replied, "Orenthal James. But my friends call me O.J."

Indeed, O.J. Simpson would break all but three of Jim Brown's records. It was made possible because he set a goal, and he committed everything he had to meet that goal. How do you respond when someone breaks your record or steals your spotlight?

In the story of the Prodigal Son, remember, the older boy had his issues, too.

"The older brother became angry and refused to go in. So his father went out and pleaded with him."

Luke 15:28

October 24

Two Kinds of People

How many kinds of people are there? Some may say Longhorns, Aggies, Sooners, etc. Others might say Republicans, Democrats, and Independents. Some might say young and old or male and female. I would argue the answer is two. There are two kinds of people. Consider the words of the poet.

"There are only two kinds of people on earth today,
two kinds of people, no more, I say;
not the good and the bad,
for 'tis well understood,
that the good are half bad and the bad are half good.
No, the two kinds of people on earth I mean
are the people who lift and the people who lean."

Those words of Ella Wheelcox ring ever true. Indeed, "The good are half bad and the bad are half good."

We all have strong hints of good and evil in us. But the end of Ella's poem says it brilliantly. "There are the people who lift and the people who lean." So which kind are you?

Jesus told the story of the widow who gave all she had. It would have been so easy for her to be a leaner, but she determined to be a lifter. Those are your only two choices. Will you lift someone today, or just be a leaner?

> *"They all gave out of their wealth; but she,
> out of her poverty, put in everything – all
> she had to live on."*

Mark 12:44

October 25

Loneliness

An old mountaineer and his wife were sitting in front of the fireplace. After a long silence, the wife said, "Jed, I think it's raining. Go outside and see."

The old mountaineer responded by gazing absently at the fire, and then he sighed and said, "Aw, Ma, why don't we just call in the dog and see if he's wet."

It's hard to say who was lonelier, the dog, Ma, or Pa.

Benito Mussolini said, "It seems my tragic destiny that in all the important moments of my life I find myself alone."

Marilyn Monroe commented to a friend, "Sometimes I think the only people who stay with me and really listen are people I hire."

Actress Inger Stevens said, "Sometimes I get so lonely I could scream."

Albert Einstein said, "It is strange to be known so universally, and yet to be so lonely."

Are you ever lonely? Remember, you don't have to be alone to be lonely. It is the condition of the mind and the heart.

The answer, in the words of F.B. Meyer, is to recognize that "loneliness is an opportunity for Jesus to make himself known."

If you are lonely, try Jesus. He is more dependable than a wet dog.

"All my longings lie open before you, Lord; my sighing is not hidden from you."

Psalm 38:9

October 26

An Army of the Lord

A man was walking out of church one day, and the minister was standing by the door shaking hands. The minister recognized the man as someone who only attended church on special days. The pastor pulled the man aside and encouraged him. "You need to join the army of the Lord," he said.

The man responded, "But I'm already in the Lord's army."

"Then how come I only see you in church three or four times a year?" asked the preacher.

The man answered, "I'm in the secret Service."

I joke that we can't find some of our church members with a search warrant. I have concluded that about half of the people who say they are members of a church are in the FBI Witness Protection Program.

But did you know that people who go to church are 25 percent more likely to live a long life? Did you know people who attend church every Sunday make for a happier pastor? But it's really not about church attendance. It's about joining the army of the Lord. I encourage you to sign up for battle.

There is work to be done, building God's kingdom on earth. We don't need you in the Secret Service.

"They devoted themselves to the apostles' teaching, and to fellowship, to the breaking of bread, and to prayer."

Acts 2:42

October 27

Hypocrisy

There once was a man who came down from the Carolina mountains one day. He was all dressed up and carrying his Bible. A friend saw him and asked, "Elias, what's happening? Where are you going all dressed up like that?"

Elias said, "I've been hearing about New Orleans. I hear that there is a lot of free-runnin' liquor and a lot of gamblin' and a lot of real good, naughty shows. I'm headed down there for a couple days of fun."

Elias' friend looked him over and asked, "But Elias, why are you carrying your Bible under your arm?"

Elias shrugged, "Well, if it's as good as they say it is, I might stay over until Sunday."

One day a pastor fell on his knees in dramatic fashion. "I am nothing! I am nothing!"

His associate heard him, and did the same. "I am nothing! I am nothing!" he repeated.

The church janitor walked by, then joined in, falling on his knees, as well. "I am nothing! I am nothing!" said the janitor.

The pastor turned to his associate and said, "Can you believe the gall of the janitor, saying he is nothing?"

Let's be genuine and honest. We all are nothing, apart from Christ.

> *"Turn my eyes away from worthless things;*
> *preserve my life according to your Word."*

Psalm 119:37

October 28

Parking Tickets

I went to the store the other day. I was only in there for about five minutes, and when I came out there was a motorcycle cop writing a parking ticket. So I went up to him and said, "Come on officer, how about giving a guy a break?"

He ignored me and continued writing the ticket. So I called him a pencil-necked Nazi. He glared at me and started writing another ticket for having an expired inspection sticker. So I called him a horse face. He finished the second ticket and put it on the car with the first. Then he started writing a third ticket! This went on for about 20 minutes.

The more I abused him, the more tickets he wrote. But I didn't care. My car was parked around the corner.

Or course, none of this really happened. But I tell it to make a point. Sometimes our anger is aimed at the wrong person.

In my story, the officer took out his frustration on the wrong guy. I've learned two things in my 29 years of life. Hurting people hurt people, and the issue is never the issue. And now I've actually learned a third thing. If I park on Cochran Street, in front of my office, for more than two hours, I get a ticket.

"Human anger does not produce the righteousness that God desires."

James 1:20

October 29

A Sure Bet

A strong young man at the construction site was bragging that he could outdo anyone in a feat of strength. He made a special case of making fun of Morris, one of the older workmen. After several minutes, Morris had enough.

"Why don't you put your money where your mouth is?" he said. "I will bet you a week's wages that I can haul something in a wheelbarrow over to that outbuilding that you won't be able to wheel back."

"You're on, old man," the braggart replied. "It's a bet! Let's see what you've got."

Morris reached out and grabbed the wheelbarrow by the handles. Then, nodding to the young man, he said, "All right. Get in."

The wheelbarrow provides a metaphor on life. There are a lot of things we can haul around that weigh more than we do. But getting ourselves where we need to be is always the struggle.

John Maxwell says it this way: "The key to being a great leader is to learn how to lead one person. That is yourself."

It is much easier to tell someone else what to do. It is easy to push the wheelbarrow until you get in it. The hardest thing you will ever have to move is yourself.

"My son, do not despise the Lord's discipline, and do not resent his rebuke."

Proverbs 3:11

October 30

The Fire Upstairs

One evening a few months ago, Marcos Ugarte was doing homework. His father, Eduardo, a teacher, was busy preparing lesson plans. They heard yelling from outside. They stepped onto the porch and saw the problem. Four doors down, they saw a glow coming from inside a neighbor's house.

"The house is on fire!" exclaimed Marcos to his dad.

They raced over to the house, as the neighbor, Yim Ma, stumbled out, nearly overcome with smoke.

"Is there anyone else in the house?" asked Eduardo.

"Yes, my son Cody!" cried Mr. Ma.

Eduardo ran into the house in search of the boy, but to no avail. Little did he know what his own son was doing.

Marcos heard a noise from the second floor. He grabbed a ladder and raced up to the window. He grabbed onto the infant boy, Cody. And he carried him down the ladder to safety.

Mark Maunder, the Fire Chief, arrived moments later. He said, "If Marcos had not gone into the fire, Cody would have never come out."

That is what Jesus did for us on the cross. He went into the fire of temptation, death, and hell, so we could come out.

"Then they would go away into eternal punishment, but the righteous to eternal life."

Matthew 25:46

October 31

Obituary

Our church was saddened to learn of the death of one of our most valued members. His name was Someone Else. Someone's passing creates a huge vacancy. Else has been with us for many years, and for every one of those years, Someone did far more than a normal person's share of the work.

Whenever there was a job to do, a class to teach, or a meeting to attend, one name was on everyone's list. "Let Someone Else do it!"

Whenever leadership was mentioned, this wonderful person was looked to for inspiration and results. "Someone Else can work with that group."

It was common knowledge that Someone Else was among the most liberal givers in our church. Whenever there was a financial need, everyone just assumed Someone Else would make up the difference.

Were the truth known, everybody expected too much of Someone Else.

Now Someone Else is gone! Someone Else left a wonderful example to follow, but who is going to follow it? Who is going to do all the things Someone Else did?

When you are asked to help in your church, remember you can't depend on Someone Else anymore.

"A sluggard's appetite is never filled, but the desires of the diligent are fully satisfied."

Proverbs 13:4

November 1

Advice of a Dad

Heinrich Bullinger was a good pastor and a better father. He was born in 1504 to a priest who, in his old age, embraced Reformation views, such as "the just shall live by faith." Though it cost him his church, it gained him his son.

Young Heinrich fell in love with Martin Luther's writings, Melanchthon's books, and the study of the Bible. At the remarkably young age of 27, he was asked to take the place of slain Swiss Reformer Ulrich Zwingly as pastor of the Grossmunster of Zurich. He ascended the pulpit there on December 23, 1531.

Bullinger continued Zwingli's practice of preaching through books of the Bible, verse by verse. His home, like his Bible, was open from morning till night, and he freely distributed food, clothing, and money to the needy. His wisdom and influence spread across Europe. No one was more affected than his son, Henry.

When Henry packed his bags for college, Heinrich gave him this piece of advice. "Fear God at all times, and remember that the fear of God is the beginning of wisdom."

Great advice from a great man. And what worked for Henry will work for you.

"The wisdom that comes from heaven is first of all pure; then peace-loving, considerate, submissive, full of mercy and good fruit, impartial and sincere."

James 3:17

November 2

Grocery Store Religion

A lady took her young child to the grocery store. She put him in the cart and said, "I will wheel you up and down every aisle. You will see a lot of things you want, but don't touch them. They are not for you."

The military has a word for such treatment. It's called "torture."

I heard about a man who took his boy to another grocery store. The little fellow asked if he could be a dog.

"What do you mean, can you be a dog?" asked the father.

"I want to be a dog!" insisted the lad.

"Okay, you can be a dog," his dad replied.

Suddenly, the boy started barking and ran up to a stranger and started to lick his leg.

The stranger said, "What is your boy doing?"

"He thinks he's a dog," said the father.

"Well, this is just horrible," said the stranger.

The dad responded, "No, 'horrible' would be if he thought you were a fire hydrant."

We learn a lot by walking through a grocery store.

Here's the lesson I have learned. I must live by direction, not by distraction. Make a list of what to buy. Otherwise, I buy things I don't need. And when it's time to "check out," I realize some things cost a lot more than I thought they would.

*"Meaningless! Meaningless! Utterly meaningless!
Everything is meaningless!"*

Ecclesiastes 1:2

November 3

Power of the Saw

A man had a firewood factory that employed prisoners. He gave them a place to live, specific directions on what to do, and he paid them good wages, but they were unproductive. Eventually the man had no choice. He fired them and purchased a circular saw powered by a gas engine. In one hour, the new saw did more than all the men had done in a week.

The man talked to his new saw. "How can you turn out so much work?" he asked it. "Are you sharper than the saws my men were using?"

The saw answered, "No, I am not any sharper than the others saws. The difference is the gas engine. I have a stronger power behind me. I am productive because of the power that is working through me, not because my blade is any sharper."

Many of us work for God in the power of the flesh. We use our best intellect, charming personality, and enthusiasm to its fullest. We are like the saw. We're really pretty sharp. The problem isn't our blade. It's our power source.

Until we are plugged into the right power, we will never produce the right results, no matter how sharp we may be.

"You will receive power when the
Holy Spirit comes on you."

Acts 1:8

November 4

Parachutes

A group of soldiers from Nepal fought on the side of Britain against Indonesia. This regiment was not trained to be paratroopers, but a particular mission required that they parachute into a remote location.

The British asked them to volunteer to jump for this mission, but they refused. Later, they sent word to the British that they would accept the mission under certain conditions. The first condition was that the area in which they were to land be reasonably soft, and the second was that the plane would have to fly as slowly as possible and at an altitude of only 100 feet.

The British said the planes always fly as slowly as possible during jumps, but they wouldn't be able to fly 100 feet from the ground because at such a low altitude there is not sufficient time for the parachutes to open.

"Parachutes?" they exclaimed. "We get parachutes?"

Think about how much more confidently we would soar in life if we had parachutes! The fact is, we do. God has promised that when we fall, he will catch us. His grace is sufficient.

So go ahead. Soar! And if you fail (sometimes you will), remember your Parachute.

> *"The Lord said, 'On the day when I act, they will be my possession. I will spare them, just as a father spares a son.'"*

Malachi 3:17

November 5

John Livingston

Let me tell you the story of a common man named John Livingston. It is the story of what happens when God's sovereignty and man's willingness to be used come together. It happened on June 30, 1630.

An unusual communion service was held at the Kirk of Shotts in Scotland. Well known ministers from all over the area were invited to assist in the service. The number of worshipers gathered was so large that the service had to be moved outdoors. The ministers had chosen one of their own to deliver the sermon, but when he became too ill to preach, 27-year-old John Livingston was asked to replace him.

Livingston was not yet ordained, nor did he have his own congregation. He was so intimidated about speaking to such an august gathering that he thought seriously about fleeing the responsibility. Finally, he resolved to preach from Ezekiel 36:25-26.

As he delivered his message, rain began to fall. Yet, Livingston continued. Suddenly there was an outpouring of the Holy Spirit and people were overcome by the weight of their sin. Over 500 people were converted that day.

"I will sprinkle clean water on you and you will be clean."

Ezekiel 36:25

November 6

Pumped

The famous Boston pastor, A. J. Gordon, visited the World's Fair in Chicago. From a distance he saw a man robed in bright, gaudy Oriental clothes, who appeared to be laboriously turning the crank of a pump and thereby creating a mighty flow of water.

Gordon was impressed with the man's energy, his smooth motions, and his obvious physical conditioning. He was pumping a tremendous amount of water. Drawing closer, Gordon was surprised to discover that the man was actually made of wood. Instead of turning the crank and making the water flow, the flow of the water was actually turning the crank and thereby making him go!

Are you tired? Most of us are. Half the population doesn't get enough sleep. That is probably because the other half snores. But either way, we are tired.

One reason may be that we have been doing all the pumping. When you decide to generate all the power, you will always be exhausted. But when you plug into the real Source, you will experience a power you never imagined before. The choice is yours. You can pump or be pumped.

If you are tired of being the pumper, I suggest you become the pumpee.

"The Advocate, the Holy Spirit, whom the Father will send in my name will teach you all things and remind you of all I have taught you."

John 14:26

November 7

Your Cheatin' Heart

According to *Psychology Today*, a survey of 2,153 juniors and seniors from colleges across the nation found that 70 percent of men and women confessed to cheating during high school. Nearly half of all college students surveyed cheated.

According to polls reported by *USA Today*, Americans lie more than we realize. Citing statistics from the book, *The Day America Told the Truth*, the newspaper reported that 91 percent of Americans lie routinely. Here are the specifics: 36 percent tell big lies, 86 percent lie to their parents, 75 percent lie to their friends, 73 percent to their siblings, and 69 percent to their spouse.

What are we lying about? 81 percent lie about their feelings, while 43 percent lie about their income. And 40 percent lie about sex.

A study by the American Management Association indicates that U.S. businesses lose over $10 billion to employee theft each year, $4 billion to embezzlement, $2.5 billion to burglary, and $2 billion to shoplifting.

Here's what the Bible says. "Do not lie." "Let he who stole, steal no more."

There is really only one solution for those who lie. It's called repentance. It's not easy. If it was, everyone would do it.

"There are six things the Lord hates . . . haughty eyes, a lying tongue."

Proverbs 6:16-17

November 8

Mediocrity

I love the words of Isaac D'Israel "It is a wretched taste to be gratified with mediocrity when the excellent lies before us."

True, competitive excellence requires 100 percent effort all the time. People figure they are getting by when they merely get close to it. And then, excellence gets reduced to acceptable, and before long, acceptable doesn't seem worth the sweat if you can get by with adequate. After that, mediocrity is just a breath away. Let's consider the real consequences of mediocrity, of only getting it right most of the time.

Natalie Gabal has done the research. If 99.9 percent was considered acceptable, in one year the IRS would lose two million documents, and 12 babies would be given to the wrong parents each day. Two-hundred-ninety-one pacemaker operations would be performed incorrectly, 20,000 incorrect drug prescriptions would be written, and 114,500 mismatched pairs of shoes would be shipped.

We have a man in our church who points out every tiny mistake in the worship guide or PowerPoint on Sundays. You know what I tell him? "Thanks!"

God wants our best. Mediocrity is not an option. Can we achieve perfection in this life? Of course not! But we can achieve excellence.

"No one who is born of God will continue to sin, because God's seed remains in them. They cannot go on sinning."

1 John 3:9

November 9

Game Shows

I grew up watching game shows. If you remember the original *Newlywed Game* and *The Dating Game*, you are old. If you remember *Match Game* and *The $64,000 Question*, you are really old. I love game shows because it's fun to watch someone other than me make a fool of himself.

My favorite was an episode of *Family Feud*. The question was, "In which month do most pregnant women begin to show?"

The first answer was "September."

On *The Weakest Link*, host Anne Robinson asked, "In which H.G. Wells novel does an inventor travel in a machine of his own making?" Answer: *The Simpsons*.

On another episode, Robinson asked, "Who wrote *Cat on a Hot Tin Roof*?" Answer: "Dr. Seuss."

Then there was the old *Family Feud*, with host Richard Dawson. He said, "Name a famous 'Willie.'" The contestant replied, "Willie the Pooh."

I'll never go on a game show, as I ascribe to the old adage, "Better to keep your mouth shut and let others think you are stupid than to open your mouth and remove all doubt."

Let others do the talking. You do the listening. Especially when God is speaking. The world will be better for everyone.

"Whoever belongs to God hears what God says."

John 8:47

November 10

Screwtape

In his classic novel, *The Screwtape Letters*, C.S. Lewis composes advice coming from Screwtape, a high-ranking demon, to his nephew Wormwood, on how to trip up a young Christian. Chapter 14 is devoted to trying to inflate the subject's pride.

Screwtape writes, "Your patient has become humble; have you drawn his attention to this fact? All virtues are less formidable to us once the man is aware that he has them, but this is especially true of humility. Catch him at the moment when he is really poor in spirit, and smuggle into his mind the gratifying reflection. 'By jove! I'm being humble,' and almost immediately pride, pride at his own humility, will appear. If he awakes to the danger and tries to smother this new form of pride, make him proud of his attempt, and so on, through as many stages as you please."

The Bible says it more clearly. "Pride comes before fall."

I have learned that ego is unattractive to men, really unattractive to women, and downright repulsive to God. Do you think you're humble? If you said "yes," you probably aren't.

"Humility is the fear of the Lord. Its riches are honor and life."

Proverbs 22:4

November 11

Perspective

A woman who was nine months pregnant with twins bellied up to the supermarket meat market in search of the perfect pot roast. The butcher appeared from the back and asked, "May I help you?"

"No, thank you," said the lady. "I'm just looking."

A minute later, the butcher returned. "May I help you?"

"No, I'm just looking," she repeated.

A few minutes passed, and the butcher returned again, this time with a look of annoyance. Before he could say anything, the pregnant lady said sternly, "I am just looking!"

To that the butcher responded, "Then please step back a bit. Your stomach keeps pressing against our service bell."

A 10-year-old boy drank a half glass of milk then announced, "I am an optimist. The glass is half empty!"

His mother answered, "Looking at the glass as half empty is a sign of pessimism, not optimism."

"Not if you don't like what's in it," the boy replied.

Life is a matter of perspective, whether you are nine months pregnant or a 10-year-old boy. I must agree with the boy's point. What matters isn't how much you have in your glass. What matters most is what you've put in it.

"It is for freedom that Christ has set us free. Stand firm, and do not let yourselves be burdened by sin."

Galatians 5:1

November 12

Not Home Yet

A missionary couple came home aboard a ship after many years of faithful service in Africa. It so happened that there was a very important diplomat also on the same ship who got special treatment and special attention. When the ship arrived, this couple stood back and watched from the deck as the band played and the people had gathered and there was great applause. As the diplomat walked down the gangplank and was whisked off in a limousine to the sound of applause, this dear saint put his arm around his wife and he walked off with her into the streets of New York.

"Honey," he said, "it just doesn't seem right after all of these years that we would have this kind of treatment when we came home, and here this fellow gets that kind of special treatment."

And she put her arms around her husband and said to him, "But, honey, we're not home yet."

Is life tough for you sometimes? Is your road hard to travel? Do others seem to have the gain while you get the pain? Don't ever forget, you aren't home yet. There is a celebration waiting. But until your ship comes in, keep trusting. The best is still ahead.

"He will wipe every tear from their eyes. There will be no more death or mourning or crying or pain, for the old order of things has passed away."

Revelation 21:4

November 13

Tiruchchirappalli

It is a city with a quarter of a million people, located in the state of Tamil Nadu, in India. Tiruchchirappalli is situated on the Cauvery River, 190 miles southwest of Madras. The city has not always been so difficult to say or spell. It used to be known simply as Trichinopoly.

Known for being an important rail junction with a large railroad workshop, Tiruchchirappalli has numerous businesses that manufacture textiles, cement, and cigars. It is the chief market for the produce of the Cauvery delta. Of course, Tiruchchirappalli was once the capital of the Chola Empire.

But none of that is the reason for today's lesson on Tiruchchirappalli. The next time you visit, you will notice that the city is dominated by "The Rock," a natural formation that rises 273 feet above street level. It is an amazing thing to see. Many have begun to refer to Tiruchchirappalli as "The Rock."

That's not a bad parable on life. The New Testament speaks of Christ as "The Rock."

When you walk with the Lord, people won't notice you so much. But they will notice "The Rock." Just ask your friends in Tiruchchirappalli.

"I will stand there before you by the rock at Horeb. Strike the rock and water will come out of it for the people to drink."

Exodus 17:6

November 14

Baxter and Boston

Richard Baxter was one of England's most famous pastors. In early life, he went to a large church that was comprised mostly of rich, cultured people. Though the congregation was cold, they were influential, because of their heritage, size, and wealth. Baxter ministered there for many years, as the church slowly eroded and lost its zeal.

Across town was a man named Thomas Boston, another minister. Boston lacked education and training. He was a novice, virtually unknown. He also stepped into a church as pastor, about the same time as Baxter.

Boston spent hours among the poor and in the slums. He fed the hungry and ministered to the downtrodden. He went unnoticed by the media and the elite. But quietly and steadfastly, Boston continued his work.

Within a few years, while Baxter's church was still well-recognized, it was through the ministry of Rev. Boston that a revival swept the land. What was the difference?

"I did one thing every day," said Boston. "I got up and asked the Lord to show me one person who was desperate for food, then I introduced him to the Bread of Life."

"Jesus declared, 'I am the bread of life.'"

John 6:35

November 15

Priorities

You've seen the bumper stickers. "He who dies with the most toys wins." Maybe you've seen the follow-up version. "He who dies with the most toys is dead."

It's not hard to see through the emptiness and superficiality of materialism. The idea that the meaning of life is to be found in the things acquired, the trophies accumulated, and the amount of money made loses its credibility in the emergency room and the funeral parlor. As one wise older person once put it, "I've never heard anyone on his deathbed say, 'I sure wish I'd spent more time in the office.'"

What is it you are pushing so hard to acquire or accomplish? Is it truly important, or merely something to gratify your ego or impress your peers? Will it come at the expense of your family or your own relationship with God?

How do you benefit if you gain the whole world but lose or forfeit your own soul?

If you are under 40, you probably care a lot about success. If you are over 40, you may care more about significance. We all like toys. That's fine. It's okay to own toys. What's not okay is for those toys to own you.

"I desire to do your will, my God; your law is in my heart."

Psalm 40:8

November 16

Hold On!

How do you break a world record for the largest raft? *Readers Digest* tells the story. "You break the world record for the largest raft by holding hands for at least 30 seconds."

Here's what happened. A rather impressive 1,902 paddlers did just that for charity on a lake in New York's Adirondack Mountains. Canoers and kayakers united and stole the title from Pittsburgh, where 1,619 boats had bobbed together in 2010. Word is, the Pittsburgh folks are mounting a comeback. They are busily recruiting the extra 284 paddlers needed to break the new record. Stay tuned to ESPN for breaking paddler news.

Actually, it is news. Anytime you can get a couple thousand people to work together, that is news. What both groups discovered is revolutionary. "All of us" is better than "any of us."

That's true in the world of rafting, sports, church, family, and life.

So go find someone with a similar passion as yours. Then work together. You may never do something that alters the course of mankind, such as hand-holding rafting, but it will change the part of the world you live in.

"Make my joy complete by being likeminded, having the same love, being one in spirit and of one mind."

Philippians 2:2

November 17

How Far Will You Go?

How far will you go in life? Today, let's talk about the single most important factor in determining your worth and destiny.

Doug Firebaugh said it this way: "Achievement to most people is something you do. But to the high achiever, it is something you are."

Professors James Kouzes and Barry Posner have spent more than 25 years surveying leaders in virtually every type of organization, in which they ask, "What values, personal traits, or characteristics do you look for and admire most in a leader?"

During those years, they have administered a survey questionnaire called "Characteristics of Admired Leaders" to more than 75,000 people on six continents.

"The results," they report, "have been striking in their regularity over the years, and they do not significantly vary by demographical, organizational, or cultural differences."

And what quality is most admired in leaders? The answer is honesty.

Norman Schwarzkoft said, "99 percent of leadership failures are failures of character."

The good news is, you can go really far in life and achieve great things. But you must come by it honestly.

"Better the poor whose walk is blameless than a fool whose walk is perverse."

Proverbs 19:1

November 18

Why God Responds

Legendary pastor John Bisagno once described why God responds to faith. He told of the time when his daughter Melodye Jan, age five, came to him and asked for a doll house. John promptly nodded and promised to build her one, then went back to reading his book.

Soon, he glanced out the study window and saw her arms filled with dishes, toys, and dolls, as she made trip after trip until she had a great pile of playthings in the yard. John asked his wife what Melodye Jan was doing.

His wife responded, "Oh, you promised her a doll house, and she believes you. She is just getting ready for it."

Bisagno reflected, "You would have thought I had been hit by an atom bomb. I threw aside that book, raced to the lumber yard for supplies, and quickly built that little girl a doll house. Now why did I respond? Because I wanted to? No. Because she deserved it? No. Her daddy had given his word, and she believed it and acted upon it. When I saw her faith, nothing in the world could keep me from carrying out my word."

What John did for Melodye Jan, your Father does for you!

"The righteous will live by faith."

Romans 1:17

November 19

Self-Improvement

James Allen said, "People are anxious to improve their circumstances, but they aren't anxious to improve themselves."

Let's talk about how to improve ourselves. It's not easy, but it is simple. You must be intentional.

Charlie Brown said, "I've discovered the secret of life. Hang around until you get used to it."

But Bruce Springsteen has a better plan. "A time comes when you need to stop waiting around for the man you want to become and start being the man you want to be."

This involves intentionality. You will never find success by good intentions. You must have good follow-through.

Where does this begin?

Jim Rohn said it well: "You cannot change your destination overnight, but you can change your direction overnight."

We all want self-improvement. But tomorrow's destiny is the result of today's choices.

Eleanor Roosevelt said, "Your philosophy is not best expressed in the words you speak. It is expressed in the actions you take."

So go ahead. Set goals. Order your priorities. Frame your dreams. But let me say it again. Tomorrow's destiny is the result of today's choices.

"If serving the lord seems undesirable to you, then choose for yourselves this day whom you will serve."

Joshua 24:15

November 20

Gainesville State School

Kris Hogan coaches the football team at Faith Christian High School in Grapevine, Texas. They took their 7-2 record into a contest with Gainesville State School, who was 0-8. Gainesville plays no home games, as they have no field. Parents don't travel with the team; correctional officers do. You see, they are a maximum-security correctional facility.

Their team was severely outplayed and out-coached every game. And the Faith Christian game would surely be no different.

Or would it?

Coach Hogan, knowing the visiting team would have no fans or support, asked his fans to sit on their side and root for Gainesville. Two hundred volunteered. Faith's cheerleaders cheered for Gainesville. When the game was over, Faith parents greeted each player from Gainesville at their bus, with a burger and fries, a Bible, and a round of applause.

One Gainesville player said, "Lord, I don't know how this happened, so I don't know how to say thank you, but I never knew so many people cared about us."

The team boarded their bus and left in tears. As for the game, who won? I have a better question. Who cares?

"Peter asked, 'Lord, why can't I follow you now? I will lay down my life for you?'"

John 13:37

November 21

Climbing Trees

Stephen Covey says, "A leader is the one who climbs the tallest tree, surveys the entire situation, and yells, 'Wrong jungle!'"

Life is a jungle, and there are a lot of tall trees. If you want to be a leader, you need to understand the Pareto Principle. The idea is this. Focus your attention on the activities in the top 20 percent in terms of importance, and you will have an 80 percent return on your effort.

You should have a to-do list, unless you don't mind wasting time. On that list, let's say you have ten items for the day. You need to spend 80 percent of your time on the two items that will produce 80 percent of the results.

I basically do two things in my job that I am uniquely called to do: lead and feed. All the other stuff goes into my 20 percent category.

That doesn't mean they aren't important, but I can't do everything. So I choose to focus on a) what I do well, and b) what only I can do.

That is what Jesus did. He spent 80 percent of his time with 12 men. He didn't visit hospitals, write books, or teach seminary. He did a few things very well.

And every now and then, he had to look at the disciples who wanted to do too much, and say, "Wrong jungle!"

"But those who hope in the Lord will renew their strength. They will soar on wings like eagles; they will run and not grow weary, they will walk and not be faint."

Isaiah 40:31

November 22

It Happened This Day

He died on this day, November 22, 1963. He was one of the most significant figures of the twentieth century. His impact was felt throughout the world, and his influence continues today. The world mourned the death of this giant of a man who left us far too early.

Did you know he published nine best-selling books? Did you know he was esteemed in the Church of England, where a statue was erected in his honor? Did you know he was a published poet? I bet you didn't know he knew ancient Greek and was a student of Irish mythology. He cherished his faith. His brother, who also died too young, just a few years later, shared this deep faith.

Do you remember where you were November 22, 1963 (if you were alive then)? On this anniversary of his death, I encourage you to pause and thank God for his life.

Is it even necessary to mention his name? Clive Staples Lewis, better known as C.S. Lewis, died on November 22, 1963.

Sure, this great theologian, philosopher, and writer wasn't the only significant figure to die that day. But his legacy may be the most profound.

"Until the ancient of days came and pronounced judgment in favor of the Most High, and the time came when they possessed the kingdom."

Daniel 7:22

November 23

Southwest Airlines

Leaders impress people from a distance, but they influence up close.

Take Herb Kelleher, for example. The CEO of Southwest Airlines was such an influence on his employees that on Boss's Day in 1994, they paid for a full-page ad in *USA Today*. The ad consisted of a letter addressed to their boss, Herb Kelleher.

As you read the letter, think about the kind of leader you are, and how you treat those who look to you as their "boss." Think about what others might say about you.

"Thanks, Herb, for remembering every one of our names. For supporting the Ronald McDonald House. For helping load baggage on Thanksgiving Day. For giving everyone a kiss (and we mean everyone). For listening. For running the only profitable airline. For singing at our holiday party. For singing only once a year. For letting us wear shorts and sneakers to work. For golfing at the LUV Classic with only one club. For outtalking Sam Donaldson. For riding your Harley Davidson into Southwest headquarters. For being a friend, not just a boss. Happy Boss's Day from each one of your 16,000 employees."

"Above all, love each other deeply, because love covers over a multitude of sins."

1 Peter 4:8

November 24

Edison & Pedrick

I'm guessing you have heard of a fellow named Thomas Alva Edison. Thanks to his genius, we have a light over our heads, movies that include sound tracks, and microphones.

But have you heard of that other great inventor, Arthur Pedrick? Between 1962 and 1977, he patented 162 inventions. But not one of them was taken up commercially. And that is really odd, when you consider his brilliant inventions, such as a bicycle with amphibious capability. He invented a car that could be driven from the back seat, and several golf inventions, including a golf ball that could be steered in flight.

My favorite invention was Pedrick's answer to the irrigation problem. Pedrick, who described himself as the "One Man Think Tank Research Laboratory," had a plan to irrigate deserts of the world by sending a constant supply of snowballs from the polar region through a massive network of giant peashooters.

I'm not making this up!

You can read about it in Stephen Pile's, *The Book of Failures*. But don't feel too bad for Arthur Pedrick. Sure, he failed. But at least he tried.

To not try is the greatest failure of all.

"Whatever your hands find to do, do it with all your might."

Ecclesiastes 9:10

November 25

Useless Trivia

I used to love to play *Trivial Pursuit*. I love meaningless information.

For example, did you know that adults watch twice as much TV as teens? Did you know that at any given time, half of all adults are on a diet? Here's some more for you. The can opener was invented 48 years after they invented the can. The most common first name in the world is Mohammed. Every year, 2,500 left handed people die while using products designed for right handed people. The most productive work day is Tuesday. The least productive is Friday. The average person knows 5,500 words. When the temperature hits -41 degrees Fahrenheit, it is also -41 degrees Celsius. Now, for one more, if you haven't already torn out this sheet and crammed it down your throat. The average person blinks every six seconds, or 250 million times in a lifetime.

Okay, enough for meaningless trivia.

Let's consider meaningful non-trivia. For example, did you know that God has an incredible plan for your life? He wants to bless you richly, today. He wants to bless you right now! Don't blink, or you may miss it.

"For I know the plans I have for you, plans to prosper you and not harm you, plans to give you hope and a future."

Jeremiah 29:11

November 26

Joshua Bell

At 7:51 a.m., January 12, 2007, a young musician took his position against a wall in a Washington, D.C. metro station. He wore jeans, a long-sleeved t-shirt, and a Washington Nationals baseball cap. He opened his violin case, removed his instrument, and began to play.

For the next 43 minutes, he played six classical pieces. One thousand ninety-seven people passed by. Only seven tossed money into his can. He made a total of $32.17.

Three days earlier, the man played to a full house in Boston's Symphony Hall. Tickets sold for $100 apiece. Two days after the Washington, D.C. experiment, he played at Bethesda, Maryland, for $1,000 a minute.

His name is Joshua Bell. His instrument is a Stradivarius, worth $3.5 million. His music was written by Bach. So how do we explain the poor response in the metro station of Washington, D.C.?

It's rather simple. Nobody expected such majesty in such a context. Think about it. Who expected the Messiah to be born in the stable? God still does today, what he did then. He shows up in the most unexpected places and goes unnoticed by the crowds.

"And she gave birth to her firstborn, a son, and wrapped him in swaddling clothes, and laid him in a manger, because there was no room for them in the inn."

Luke 2:7

November 27

Historical Figures

You know you've made it big when they write a book about you. And you have really made it big when they make a movie about you. I asked a movie producer if he could make a good movie about my life. He said, "It depends. Can it be fiction?"

We've all seen a lot of great movies. Some of my favorites tell the stories of historical figures. Can you guess the three historical figures that have been the focus of more movies than any others? Let me help. They were all profound leaders. They all changed the course of history. Two of them lived in the 1800s, while the other is still alive.

The two from over a century ago are Abraham Lincoln (137 movies) and Napoleon Bonaparte (194). But who is the one who is still living? Let me help with that one. He is a personal friend of mine. Most of my closest friends have met him. He comes in second, behind Napoleon, with 152 movies. He would come in first, but he is a man of peace, and movie-goers like violence.

Figured it out yet? His name is Jesus Christ. And the best thing is that no fiction is needed. You see, all history is really his story!

> *"In the beginning God created the heavens and the earth."*
>
> Genesis 1:1

November 28

The Tongue

On a windswept hill in an English country churchyard stands a drab, gray slate tombstone. Bleak and unpretentious, it leans slightly to one side, beaten slick and thin by the blast of time. The quaint stone bears an epitaph not easily seen unless you stoop over and look closely.

The faint etchings read: "Beneath this stone, a lump of clay, lies Arabella Young, who, on the 24th of May, began to hold her tongue."

The tongue. What a study in contrasts! To the physician it's merely a complex array of muscles and nerves that enable our bodies to chew, taste, and swallow. How helpful! Equally significant, it is the major organ of communication that enables us to articulate sounds so we can understand each other. How essential!

The tongue is as volatile as it is vital.

Washington Irving said, "A sharp tongue is the only edge tool that grows keener with use."

And James said, "The tongue is a fire, a restless evil and full of deadly poison."

I have had to apologize for my words many times. But I have never had to apologize for my silence.

"The mouths of fools are their undoing, and their lips are a snare to their very lives."

Proverbs 18:7

November 29

Creation

One day a group of scientists got together and decided that man had come a long way and no longer needed God. So they picked one scientist to go and tell him that they were done with him.

The scientist walked up to God and said, "God, we've decided that we no longer need you. We're to the point that we can clone people and do many miraculous things, so why don't you get lost!"

God listened patiently to the man. After the scientist was done talking, God said, "Very well, let's have a man-making contest."

The scientist replied, "Okay, great!"

Then God added, "Now, we're going to do this just like I did back in the old days with Adam."

The scientist said, "Sure, no problem," and bent down and grabbed himself a handful of dirt.

God said, "No, no, no. Go get your own dirt!"

We are funny, the way we think we can live without God. But the only thing man ever created all on his own was chaos. The Hebrew word used in the Bible, for creation, means to create something out of nothing.

So go ahead, Mr. Scientist. Get your hands dirty. But you are no God.

"Remember that at that time you were separate from Christ, excluded from citizenship in Israel and foreigners to the covenants of God."

Ephesians 2:12

November 30

Ben Franklin's Death

Benjamin Franklin died from sitting in front of a window. It happened on April 17, 1790. Franklin was a big believer in fresh air, even in the middle of winter. Every night, he slept with the window open, no matter how cold it might be.

He wrote, "I rise almost every morning and sit in my chamber without any clothes, whatsoever, regardless of the season."

April of 1790 was no different for the 84-year-old statesman. He developed an abscess in his lungs, which his doctor attributed to his many hours before the open window. The abscess burst on April 17, sending Ben into a coma. He died a few hours later.

I'm sure that Ben would have closed the window if he knew then what we know now. After all, he was a very healthy man. We could have used his wisdom today.

Think of it. Franklin would be over 200 years old now, if only he had closed the window.

Actually, the Bible says, "It is appointed to man once to die, and then the judgment."

You don't know when or how you will die. So concentrate on how you will live, instead. And close the window before you go to bed.

"Just as people are destined to die once, and after that they face the judgment."

Hebrews 9:27

December 1

Wheaties

Putting great athletes on the front of Wheaties boxes is a time-honored tradition in our country, right up there with crossing our heart during the National Anthem, honoring mothers the second Sunday of May, and watching 27 football games on New Year's Day. Do you know the first athlete to appear on a Wheaties Box? I'll give you two hints. The year was 1924. His name was Lou Gehrig. Can you guess who it was now?

Here's another question for you. Which athlete has appeared on a Wheaties box the most? That would be Michael Jordan, with 18 such appearances.

But here's my favorite Wheaties trivia. In 1937 they sponsored baseball broadcasts on 95 stations. They held a nationwide contest to find their "most popular announcer." The winner was a play-by-play announcer from Des Moines. His reward was a trip to California. When he was there, he was spotted by Warner Brothers, who gave him a screen test. His name was Ronald Reagan.

He was asked the key to his success. "I learned as a kid, to be where I was supposed to be when I was supposed to be there."

Location is everything when it comes to your spiritual walk. Be in the right place with the right God, and your potential is unlimited.

"Many will be purified, made spotless and refined, but the wicked will continue to be wicked. None of the wicked will understand, but those who are wise will understand."

Daniel 12:10

December 2

Get Ready

He was "the prince of preachers," still considered the best since Paul, 100 years after his death. His name was Charles Haddon Spurgeon, the incomparable orator, author, and pastor of England. He would speak to 20,000 people every Sunday, without the use of a microphone.

While Spurgeon was best known for his preaching, he always had the heart of a pastor. One day, he went to visit a widow in his church, to see how she was doing after the loss of her husband. Arriving by horse and buggy, Spurgeon approached her front door and then knocked.

The woman responded with full embarrassment. "I look awful!" she declared. "I have been sweeping and cleaning. If I knew you were coming, I would have cleaned myself up."

"Far better," said Spurgeon, "that I find you working upon my arrival, than to find you in the idleness of the devil's pleasure."

Well said, Mr. Spurgeon! Someone even greater than Charles Spurgeon is coming one day soon. His name is Jesus. And when he comes, may he "find you working upon his arrival, rather than to find you in the idleness of the devil's pleasure."

God's will for you is simple: full devotion all the time.

"They devoted the city to the Lord and destroyed every living thing in it."

Joshua 6:21

December 3

The Wages of Sin

Born in 1891, he stood just 5'5" and weighed 155 pounds. But "Rabbit" Maranville was committed to his trade, which was baseball. In 1912 he made it to the Major Leagues. But "Rabbit" hit only .258 for his career. The second baseman was not good enough to stick, and no one really wanted him. So the Braves traded him to the Pirates, who traded him to the Cubs, who sent him to the Minors, then traded him to the Dodgers, who traded him to the Cardinals, who traded him back to the Braves again.

"Rabbit" was known for two things: speed and alcohol. He was the fastest player in baseball, and an excellent fielder. This kept him in the game for 23 years.

But alcohol nearly ended his career. His late night carousing ruined his marriage and his health.

Then one night in 1927 he woke up and determined to give his life to a higher power. And he quit drinking. Then he had his best year in baseball. He played so well, in fact, that he became a spokesman for baseball. In 1935 he broke his leg, and his career was over. In 1954 he died of illnesses brought on by the sins of his youth.

Two weeks later, he was elected to baseball's Hall of Fame. Sin always comes with a price. But grace comes with a reward.

"The wages of sin is death, but the gift of God is eternal life in Jesus Christ our Lord."

Romans 6:23

December 4

Potato Chips

Did you know that Mr. Potato Head was the first toy advertised on television? But nobody put "potato" on the map like Herman did.

You see, in 1853, a customer walked into a place called Moon's Lake House in Saratoga Springs, New York. He ordered potatoes, to be prepared by head chef George Crum. When the potatoes were served, the customer complained that they were too soggy and not salty enough. Crum was filled with rage, and responded by thinly slicing the potatoes, frying them until they were brown, and pouring salt all over them.

The new "Saratoga Chips" were a big hit for the customer, and then his friends. So Mr. Crum kept making them.

One day, the customer brought in a fellow named Herman, who bought a plate of "Saratoga Chips." He loved them, and packaged them with his name out front. Herman's last name was Lay. Thus, we see the beginnings of the "potato chip," as he renamed them, and more specifically, Lay's Potato Chips.

The next time you eat a potato chip, remember that great things (and people) often come from humble beginnings. We were born in sin. The Bible makes that clear. But God is bigger than that.

"Surely I was sinful at birth, sinful from the time my mother conceived me."

Psalm 51:5

December 5

Run!

Danielle Barnes is like a lot of 24-year-old women. She likes to drive fast. But unfortunately for Danielle, the police of Burlington, Vermont are a lot like other police. They like to stop cars that drive fast. And when those drivers decide a high-speed chase would be more fun, most police are happy to oblige.

Eventually, Danielle gave up. The kind officers wrote her up for excessive speed and for eluding the police. When asked why she was speeding and would not pull over, Danielle had only a moment to think of a good excuse. Did she claim illness or a family emergency? Nope. Give Danielle credit. She was honest.

"The reason I was driving so fast," she said, "was that I have some drugs here that I need to deliver. I am running late."

Vermont law is pretty strict about speeding and dealing illegal drugs. In fact, in reward for her honesty, she was arrested for dealing drugs.

Before the judge, Danielle complained, "I was honest with the officer. Doesn't that count?"

Of course, honesty is a good thing. But not doing anything that you may want to lie about later would be much better!

God is clear about holiness. He says we need to run from sin, even faster than Danielle drove her car.

"And when the Lord your God has delivered them over to you and you have defeated them, then you must destroy them totally. Make no treaty with them, and show them no mercy."

Deuteronomy 7:2

December 6

Popsicles

They come in all kinds of colors. They can be eaten or dissolved in one's mouth. Then their sticks can be used to build tiny boats, boxes, and other fascinating objects. I'm talking, of course, about the Popsicle.

But what is the origin of the Popsicle? Inquiring minds want to know.

The year was 1905. An 11-year-old boy named Frank Epperson mixed up some fruit-flavored soda powder and mistakenly left the glass outside overnight. When he awoke the next morning, he discovered the beverage had frozen, with the stirring stick in the middle. He shared this "soda on a stick" with his friends, and kept making them as a kid.

Fast forward Frank's life to the age of 30. After several failed attempts in business, he didn't know what to do to make money. A friend reminded him of his "soda on a stick" invention. His buddy said there might be a market for this.

Having nothing to lose, Frank patented his idea, and called it "Popsicle." The idea caught on, and Frank became rich.

Here's the point. In each of us is one great idea. What is yours? Think outside the box. Figure out what you do well. And then go for it!

"Do not conform to the pattern of this world, but be transformed by the renewing of your mind."

Romans 12:2

December 7

Space Invaders

It is where they launch rockets into space. No, not Cape Canaveral. The other place. Yes, Baikonur, Kazakhstan. A Soyuz spacecraft with two Americans and one Russian on board lifted off from Kazakhstan.

Along for the ride was American computer game millionaire Richard Garriott. Atop a Russian rocket, it soared out of sight. Guided by U.S. astronaut Mickael Fincke and Russian cosmonaut Yuri Lonchakov, the space traveler was in good hands.

But let's go back to Richard Garriott. What was he doing there? Why would a man who had millions of dollars blast off into space? Well, Richard has an answer.

"I have about everything there is in this world. But it's not enough," he said.

Wow! What a statement! He had everything of this world, and it was not enough. So off he went, chasing after other worlds.

Here's the good news. God has invaded our universe and our planet, with his love and his Son. Trust in him. Give him your life. He's out of this world!

"There is a way that appears to be right, but in the end it leads to death."

Proverbs 14:12

December 8

Pizza

Welcome to the Food Section of this devotional book. I know what you were thinking when you opened today's lesson. "Would someone please give me some pizza trivia!"

We sure will. This is just one of the things that make this such a great read. Where else can you get pizza trivia when you want it? So, here we go.

For starters, let's talk about national policy. Domino's Pizza locations in Washington, D.C. report that whenever they have a marked increase in late night deliveries to the Pentagon or White House, a major news story will be announced within two days.

Now, for trivia #2. Do you know the day that more pizza was delivered than any other in history? The date was June 17, 1994, the day that millions of Americans watched O.J. Simpson's Bronco drive across Los Angeles. Viewers weren't about to leave their television sets to make dinner.

Pizza plays a defining role in society today! You see pizza at college study groups, kids' parties, and sporting events. Why is this? We like to be fed. It's that simple. Do you like to be fed, spiritually?

"I gave you milk, not solid food, for you were not yet ready for it. Indeed, you are still not ready."

1 Corinthians 3:2

December 9

Grand Master

In 1997, a team of IBM engineers designed and developed Deep Blue, the computer that outmaneuvered chess grand master Garry Kasparov. Deep Blue was equipped with 32 processing engines that could calculate 200 million chess moves per second.

I don't know about you, but I am comfortable with up to about two options. Give me true/false, right/left, or vanilla/chocolate. But 200 million options? I might struggle with that.

Now, here's the point. Think of yourself as the pawn (chess piece) and God as the Grand Master. The pawn never tells the Grand Master where he wants to move next.

In my office I proudly display my chess trophy, representing the Sharpstown Junior High Chess Championship of 1973. It rises nearly 5" above my desk. I could plan two or three moves ahead. But 200 million?

The Grand Master sees the whole board, and he plans several moves ahead. He may be willing to take some losses (a bishop or knight) in order to win the game.

I'm guessing you aren't as smart as Deep Blue. So why not trust the Grand Master with your next move?

"If you fully obey the Lord your God and carefully follow all his commands I give you today, I will set you high, and blessing will come on you."

Deuteronomy 28:1-2

December 10

Is God in Church?

After attending church with his father one Sunday morning, a little boy knelt beside his bed to say his nightly prayers. Nothing could have made his dad more proud. He started with the typical things kids pray about: his dog, his cat, and his mean older sister.

Then the boy turned spiritual with his prayer. "Dear God, we had a really good time at church this morning. I wish you had been there."

In a related story, two ministers were arguing over minor doctrinal issues one day. Finally, one said to the other, "Look, what are we fighting over? We are both trying to serve God. You do it your way and I'll do it his way!"

Why do you go to church? Do you go to church? There have been many Sundays when I felt like the little boy. We had great services, but I didn't really feel the holy presence of the Almighty.

Maybe the problem is we are too much like the two pastors. We squabble over the little stuff when we need to just seek the presence of God.

Nothing is worse than having church without God. But he is under no obligation to show up just because it's "church."

"You will seek me and find me when you seek me with all your heart."

Jeremiah 29:13

December 11

Fire Three Shots

Two men went hunting in the woods. The game warden told them that if they got lost they should shoot three shots in rapid succession. Sure enough, they got lost.

One of them said to the other, "We better do what the game warden said. Why don't you shoot the three shots?"

So he fired three shots. Nothing happened.

The first hunter said, "You had better fire another three shots."

So three more shots were fired. They waited another hour, but still no one came to get them.

Again, the first hunter turned to his buddy and said, "I guess you had better fire three more shots."

His friend said, "I can't. I've run out of arrows."

Life is a lot like that. We find ourselves lost. We give it our best shot. We fire all the arrows in our quiver. Perhaps your "arrows" are good works, personal achievement, personality, or wealth. You have tried them all, but you're still lost.

You can give life your best shot, but until you do it the Game Warden's way, you'll never find your way home.

"Anyone who chooses to do the will of God will find out whether my teaching comes from God or whether I speak on my own."

John 7:17

December 12

Just One Road

It happened in the big city of Kingman, Arizona. A dude rancher filed a notice of appeal with federal authorities to stop the use of a bypass road to the Grand Canyon Skywalk. Nigel Turner is the owner of the Grand Canyon Ranch Resort, which supplies his total income and livelihood. His problem with the bypass road was that it was an unnecessary route into the Skywalk area because two other routes already exist.

Here's the real issue. Nigel wants all tourists to the Grand Canyon to pass by his resort. This means more business for him. He is already upset that two routes exist; he can't stand the thought of three.

Most places have multiple routes. When my wife and I drive somewhere, her smart phone tells this dumb driver about three possible routes, whether we want three possible routes or not. But that comes in handy in times of heavy traffic.

But there is one place that only has one route. That place is heaven. Jesus said, "I am the way." There is one way in and no way out.

"If you declare with your mouth the Lord Jesus, and believe in your heart that God raised him from the dead, you will be saved."

Romans 10:9

December 13

57 Rules

A sign in a small business read, "The 57 Rules of Success: Rule #1 – Deliver the goods. Rule #2 – The other 56 rules don't matter."

When I was a young boy, we had a milkman who "delivered the goods" right to our front door. The grocery store did the same thing. Mom never accepted excuses. They either delivered the goods, or they were in big trouble.

Today's generation has mastered the art of excuse. But the blame game doesn't work. God expects us to "deliver the goods."

Here's where it starts: with you. And you need to understand that you will never change your life until you change something you do daily.

John Kotter said, "Most people don't lead their lives; they accept their lives."

Benjamin Disraeli said, "The secret of success in life is for a man to be ready for his time when it comes."

Your time has come to "deliver the goods" in your personal life, your family life, and your business life. It starts with a decision, but requires more than that. To "deliver the goods," you must start with a decision, but it is discipline that will take you across the finish line.

Now is the time. "Deliver the goods!"

"No discipline seems present at the time. But later on, it produces righteousness."

Hebrews 12:11

December 14

The Proposal

Lady Gaga said, "I'm a religious woman that is confused about religion."

Lady Gaga confused? Let's talk about it.

Let's liken this religion thing to marriage. In the Bible there are scores of famous couples: Adam and Eve, Jacob and Rachel, Abraham and Sarah, David and Bathsheba. But there was another couple: Hosea and Gomer. (Gomer was the girl.) Here's what happened. God told Hosea to pursue Gomer in marriage, knowing Gomer had a checkered past and a lousy present. She was not a one-man gal.

Hosea married Gomer. Their marriage was a parable on life.

God pursues us when we are not worth it. It is not about religion, but relationship. You need to see God as the one who is pursuing you. He will keep pursuing you.

Here is his proposal. "Marry me. Commit to me."

God can change your life. But you must first accept his proposal. Turn to him and say "yes." Jesus called this "being born again."

> *"No one can see the kingdom of God unless they are born again."*
>
> John 3:3

December 15

Lucky

David was bumped while getting on the school bus and suffered a two-inch cut. At recess he collided with another boy and lost two teeth. At noon, on the playground, he fell and broke his wrist. At the hospital, his father noticed David was clutching a quarter in his good hand.

David explained, "I found it on the ground when I fell. This is the first quarter I ever found. This is my lucky day!"

I love the newspaper ad: "Lost – one dog. Very little hair on his body. Right leg broken due to auto accident. Rear left hip hurt. Right eye missing. Left ear bitten off in a dog fight. Answers to the name 'Lucky.'"

One day, I got wet on the only day it rained that I didn't have my umbrella. Bad luck.

Last year, the Astros won their game on the night I was there. Good luck. Incredibly good luck. But luck will only take you so far.

J. Paul Getty had it right. "Rise early, work late, and strike oil!"

The "oil" part is luck. But the "rise early" part is a choice. And I've noticed that the harder I work, the luckier I am.

"All hard work brings a profit, but mere talk leads only to poverty."

Proverbs 14:23

December 16

Knocking on the Door

G.K. Chesterton said, "Every man who knocks on the door of a brothel is looking for God."

Jud Wilhite is pastor of a thriving church that reaches out to the most unlikely church prospects in Las Vegas. Annie was one of those people. She endured a roller coaster life of alcoholism, drug addiction, and sexual promiscuity. She went from middle class good girl to high class call girl as part of a slow, gradual descent into the darkness of her own doubt, fear, and pain.

A string of boyfriends led to one-night stands with guys she picked up in clubs, which included lots of drinking, drugging, and partying. Then something happened. Annie got as low as a person can go. She found herself without family, friends, and peace.

Then Annie turned to God. And God radically changed her forever.

Chesterton was right. Every man knocking on the door of a brothel is looking for God. They just don't know it quite yet.

"Here I am! I stand at the door and knock. If anyone hears my voice and opens the door I will come in and eat with that person, and they with me."

Revelation 3:20

December 17

Four Boys in the Corner

A school principal received a phone call. The voice said, "Thomas Bradley won't be in school today."

The principal was a bit suspicious of the voice. He asked, "Who is speaking?"

The voice came back, "My father."

The locus classicus on the flushing out of the deceitful heart of man is the oft-quoted story about the four boys who cut class one morning and didn't get to school until noon. They said that they'd had a flat tire.

The teacher said, "That's ok. You missed a test, but you can make it up now on your lunch time."

Then she seated them in the four corners of the room and gave them each one question for the test: "Which tire was flat?"

The Bible says our sins will find us out. You may think you are getting away with something for awhile. But your sins will find you out.

So ask yourself this question. "How honest am I, really?"

There is a famous movie line that says, "You can't handle the truth!" That's Hollywood. There is another line that says, "Thou shalt not lie." That's the Bible.

"Do not lie to each other, since you have taken off your old self with its practices."

Colossians 3:9

December 18

Shot in the Dark

Have you heard the phrase, "a shot in the dark"? That has new meaning for Tina Owens, of Morgantown, West Virginia. It seems the 57-year-old woman awoke to strange sounds outside her house one night. Suspecting intruders were trying to break into her home, she grabbed her gun. She then fired several shots in an attempt to scare them off.

Tragically, one of her shots pierced the wall of her son's home, 200 yards away. And the bullet hit her 11-year-old grandson William. The boy died instantly.

There are so many lessons from this horrible story. Be careful with guns. Make sure there are really intruders before you fire your gun. Call the police instead.

But I think it serves as a larger parable. "A shot in the dark" refers to one's decision to throw up a feeble effort, then hope for the best.

God has a better plan. The wisdom of Scripture teaches us to fear and follow God. It is what Rick Warren calls the "purpose-driven life."

Find your purpose. It sure beats "a shot in the dark."

"Now all has been heard; here is the conclusion of the matter: fear God and keep his commandments, for this is the duty of mankind."

Ecclesiastes 12:13

December 19

Growing Up

Let's talk about growing up. Let's talk about spiritual maturity. Someone noted, "It seldom occurs to teenagers that some day they will know as little as their parents."

Another said, "We can only be young once, but we can be immature indefinitely."

I love the story of the little boy. He heard the phone ring. He ran to the phone, picked it up and answered it. The caller was a telemarketer. "Is your mother home?"

"Nope," replied the little boy.

"Well then, is your father home?"

"Nope."

"Do you have a sister I can speak to?"

"Yep."

"May I speak to her now, please?"

The telemarketer waited. Finally, the boy returned. "I'm back," he said.

"Where is your sister?"

He responded, "I can't lift her out of her playpen."

The Bible says a lot about maturity. It says we should desire the meat of the Word.

A church member once told her pastor, "I don't feel like I'm being fed at this church."

He wisely responded, "If you are dependent on others to feed you, you will starve anyway."

Let me restate it this way. It's time to grow up. Learn to feed on the Word of God every day, with the help of one person: the Holy Spirit.

"When I was a child, I talked like a child, I thought like a child, I reasoned like a child. But when I became a man, I put the ways of childhood behind me."

1 Corinthians 13:11

December 20

What's an Idol?

John Calvin said, "Every one of us, even from his mother's womb, is a master craftsman of idols."

When you were growing up, did you ever stick up a poster of someone you idolized, on the wall in your room? Maybe it was Michael Jackson or Madonna or Patrick Swayze from *Dirty Dancing*. If you are from my generation, you will recall the best-selling poster of all time, the 1976 *Life* magazine cover featuring Farrah Fawcett.

If that was before your time, maybe it was the Backsteet Boys, N Sync, Michael Jordan, Lance Armstrong, Britney Spears, or Taylor Swift.

The flavor of the month is Justin Bieber. I'm not sure I've ever seen someone come on the scene so young, with such a wide appeal to the current generation of young people. He has become an idol to millions.

Here's a quick Bible question for you. Which commandment was about idols? Answer: all of them. You see, putting anything before God makes that an idol.

What consumes your money and your time? That is your God. And that will be your undoing if you don't get it under control.

"Dear children, keep yourselves from idols."

1 John 5:21

December 21

Don't Tell Bill

A counselor from a seventh grade camp was talking to 12-year-old Scott about his experience, trying some "snuff" with some other boys the night before.

The counselor asked, "What did you think of the whole experience? What do you have to say for yourself?"

Scott replied, "I won't ever try it again, but please don't tell Bill, the camp director."

The counselor questioned Scott further. "God knows what you did. What's the difference between God knowing and Bill knowing?"

Scott explained, "God won't tell my parents!"

I can relate to that. When I did something wrong, my dad was the last one I wanted to find out. I wish I could say I was as mature as the boy who was mocked for his refusal to disobey his dad. The other kids said, "You're afraid he will find out and hurt you, aren't you?"

The boy replied, "No, I'm afraid he will find out, and that will hurt him."

The fact is, anytime we sin, our Father finds out, whether our parents do or not. And the last thing we should want to do is to hurt him.

"Jesus said, 'If you love me, keep my commands.'"

John 14:15

December 22

Bing

Late one Christmas Day, a man living in a posh California neighborhood, accompanied by his wife and children, set out to sing carols for the neighbors. As they approached their first stop, the woman of the house came to the door, looking distraught.

"Look fella," she said, "I'm just too busy right now. I have cooking to do and things to put up. Come back some other time, okay?"

"Yes, ma'am," replied the gentleman, respectfully, as he herded his group elsewhere. The name of the scorned caroler was Bing Crosby, an American icon.

I'm sure that if the lady had recognized who it was who was knocking on her door that day, she would have let him sing.

Jesus said, in the Book of Revelation, "Behold, I stand at the door and knock. Whoever opens the door, I will come in and dine with him."

Indeed, someone is knocking on your door. You may not recognize the knock. It may be coming from the manger of Christmas. Or the knock may be coming from the direction of the cross. Either way, he is knocking. And you have no idea of the blessings on the other side of the door.

On the other side stands a gentleman. He wants to come in. The next move is yours.

"My sheep listen to my voice; I know them,
and they follow me."

John 10:27

December 23

Mezuzahs

Rabbi Chaim Bruk has set his sights on making sure each Jewish home in Montana has a mezuzah at its entrance, and that the ones already there are kosher. Montana's only orthodox rabbi says the mezuzahs, small parchments of handwritten biblical verses rolled into 4-inch cases and fastened to door frames, are a reminder that God is the ultimate home protection, in a state where many people believe that such security begins and ends with a gun.

Bruk states, "I'm young (age 31), so I hope to get to every home in Montana to make sure every Jewish house has a mezuzah."

Bruk continued, "Montana should be the most protected state in the union, not only because of our weapons, but because of our mezuzahs. We'll be protected by the Second Amendment and by the mezuzahs."

Bruk's mission is an ambitious one, as Montana is the fourth largest state in the country, based on land mass. But he will stay at the task, because he believes in the protection of God's Word.

You may not be Jewish, but you can still honor God's Word in your home. Nothing will do more to provide protection from the enemy.

"For everything that was written in the past was written to teach us, so that through the endurance taught in the Scriptures, and the encouragement they proved we might have hope."

Romans 15:4

December 24

Christmas Truce

It was called "the most famous truce in military history" by British television producer Malcolm Brown and researcher Shirley Seaton in their book, *Christmas Truce*, published in 1984.

It happened on December 25, 1914, the first Christmas of WWI. British and German troops put down their guns and celebrated peacefully together in the no-man's land between the trenches. The war, ever so briefly, came to a halt. Festivities began when German troops lit candles on Christmas trees so the British could see them.

Private Oswald Tilley, of the London Rifle Brigade, wrote to his parents, "Just you think that while you were eating your turkey, etc., I was out talking and shaking hands with the very men I had been trying to kill a few hours before! It was astounding!"

On this Christmas Eve, think about someone with whom you have had a conflict. Jesus said to forgive them "seventy times seven" times.

But you start with one. You can start today. Maybe you aren't ready to forgive them 490 times yet. But can't you, on this sacred day, call a "Christmas Truce"?

I can't think of a better way to honor the birth child!

"And there were shepherds living out in the fields nearby, keeping watch over their flocks at night."

Luke 2:8

December 25

Follow the Star

Today is the most special day of the year. I'm sure you have your family traditions, without which Christmas would not be Christmas: big family breakfast, opening the stockings, reading the Christmas Story, and opening your presents. Then you save the best for last, as you gather the family around your *Daily Walk* devotional book to read the day's message. No Christmas would be complete without it.

So let's talk about tradition. When I was a child, mom made bacon-wrapped scallops for Christmas Day. (What says Christmas like scallops?) Then we would open our stuff. Dad would put our toys together, and we'd play the rest of the day. I'll never forget the Christmas when my brother and I played tennis all afternoon, with our new Wilson T-2000 aluminum rackets.

Let me suggest another tradition. Pray. That's it. Pray. Take just ten minutes sometime today, and pray. Tell God you are grateful for the gift of his son. Pray. Rejoice in the blessings you enjoy. Pray. Confess your sins. Pray. Commit your heart, your life, yourself to the Christmas Child. Pray.

Merry Christmas!

"Where is the one who has been born king of the Jews? We saw his star when it rose and have come to worship him."

Matthew 2:2

December 26

Football and Church

Note the contrasts between the average football fan's worship of a pigskin and the average Christian's worship of God. Football fans pay a hefty sum to park their cars and walk a long distance to the stadium. The churchgoer expects free parking close to the building. Football contests are noisy with loud cheering and the enthusiasm of the fans. The churchgoer sits in grim silence, and objects to loud music. Football stadium seats are narrow, backless, and assigned. The churchgoer hates a hard pew and insists on a particular seat.

Football games always last well past three hours, and if they go into overtime, fans consider it a bonus. The churchgoer expects worship to take only an hour. If the service goes into overtime, the churchgoer displays great movements of agitation and frustration.

Actually, things don't have to be that way. At my church, season tickets are free, and if you come early enough, you can sit in the same seat every week. Our seats are comfortable, the music is excellent, and the home team (Jesus) wins every time. And we try to keep it to an hour. By any measure, the best arena you will ever attend is the one down the street, with the steeple.

With the new year dawning, find a place of worship this Sunday.

"Let everything that has breath praise the Lord."

Psalm 150:6

December 27

Two-by-Fours

A fellow at the lumber yard asks for some four-by-twos. The clerk says, "You mean two-by-fours?"

He says, "Just a moment. I'll check."

He goes back to his car where his friends are waiting for him, and he has a short conversation with them. He returns and says, "Yes, I mean two-by-fours."

The merchant asks, "How long do you want them?"

The fellow says, "Just a minute. I'll check." And he confers with his friends in the car once again, and comes back and answers, "A long time. We're building a house."

One day Jesus talked about building a house that would last for a long time. He said there are two ways to go about it. You can build on whatever foundation is readily available and get it done quickly. Or if you want it to last a long time, you must build it on a solid foundation. Your home will encounter storms. How your home stands in the midst of the storms is dependent on the foundation on which it is built.

Only when you build on Christ can your house last "a long time."

"Everyone who hears these words of mine and puts them into practice is like a wise man who built his house on the rock."

Matthew 7:24

December 28

Driving on Empty

Larry had a lot on his mind when he noticed that his fuel gauge was on empty. Quickly finding the closest gas station, he pulled in. At this particular station, the "pay at the pump" feature was not working. So he went inside and paid the cashier ten dollars. Then he walked out to his car, got in, and drove off without ever filling up.

He kept running errands until finally pulling into his driveway when he looked down at his gas gauge, which was now well below "E." He had stopped at the gas station, paid, but never pumped.

Talk about distracted! Bill was literally driving on fumes.

This is a picture of most of our lives. We need a fill-up. The price has already been paid. We may be at church, God's filling station. But we drive off without truly filling up.

Sometime today, slow down. Return to the pump, in prayer. Remember, the fuel is already paid for.

"Be filled with the Holy Spirit."

Ephesians 5:18

December 29

Lost Wallet

It happened in Wilkes-Barre, Pennsylvania. A man was simply walking down the street. We don't know where he was going or even who he is. But then he saw it. Laying on the pavement in front of him was a wallet. He did what we all would do. He picked it up. Then he looked inside. He found some money, some credit cards, and a driver's license.

To his shock, the wallet belonged to Steve Martin, famed actor and comedian. Mr. Martin was in town to play a bluegrass concert. He had been riding a bike down that street just moments before when his wallet fell out.

Now the stranger had a dilemma. Would he simply turn the wallet in to the authorities? Or would he keep the cash and throw it back down? Or maybe he would seek a hefty reward from the wealthy actor. Nobody was looking. If he took the money, no one would know. What did he do?

To his credit, he turned in the wallet, refusing any possible reward. That is the definition of character. It's doing the right thing, and waiting on God to bless our obedience according to his plan. It's what you do when no one is watching.

What would you have done?

"Wait for the Lord; be strong and take heart and wait for the Lord."

Psalm 27:14

December 30

Babe Ruth

In 1926, Johnny Sylvester got kicked in the head by a horse. The wound got badly infected. Doctors told his parents the bad news. Johnny would die.

"I wish I could see Babe Ruth wallop a homer before I die," Johnny told his parents.

So they sent a telegram to the great slugger of the New York Yankees. And Babe Ruth sent an answer. He would hit a homer just for Johnny in the next game.

Johnny Sylvester instantly became one of the most famous boys in baseball history. Did Babe Ruth slug one for Johnny? Yes! In fact, he hit three homers in that game. It was an incredible gift for young Johnny.

But let's get back to his injury. Were the doctors right? Did Johnny Sylvester die?

Yes, they were right. Johnny did die. But not until he was 74.

The Bible says, "It is appointed to man once to die."

Babe Ruth was a legend. He still is. Perhaps it was his inspiration that led Johnny Sylvester to become one of America's great business executives.

We can learn from that. Inspire someone today. You never know when their last days will come. But God does.

"Blessed are the dead who die in the Lord."

Revelation 14:13

December 31

Cleaning Up the Mess

We used to have a Cocker Spaniel named Duffy. She was one happy mess. Every time a guest would come over to our house, she would lick them to death and then wet the floor. Duffy's bladder was unable to control her joy.

We were always cleaning up after her. She slobbered horribly. When she would run or shake her head, slobber flew everywhere, and we'd clean it up.

But we loved her anyway. She was incredibly loving, loyal, and fun. And messy.

One day, due to a back problem that is common among Cockers, Duffy became paralyzed. She couldn't walk or get to her food dish. We spent a king's ransom on her back surgery, knowing it may not be successful. Then we just had to wait and see. We fed her by hand and carried her outside where she could at least enjoy the view.

One day, she began to move again, and she fully recovered, though she remained a mess. But she was our mess. We loved that dog. We didn't like the messes, but we were willing to clean them up because we loved Duffy more than we hated the mess.

The truth is, we are all a mess. You are a mess. But God loves you more than he hates your mess.

And as you enter the New Year, know this. God loves you enough to clean up after you.

"Their sins and lawless acts I will
remember no more."

Hebrews 10:17

About the Author
Mark Denison

Mark has served as a church planter and senior pastor for 30 years. His passion in ministry is to connect the Gospel with the community. He does this with his daily radio devotions, daily newspaper columns, and daily email devotions.

In addition to his ministry as pastor of First Baptist Church in Conroe, Texas, Mark serves as a chaplain for the Houston Rockets and as chairman of the Board of Trustees at Houston Baptist University. Mark holds degrees from HBU and Southwestern Baptist Theological Seminary. He is a sports enthusiast, with an extensive collection of hundreds of autographed memorabilia from the greats of each sport.

Dr. Denison wrote *The Daily Walk* to encourage others in their walk with Jesus. These daily devotions reflect the relationship Mark has had with the Lord since he came to Christ as an eighth grade student growing up in Houston. Mark has been married to Beth, his beautiful wife and partner in ministry, since 1983. Their son, David, is a talented musician and communicator, who is also pursuing a life in ministry.

To contact Dr. Denison, or to receive his daily online devotions, email him at mark@fbcconroe.org.

CPSIA information can be obtained at www.ICGtesting.com
Printed in the USA
BVOW03s0751231113

336797BV00003B/3/P